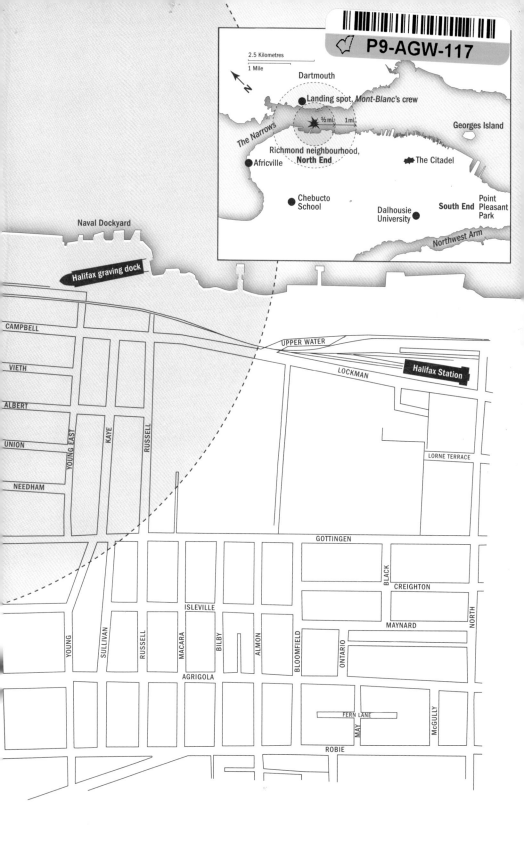

P9-AGW-117

2.5 Kilometres
1 Mile

N

Dartmouth

Landing spot, *Mont-Blanc's* crew

The Narrows

½ mi.   1 mi.

Georges Island

Richmond neighbourhood, **North End**

Africville

The Citadel

Chebucto School

Dalhousie University

South End   Point Pleasant Park

Northwest Arm

Naval Dockyard

Halifax graving dock

CAMPBELL

VIETH

ALBERT

UNION

NEEDHAM

YOUNG EAST

KAYE

RUSSELL

UPPER WATER

LOCKMAN

Halifax Station

LORNE TERRACE

GOTTINGEN

BLACK

CREIGHTON

ISLEVILLE

MAYNARD

NORTH

YOUNG

SULLIVAN

RUSSELL

MACARA

BILBY

ALMON

BLOOMFIELD

ONTARIO

AGRIGOLA

FERN LANE

MAY

McGULLY

ROBIE

THE HALIFAX EXPLOSION

THE HALIFAX EXPLOSION

CANADA'S WORST DISASTER

KEN CUTHBERTSON

PATRICK CREAN EDITIONS
HarperCollins*PublishersLtd*

Published by Patrick Crean Editions, an imprint of HarperCollins Publishers Ltd

First edition

Maps (endpapers and p. 177) by Larry Harris.
Title page photograph courtesy of the City of Toronto Archives.

HarperCollins books may be purchased for educational, business,
or sales promotional use through our Special Markets Department.

HarperCollins Publishers Ltd
2 Bloor Street East, 20th Floor
Toronto, Ontario, Canada
M4W 1A8

www.harpercollins.ca

Library and Archives Canada Cataloguing in Publication
information is available upon request.

ISBN 978-1-44345-025-6

Printed and bound in the United States
LSC/H 9 8 7 6 5 4 3 2 1

For Grandfather Hubley (1888–1975) and
my mother, Dorothy (née Hubley) Cuthbertson (1921–2015),
proud Nova Scotians

CONTENTS

INTRODUCTION

I t was a blast heard 'round the world. News of what happened when two ships collided in the harbour of the historic port city of Halifax, Nova Scotia, on December 6, 1917, made headlines worldwide. In times of war, accidents happened in busy seaports, and life went on. But this time, things were different.

One of the vessels involved in the collision was the SS *Imo*, a Norwegian war-relief ship. The other was the SS *Mont-Blanc*, a rusting French tramp steamer that was loaded to the gunwales with high explosives—almost 3,000 tons of picric acid, TNT, and gun cotton—while piled high on her deck were hundreds of barrels of high-octane benzol fuel. The *Mont-Blanc* was a floating bomb. As one veteran Royal Navy officer would later marvel, "I'm surprised the people on the ship didn't leave in a body when they saw the nature of the cargo she had been ordered to carry." [1]

The chain of events that put the *Imo* and the *Mont-Blanc* on a collision course was as improbable as it was bizarre. It defied logic. The weather was clear and mild. The sea was calm. Veteran harbour pilots were guiding each ship. The two captains involved were experienced mariners.

Those eyewitnesses who lived to tell the tale reported that they had seen trouble coming long before it ever happened. It was as if events on the water were happening in slow motion. That cliché is a cliché for a reason.

In the moments after the crash, it appeared as if no great damage had occurred. Then, as the ships were disengaging, the grinding of metal on metal sparked a small fire aboard the French ship. The wispy flames that began to flicker and dance on the *Mont-Blanc*'s foredeck quickly took on a life of their own. They became a raging, angry inferno.

Few people in Halifax on this sleepy, sunlit Thursday morning knew the awful secret that the *Mont-Blanc*—the stricken ship that was on fire and drifting toward the Halifax shoreline—was carrying munitions. The curious flocked to the water's edge to watch the excitement as the *Mont-Blanc* burned. For twenty minutes, spectators stood spellbound. A succession of small explosions, the pyrotechnics' soundtrack, echoed across the harbour, drawing collective gasps from awed onlookers. The show was something to behold. But then . . . in a nanosecond, the show ended, as the unexpected, the unthinkable, happened.

At 9:04 a.m., there erupted an apocalyptic blast the likes of which had never before been seen or heard. The biggest man-made explosion prior to the 1945 atomic bomb blasts unleashed an incendiary firestorm. A split second later, there followed a deadly shock wave and then a killer tsunami. The destructive energy that radiated outward from the blast would claim 2,000 lives. It would also injure 9,000 people, level half the city of Halifax, and shatter windows for miles around. Those who heard the thunderous rumble from afar described it as being "a sound for God to make, not man."

So great was the devastation around ground zero—on the water beside Pier 6 in Halifax harbour—that a quarter century later, physicist Robert Oppenheimer, the father of the atomic bomb, reportedly studied aspects of the explosion in hopes of gaining understanding of the destructive power of such a huge blast at ground level.[2]

The Elizabethan playwright Christopher Marlowe mused in his play *Doctor Faustus*, "Hell hath no limits, nor is circumscribed." There is no more vivid example of the truth of those words than the great Halifax harbour explosion of 1917. The story of the disaster has become an integral element of the city's self-identity and of Canada's national mythology.

The explosion that devastated Halifax on December 6, 1917, is one of the few Canadian historical events that the world—and, indeed, Canadians themselves—remember. The disaster is unforgettable for many reasons, not the least of which is that it was so quintessentially Canadian.

It was a forty-three-year-old family man who emerged as one of the iconic figures involved in the disaster. Vincent ("Vince") Coleman, a railway telegraph operator, ignored his own safety when he stayed at his desk to telegraph a Morse code message—a warning to an approaching passenger train. "Hold up the train," Coleman tapped out. "Ammunition ship afire in harbour making for Pier 6 and will explode. Guess this will be my last message. Good-bye boys." Coleman's heroism may have saved hundreds of lives, but it cost him his own.

Vince Coleman was depicted as the central figure in a 1991 Halifax explosion segment of the popular Heritage Minute series, the historical infomercials produced by Historica Canada (available for viewing online at www.historicacanada.ca). A 2012 survey done by the Ipsos Reid polling firm identified that mini-drama as being one of the most memorable of the eighty-three Heritage Minutes aired to that time. The well-known Montreal businessman and philanthropist Charles Bronfman, who provided money to help produce the series, has a theory as to why. Bronfman has hailed Coleman as "the Canadian paradigm of a hero. He was an ordinary guy, who when extraordinary circumstances came along, did the thing he was supposed to do. That's what [Canadians] are about."[3]

In many regards, that is the essence of the story of the great Halifax harbour explosion of 1917. The people of that historic port city—ordinary, hard-working men and women—suffered a staggering, catastrophic blow. Yet, incredibly, life in Halifax began to resume within days of the disaster. As one elderly explosion survivor observed many years later, the people of Halifax, like all Canadians, are "made from pretty strong stuff."[4]

Over the years, countless articles, stories, and books—both fictional and non-fictional—have chronicled aspects of the great Halifax harbour explosion of 1917 and its tragic aftermath. There is even a play about the disaster, as well as a 2003 television miniseries called *Shattered City: The Halifax Explosion*, and, of course, that memorable Heritage Minute.

As Canada and the world mark the centenary of the tragedy, this book offers a fresh look at the remarkable story of Canada's worst-ever disaster. Here are the untold backstories of some key figures who were involved as well as answers to some of the questions that have always lingered.

Was the disaster the result of negligence on the part of the ships' pilots, the captains, or the naval officials who were in charge of the port of Halifax? Was the collision of the *Imo* and the *Mont-Blanc* the inevitable result of shortcomings in harbour practices and protocols? Or was the blast—as many people at the time believed—the result of wartime sabotage carried out by German agents?

A superstitious person well might wonder if the great Halifax harbour explosion of 1917 was the capper in a quartet of epic North Atlantic maritime disasters that shocked the world in the first two decades of the twentieth century.

On April 15, 1912, "the unsinkable" Royal Mail Ship (RMS) *Titanic*, the pride of Great Britain's White Star Line, took 1,517 passengers and crew to a watery grave after hitting an iceberg off Newfoundland.

Two years later, on the morning of May 29, 1914, the RMS *Empress of Ireland* ocean liner carried 1,012 victims with her when she went to the bottom of the St. Lawrence River after colliding with a Norwegian collier.

Then a year after that, 1,962 innocent people perished when a German U-boat torpedoed the Cunard luxury liner RMS *Lusitania* off the west coast of Ireland on May 7, 1915.

Then came the December 6, 1917, explosion in Halifax harbour.

It was no coincidence that all these disasters took place within a five-year period. All occurred near the tail end of a time of tremendous change and upheaval, when Western society was still transitioning from being rural and agrarian to being urban and industrialized. The rate this happened was fast-paced, and it was profound. Science and technology, the "engines of progress," were proving to be a mixed blessing. Being bigger, faster, and more powerful were not always desirable traits. There is an argument to be made that the disaster at Halifax—like the accidents that claimed the *Titanic* and the *Empress of Ireland* and the deliberate sinking of the *Lusitania*—was the result of collective bungling, hubris, and the foolishness of men.

The real story of the Halifax disaster is not the one you may have heard or that you think you know. Rather, it is a multi-layered tale of tragedy on an epic scale. It is a story of senseless death and suffering, and it is a story of clumsy attempts by government and military officials to cover up their own incompetence. However, above all, the essence of the true story of the great Halifax harbour explosion of 1917 is one of the courage, strength, and grit of ordinary Canadians—men, women, and children—who not only endured but who also triumphed over adversity and suffering to ultimately emerge with renewed strength, determination, and sense of purpose.

The real story of the great Halifax harbour explosion of 1917 is also one that all Canadians should know and should understand. The impacts of the disaster were myriad. Some were immediate and transitory; others took longer to unfold.

In the aftermath of so much death and destruction, government officials, naval commanders, and port authorities in Canada, the United

States, and Great Britain began re-examining the regulations that governed the shipping of dangerous goods, the reporting of maritime cargoes, and the management of harbour traffic. The tragic events at Halifax underscored the need for governments at all levels—and those in port cities especially—to have a coherent, comprehensive disaster relief plan ready to go at all times. Never has that been truer or more important than in our own post-9/11 world.

In the long term, the Halifax disaster continues to offer lessons and cautions that we would be wise to heed in these uncertain, dangerous times. A century has passed. The world has changed immeasurably, but human nature is unchanging. As historian Margaret MacMillan has noted, it is folly to "underestimate the part played in human affairs by mistakes, muddle, or simply poor timing."[5]

CHAPTER 1

"Theirs Not to Reason Why"

New York Harbour, November 30, 1917

What had he gotten himself into? Captain Aimé Le Médec had been on the job for eleven years. He had always been supremely confident of his ability to meet any challenges that man or the sea threw at him. Until now. Le Médec knew—only too well—the dangers of the voyage upon which he and his men were about to embark. There was no question this was his most dangerous assignment ever. Nor was there any question that this was one trans-Atlantic crossing he was not eager to make.

The captain was a brave man; cowards and nervous Nellies tend not to become mariners. At age thirty-nine, Le Médec had no burning desire to be a hero, but he knew he had no say in the cargo his ship carried.

Orders were orders, and the captain accepted that he must obey them, especially in wartime. As the master of a lowly tramp steamer and an officer of the French naval reserve, Le Médec was subject to military discipline and to punishment, if ever it came to that. The punishment for insubordination, mutiny, or desertion would be prison, if he was lucky. If he was not, could it be a firing squad, he wondered? But none of that mattered. Le Médec was a patriot. He would do his duty for France.

The captain's superiors had directed him to deliver a load of munitions from New York to the killing fields of Western Europe, and he would do so. Le Médec remembered what that Englishman, the poet Lord Tennyson, had mused in his famous poem "The Charge of the Light Brigade": "Theirs not to make reply, / Theirs not to reason why, / Theirs but to do and die."

Instant obliteration. That was the terrifying prospect Captain Aimé Le Médec and his forty-man crew faced as their plodding ship prepared to steam out of New York harbour. They were bound for Halifax, Nova Scotia, and then, it would be on to their home port of Bordeaux. That is, if the SS *Mont-Blanc* was lucky enough to make it that far.

The members of the ship's crew, French citizens with a few colonials mixed in, were aware to a man that theirs were *le salaire de la peur*—the wages of fear. Besides having to run the usual wartime gauntlet of German U-boats that lurked in the depths of the North Atlantic, they faced additional danger on this trip. Packed to the gunwales, the ship was carrying more than enough munitions and barrels of high-octane benzol fuel to blow the ship and all souls on board her into eternity, and perhaps beyond, in the blink of an eye.

After more than three years of bloodletting in Europe, Germany had made a desperate and ultimately ill-advised decision to initiate unrestricted submarine warfare in the sea lanes between North America and Europe. That move had brought the United States into the war on the side of the Allies on April 6, 1917. Once that happened, New York City became a major port of embarkation for Allied troops, supplies, and munitions bound for the Western Front. The already busy waters in and around New York teemed with wartime traffic.

Most seafarers believed the harbour there was too shallow, too murky, for even the most daring of U-boat commanders to venture into. American military officials were not so sure of that; the German enemy was as devious as he was ruthless. The United States navy left nothing to chance. Following the lead of the Royal Navy in Halifax and other Allied ports, Uncle Sam's patrol boats installed an anti-submarine net across the Verrazano narrows. This effectively sealed the entrance to New York harbour and provided protection against submarine attacks in a war that became bloodier by the day.

By December 1917, the fighting in Europe was into its fourth calendar year. The carnage had dragged on much longer than Aimé Le Médec—or anyone else—had ever expected or even feared. However, after just six months of involvement, America's military and industrial muscle were already making themselves felt. Momentum in the war was beginning to tip in the Allies' favour.

The British and American navies were sinking as many as ten U-boats each month, faster than German shipyards could replace them. Despite this, the threat of submarine attacks in "U-boat alley" remained high for the captains and crews of Allied—and neutral—ships. In December 1917, for example, German torpedoes sent dozens of ships, almost 400,000 tons of cargo, and hundreds of sailors to the bottom of the Atlantic.

Captain Le Médec knew all about the threat posed by German U-boats. He understood, too, that even in ideal sea conditions his ship, which was rusting, in poor repair, and much slower than most merchant ships, was a sitting duck.

THE *MONT-BLANC* WAS a typical ocean-going cargo vessel in the early decades of the last century. She was a serviceable 325 feet from bow to stern—slightly longer than an American football field. However, at 3,121 gross tons, she was a minnow compared with the elite passenger liners that plied the waters between Europe and North America. The RMS *Olympic*, the sister ship of the RMS *Titanic*, was a prime example.

Three massive propellers powered the *Olympic* through the waves at a top speed of twenty-one knots—about twenty-five miles per hour. The *Mont-Blanc* crawled along at a relative snail's pace. Her three-cylinder, 247-nominal-horsepower "single-screw steam engine" cranked a solitary propeller. Going all out, even when she was shiny new, the ship could only have reached eleven knots—a little under thirteen miles per hour—"in ballast," as old salts say when describing a ship that is sailing with empty cargo holds.

Launched in June 1899 at the Raylton Dixon & Company shipyards in Middlesbrough, England, the *Mont-Blanc* was a for-hire "tramper," a packhorse of the sea that carried goods and passengers for money. Yet she was built "to Lloyd's [Register] highest class," a complex set of standards that had as much to do with pegging the level of insurance premiums a ship's owner paid as they did with the quality of the vessel's construction.

In her first year afloat, the *Mont-Blanc* was owned by the Société Générale des Transports Maritimes à Vapeur shipping line. As such, she travelled between Marseille, on France's Mediterranean coast, and sundry ports of call in Brazil and Argentina. However, owing to the ever-shifting financial tides of maritime commerce, title to the *Mont-Blanc* passed through various hands. By 1906, the ship had seen too much hard use, hauling bulk shipments of ore. Her centime-pinching French owner was intent only on wringing as much profit as possible from his investment. Thus, he scrimped on upkeep and maintenance, with predictable effect. After just seven years in service, the *Mont-Blanc*'s glory days were already in her wake. She was old before her time.

THE SS *MONT-BLANC* IN THE PORT OF MARSEILLE PRIOR TO HER MAIDEN VOYAGE ON
SEPTEMBER 23, 1899. (COURTESY OF M. ALAIN CROCE)

IN DECEMBER 1915, the Compagnie Générale Transatlantique (CGT)—popularly known as "the French Line"—purchased the *Mont-Blanc*. As the French government's preferred carrier, CGT ships hauled mail and provided other public services. When the *Mont-Blanc* joined the CGT fleet, it was a given that she would serve the needs of France. With that in mind, the new owners sent the ship into dry dock for the repairs and updating she needed to ensure her continued seaworthiness. As one observer noted, the *Mont-Blanc* had been "pushed to the very limits of safety and sea-worthiness."[1]

The ship had undergone a facelift, a refit, at Bordeaux in September 1917. Workers there had serviced the engine and carried out other essential upgrades. In addition, the workers had painted the *Mont-Blanc* a sombre camouflage-grey and had fitted her with two cannons—a 90-mm one on the foredeck, another astern. There was room on deck to store a few shells for each weapon, "ready to be fired in case of necessity," as Aimé Le Médec noted.[2] The rest of the ammunition, 300 rounds, was stowed below-decks; if the ship's gunner needed shells, someone ran to fetch them.

Deck guns had become standard additions to Allied merchant ships in World War I. The crews were under orders to shoot it out with any German U-boat that was bold enough to surface before launching its attack; that had happened often in the early months of the war. Not so much by December 1917. Regardless, the *Mont-Blanc's* armaments added an element of military muscle to her profile. The weaponry was intended to deter an enemy attack rather than to defend against one.

IN THE SUMMER OF 1914, the CGT fleet had included just twenty-five vessels. When, on July 28, the opening salvos of "the War to End All Wars" shattered the peace in Europe, the French government decreed that henceforth all large French cargo ships were under the direction of the French Admiralty and were subject to military orders. The navy did not commandeer them; instead, it mobilized the officers of the country's merchant marine, drafting the vessels into the French naval reserve. No ship sails without a master and officers.

CGT captains were told what cargoes their ships would carry, when they would carry them, and to what ports of call. "I was then under the orders of the French government," said Aimé Le Médec.[3]

Even after her refit, when carrying a full load of cargo the *Mont-Blanc's* top speed was a glacial eight to eight and a half knots. That being so, she had been fortunate to survive the first three years of the war unscathed. However, by late 1917, with the German navy expanding the range and intensity of its U-boat campaign, the chances of a lumbering vessel such as the *Mont-Blanc* falling victim to a torpedo had increased dramatically. In the autumn of 1917, she had defied the odds yet again to make an incident-free, but nerve-racking, passage from Bordeaux to America. The

Mont-Blanc had been carrying just a few crates of machine parts when she arrived in New York City on November 9[4] after being at sea for three weeks and enduring the bone-numbing cold of the North Atlantic.

As was generally the case when a tramp steamer delivered her load, the captain and crew had no idea where their next assignment would take them or what their ship's next cargo would be. Such matters were for the shipping company's local agent to arrange. It was the agent's job to represent the vessel's owner in customer dealings. In the case of the CGT line in 1917, the customer was invariably the French military.

In New York City, Captain Le Médec's orders were to proceed to the CGT's Hudson River pier, at the foot of West 14th Street. There, he was to take on another small load of machinery parts and then wait for further instructions. The *Mont-Blanc*'s crew members were fine with that. Once the men had finished their daily tasks, they had some time to explore the streets of New York City and savour the earthy pleasures that sailors on the prowl seek out. Meanwhile, Captain Le Médec could only cool his heels and wonder about his next assignment. When finally he learned what it was, he had cause for concern.

TWICE DURING THE *MONT-BLANC*'s three-week stay in New York City, Le Médec and Edward Flower, the assistant maritime inspector in the French government's office and the CGT's local agent, visited the offices of the British Admiralty. There the two men met with Commander Odiarne Coates, the senior Royal Navy (RN) officer in New York who was the port's convoy officer. The forty-nine-year-old Coates had retired in 1913 after a twenty-nine-year naval career, but like many other RN veterans, he had returned to duty when the war began.[5] It was Coates' job to see to it that the *Mont-Blanc* was included in a naval convoy for her return voyage to Bordeaux. Flower served as the interpreter in conversations between Coates and Le Médec, whose grasp of English was iffy at best.

When the commander queried the Frenchman about his ship's technical specifications and nautical capabilities, Le Médec was chagrinned. "*Je ne sais pas*," he said repeatedly. "I don't know."

That was true. The voyage from Bordeaux had been his first aboard the *Mont-Blanc*. After signing on with the CGT in 1906 as a second officer, it had taken him a decade to work his way up to become a captain. Le Médec had persisted. Being just five feet, three inches tall and a shade over 125 pounds, he was used to big challenges, both in the physical environment of the sea and in life. However, whatever the captain lacked in physical stature, he more than made up for with his courage and strength of character.

Back home in France, members of the Le Médec family knew their Aimé as a man of steely determination with a nimble, inquisitive mind. He was detail-oriented and when at sea insisted on doing things "by the book." At home, he was more relaxed and easygoing. Le Médec collected souvenirs of his voyages to exotic ports of call—artifacts such as spears, native masks, and baubles—and decorated his house with them.

Although Le Médec was Roman Catholic, he was not especially devout; like many mariners, the captain's peripatetic ways and myriad responsibilities when he was away at sea made it difficult, if not impossible, for him to attend church with any degree of regularity.

On occasion, Aimé Le Médec could be as personable as a saloon-keeper. However, most of the time, he was reserved and even aloof. The personnel file his employer kept on him in their Paris offices noted he was "of a serious and modest character with remarkable qualities as an active and conscientious officer."[6] There was no arguing that, yet some who knew and worked with Le Médec had a different opinion of him. It was less favourable. He was "a competent, rather than a brilliant sailor," said one, adding that the captain was "a likeable, but moody man."[7]

Le Médec was dark-haired and bushy-browed, and his eyes flashed when he felt animated; a newspaper journalist would describe him as having "a broad forehead over snapping dark eyes." In quiet moments, the captain's face hinted at a world-weariness that perhaps was the product of too many long, lonely days spent at sea.

BETWEEN VOYAGES, AIMÉ LE MÉDEC lived in the port town of Vannes, Brittany. There he shared a house with one of his sisters. Like her older brother, Marie Le Médec was unmarried, and she was a loner; the house she and Aimé shared was quiet. Anne-Marie Pocreau, a distant cousin, would recall making childhood visits to the Le Médec house with her parents. Pocreau and her brother preferred to play outside in the garden rather than spend time with the adults; it was not just children wanting to be free from parental supervision. "My brother told me that he was afraid of great-uncle Aimé," said Pocreau.[8] Given his occupation and temperament, it is not surprising that Captain Le Médec never married or that he did not relate well to youngsters—at least not where the offspring of his own extended family were concerned.

Apart from his diminutive stature, Le Médec's most noticeable aspect was his goatee. Full and bushy, the dark thicket of facial hair gave him a presence, an air of authority. When he donned his single-breasted navy-blue captain's jacket, he looked every bit like a Hollywood casting director's notion of a WWI-era French sea captain.

Born December 8, 1878, Aimé Le Médec hailed from the seaside village of Pénerf, Morbihan, in Brittany. This historic French province, distinctive owing to its cultural isolation, is renowned for its jagged, rock-strewn coast, perilous inlets, and unforgiving waters. The briny tang of the sea pervades the landscape and imbues the light there with a gentle luminescence. The abundance of oysters, mussels, sardines, and other fish in Brittany's offshore waters has always been a powerful draw for fishermen and mariners.

With its roots in the Morbihan area, the Le Médec family had a long nautical history. Many generations of the clan had wrung a living from the sea. So it was natural that young Aimé Le Médec would take after his *père* and *grand-père* and become a mariner. He was the third of six children—and the eldest son—of Marie Françoise (Pocreau) and Aimé Vincent Le Médec.[9] The elder Aimé was an *haute personnalité*—"a somebody"—in Pénerf because he held a cabotage licence. This government-bestowed benefit gave him exclusive rights to transport passengers and cargo to small ports along the coast in the Pénerf area. Business was good, and the Le Médec family was relatively well off.

CAPTAIN AIMÉ LE MÉDEC, CIRCA 1915.
(COURTESY OF ANNE-MARIE POCREAU)

YOUNG AIMÉ WAS EIGHTEEN when he went off to sea. Ships and the world of maritime commerce would become his life. Le Médec was a seasoned mariner with salt water in his veins and an insatiable wanderlust in his heart by the age of twenty-eight, when he passed his captaincy examinations and took command of the CGT passenger/cargo ship SS *Antilles*. That vessel, launched in 1903, was the product of the shipyard at Saint-Nazaire, France, the historic seaport at the mouth of the Loire River that also was Le Médec's homeport (and, coincidentally, that of the SS *Mont-Blanc*, although in 1916 Le Médec as yet had no tie to the ship).

Like many shipping lines, the CGT routinely rotated the captains of the vessels in its fleet. Thus it was that in early 1917, Aimé Le Médec took charge of another ship. The SS *Abd el-Kader* was an aging passenger/cargo ship out of Marseilles.

The *Abd el-Kader*, the *Antilles*, and the *Mont-Blanc* were all textbook examples of "three-island" ship construction. Each had a forecastle, a main deck, and a poop deck. This basic, cookie-cutter design enabled shipyards to turn out vessels economically and quickly. The architecture was common in tramp steamers of the day. That was where any comparisons of the three ships ended.

Both the *Antilles* and the *Abd el-Kader* had been better maintained than the *Mont-Blanc* and were faster ships. The *Mont-Blanc*'s sluggishness made her an unfortunate—and unlikely—choice to transport the cargo the French government ordered her to deliver to France in December 1917. Edward Flower's boss in the French government's New York offices made that decision. Once the chief of maritime transportation issued orders, it was Flower's job to carry them out. This he did without question. Flower arranged the details of the *Mont-Blanc*'s task of transporting its assigned cargo. He insisted that like Captain Le Médec, he was duty bound to accept whatever assignment came his way. This had been his situation for three years, ever since the start of the war. By 1917, the needs of the French army were dire—so much so that Edward Flower was dispatching from New York to France as many as four merchant ships each week, all laden with American-manufactured munitions.

Not surprisingly, Flower did not consult with Le Médec about the decision to have the *Mont-Blanc* transport explosives. The captain's first inkling of the cargo his ship would carry on the return voyage to France came when shipwrights came on board. The men spent a couple of days building wooden partitions in the *Mont-Blanc*'s cargo holds. The resulting compartments, Le Médec learned, were intended to hold dangerous cargo.

"It's explosives, I'm afraid, on this trip," Flower admitted. "And a rather large shipment."

The *Mont-Blanc* ordinarily would never have been called upon to carry such a volatile load, the agent explained. "But we're short of ships, and so we have no choice." [10]

Flower's explanation did nothing to quell Aimé Le Médec's unease. He had never transported explosives before and was fearful of doing so. It would turn out that the captain had ample reason to worry.

CHAPTER 2

I t was a job with serious risks. The loading of the *Mont-Blanc*'s cargo—
almost 3,000 tons of munitions worth an estimated $3 million (U.S.)—
took place at Gravesend Bay in Brooklyn. Fearful of German sabotage or
accidents, local military and government officials had decreed this the
only spot in New York harbour where workers could do this hazardous
labour. Apprehensive residents of the adjacent Bath Beach neighbourhood
who peered out their windows each day saw bobbing in the harbour "a
fleet of dingy nondescript vessels at anchor," as one observer put it.[1]

Often there were as many as six ships waiting to be loaded with cargoes
of munitions bound for the battlefields of Western Europe. The threat of
German sabotage being a constant concern, government inspectors and
armed police restricted access to these vessels and kept an eye on loading
operations. Overseers from the munitions manufacturers supervised both
the lightermen who delivered the cargo to the ships and the stevedores who
actually did the heavy lifting. "In strongly bound cases, each one as carefully constructed as a high-grade storage chest, the [cargo] is lifted about as

gingerly as if the stevedores were afraid of scratching the varnish," a writer for the *Brooklyn Daily Eagle* reported.[2]

The cargo containers used aboard the *Mont-Blanc* when loading began were new. The shipwrights who had come on board a few days earlier to construct them had used dunnage lumber and copper nails, which were less likely to spark as they were being hammered into place. The incongruously dainty footwear worn by the burly stevedores who were doing the loading also underscored the perils of the operation and of the cargo the *Mont-Blanc* would carry. The linen bags the men wore on their feet were a further precaution taken to lessen the danger of hobnails in the soles of the men's boots causing sparks on the ship's metal deck. Hard experience had repeatedly proven that sparks and explosives are a bad mix.

While workers were busy stowing the *Mont-Blanc*'s volatile cargo, a red swallowtail pennant, an internationally recognized symbol that explosives were being handled on board, fluttered in the breeze atop the ship's yard-arm, where it was highly visible. Captain Aimé Le Médec had tasked Jean Glotin, his first officer, with observing the loading operation; afterward, when Glotin recalled the details of what he had seen, Le Médec listened with growing bewilderment. The stevedores had packed the ship's four cargo holds, and a like number of 'tween deck holds, with thousands of crates filled with an alarming variety of high explosives. According to the *Manifest de Frêt*—the freight manifest—the *Mont-Blanc*'s cargo included 5,000 kegs and cases of TNT, 682 cases of gun cotton, 12,000 kegs of dry picric acid, and 9,830 barrels of the wet variety.[3] Le Médec, having no experience transporting munitions, was understandably fearful.

DESPITE THE BLOODLETTING proficiency of the armies that were battling it out on the Western Front in Europe, the reality was that in 1917 munitions science was still in its infancy.[4] It had been just a half century since Swedish chemist Alfred Nobel invented dynamite. The ingenious

Nobel held 355 patents, but it was the one for dynamite that revolution-ized warfare. Other researchers adapted the industrial explosive for mili-tary use, and Nobel suddenly became very famous, very rich, and very disillusioned.

When he realized what a Pandora's box of death and destruction he had opened and that there was no closing the lid again, Nobel was dis-mayed beyond measure. In hopes of redeeming himself, in his will he directed that his fortune be used to fund a series of prizes that would fur-ther the cause of international peace and understanding—the Nobel Prizes.

During his lifetime (1833–1896), Nobel's lamentations about the destructiveness of high explosives had little effect; the quest to create ever more lethal and ingenious military munitions continued apace. In the 1880s, French chemists figured out how to use picric acid as a high explo-sive in artillery shells. Prior to this, the main use for this odourless yellow powder had been as a commercial dye and an antiseptic.

Once a munitions maker processed picric acid and turned it into an explosive, the compound was problematic to handle or store. Kept wet, picric acid was relatively safe to work with, although it was so corrosive that it had to be stored in wooden barrels. As a result, it was illegal to include picric acid in regular cargo shipments within the United States. It was only because the *Mont-Blanc* was a French ship and was sailing in international waters that American officials were unconcerned about what it was carry-ing. Captain Le Médec was not nearly as blasé. No less problematic from his standpoint were those thousands of cases and kegs of trinitrotoluene (TNT) and hundreds of cases of gun cotton in the holds of his ship.

The original use for TNT, like picric acid, was as a commercial dye. It was German chemists in 1902 who devised ways to use it militarily. TNT-filled shells explode after contact; that is, after they have penetrated a ship's or vehicle's protective armour. This produces maximum damage and loss of life.

As its name suggests, gun cotton is cotton fibre that has soaked in a bath of volatile chemicals. Scientists developed a technique for mashing this explosive concoction into a relatively stable watery pulp that workers could safely handle. Scientific innovation knows no bounds.

WHEN THE LAST of the devil's cargo of munitions was finally stowed in the *Mont-Blanc*'s holds, the stevedores proceeded to add an exclamation point to their labours. The ship may have been full volume-wise, but the shipping agent calculated that the vessel could carry still more weight. Thus, in response to a last-minute request from the chief of maritime transportation in far-off Paris, Edward Flower had stevedores load some additional cargo: 494 barrels of benzol. This high-octane liquid, a by-product of the process that turns coal into coke, is a component in the production of motor fuel and picric acid. Highly flammable, benzol boils at a mere 176 degrees Fahrenheit (80 degrees Celsius), and it reeks strongly of petroleum. And danger.

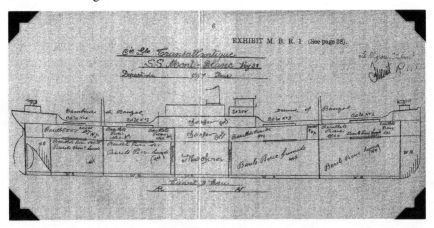

THIS SKETCH BY CAPTAIN LE MÉDEC SHOWS HOW THE *MONT-BLANC*'S CARGO OF MUNITIONS WAS LOADED. (WRECK COMMISSION EXHIBIT MBR 1)

Residents of Bath Beach and other neighbourhoods who watched from afar the loading of the *Mont-Blanc* and other munitions ships were well aware of the dangers involved in handling and transporting benzol and other hazardous cargoes. So fearful of explosions were they that they had repeatedly petitioned the state government and local municipal officials to demand that the loading of munitions ships in Gravesend Bay be subject to ever more stringent conditions. In fact, across the harbour in New Jersey, a state legislative committee was holding public hearings on the same days the *Mont-Blanc* was taking on her perilous cargo. The residents' sense of urgency was understandable. After all, the memory of the traumatic events that had shaken New Jersey the year before were still fresh in people's minds.

Although the United States was still neutral at the time, on the night of July 30, 1916, two German agents had crept into the munitions depot at Black Tom Island in New Jersey. There the saboteurs had torched eighty-seven railway cars loaded with shells and ammunition destined for delivery to British and French armies in Western Europe. The resulting explosion was catastrophic. Seven people had died in the blast, which rattled windows as far as twenty-five miles away and created a seismic shock that registered 5.5 on the Richter scale. Government officials pegged the property losses at $20 million—including $100,000 in damages to the Statue of Liberty, more than a mile across the water from Black Tom Island.[5]

That incident sparked a heated debate in New Jersey and all across the country. Politicians, military officials, the media, and angry citizens began discussing ways to prevent similar disasters. With more than 130,000 German immigrants living in the area of New York City, paranoia was rampant. And the fear of sabotage took on renewed urgency in the United States after its April 1917 entry into the Great War. Officials in New Jersey responded to the Black Tom explosion by forbidding the storage of munitions in the state and by placing tight restrictions on shipping. However, the controls were more lax in neighbouring Brooklyn, just to the east across Lower New York Bay. That borough was home to Fort Hamilton, which was a major processing centre and embarkation point for American troops and war supplies headed overseas.

The Black Tom explosion was one of the first on American soil that police and intelligence officials blamed on German saboteurs. However, by no means was it the only homeland disaster involving munitions or war matériel. World War I was destined to become in many ways a watershed historical event. This was the first mass conflict in which mechanized bloodletting made destruction and carnage possible on a nightmarish, unprecedented scale. Here was a war planned by generals who came to their tasks with nineteenth-century minds, but who now had at their disposal twentieth-century weaponry of heretofore undreamed of destructive power. It is hardly surprising that horrific accidents happened when suppliers were manufacturing, shipping, or storing munitions and other volatile military supplies.

The *New York Times* reported that in 1916 alone there were thirteen munitions explosions in the United States. Another twelve occurred elsewhere in the world; among them were two massive explosions that happened in short succession and devastated the Russian port of Archangel,[6] and two much smaller blasts in Canada—one at a military base near Niagara Falls, the other at a Montreal munitions factory.[7]

ONCE THE DEADLY CARGO was loaded and the *Mont-Blanc* was ready to sail, Captain Le Médec and Flower paid another visit to the British Admiralty Office in New York City. As before, they met with the convoy officer, Commander Odiarne Coates. The three men discussed details of the arrangements for the *Mont-Blanc*'s possible inclusion in a convoy that with any luck would offer her at least some measure of protection on the voyage home to France.[8]

There were four North American assembly points for convoys bound for Great Britain, France, and other Allied ports in Europe: New York,

Hampton Roads in Virginia, and Sydney or Halifax in Nova Scotia. Naval officers in each port grouped ships according to the speed they could maintain; twelve knots generally was regarded as being the minimum acceptable speed for inclusion in a convoy. These nautical caravans typically consisted of about two dozen cargo ships and oil tankers sailing together while a British naval escort rode shotgun. Obsolete cruisers, armed merchant cruisers, and pre-dreadnought battleships usually served as escorts in midocean. Faster, better-armed, and more modern destroyers took over when the convoys entered the primary U-boat danger zone, which was in the waters around the British Isles.

The use of convoys proved to be highly effective in thwarting U-boat attacks. By late 1917, with the convoy system fully in place, the loss of Allied ships travelling in a typical convoy dropped to ten per cent of the number of ships that fell victim to enemy attack while sailing solo. Knowing this, Captain Aimé Le Médec was understandably eager to finalize arrangements for the *Mont-Blanc* to hook on with a convoy. However, he had a problem. A big one.

Any convoy could travel only as quickly as its slowest ship. With a top speed of less than twelve knots, the *Mont-Blanc* was dead weight. When Commander Coates asked Flower for Le Médec's best "guesstimate" of how fast his fully loaded ship could go, the Frenchman fidgeted nervously. No one had bothered to consult with Le Médec when the stevedores were loading his ship. Now that he was being asked for comment, he speculated the *Mont-Blanc* would be hard pressed to make eight knots on "a good day." Hearing this, Coates stroked his beard and asked if Le Médec thought his ship could somehow make 200 miles per day; maintaining that pace would enable the *Mont-Blanc* to complete the 3,600-mile journey to Bordeaux in about eighteen days.

Captain Le Médec nodded slowly. "I think we could do that in fine weather," he agreed, although in truth, he had to wonder.

"Then I'll have to see about that," Coates replied. With the *Mont-Blanc* paperwork in hand, he rose from his desk and went to confer with his commanding officer, Commodore E.J. Wells.

When Coates returned several minutes later, he was frowning. Looking Le Médec in the eye he announced, "Captain, you shall proceed to Halifax for convoy." Coates then went on to explain that if naval officers there decided the *Mont-Blanc* was too slow to be part of the next Europe-bound convoy, Captain Le Médec would have no choice but to travel solo. In that event, he would receive a sealed envelope that would contain a letter providing the secret details of the route he should follow across the Atlantic.

This was not what Le Médec wanted or hoped to hear, and although he was dismayed, as Flower would later explain, the captain "had been given his orders, and had no choice but to comply."[9]

THE SS *MONT-BLANC* weighed anchor on the night of December 1, 1917, steaming out of Gravesend Bay on the high tide. It was a few minutes after 11:00 p.m. Standing on Captain Le Médec's right on the ship's open-air bridge was First Officer Jean-Baptiste Glotin, who shared his captain's unease about the voyage ahead. To Le Médec's left was the local harbour pilot who had come on board to guide the ship out of New York harbour, the busiest on the east coast of North America and one of the busiest in the world.

The waters of Lower New York Bay are notoriously shallow, the currents treacherous. For the captain of any visiting ship, the port loomed as an accident-rife cauldron of shoals and nautical traffic. Ocean liners large and small, cargo carriers, navy ships, and all type and manner of lesser ships—ferries, fishing boats, and scows—came and went at all hours of the day and night. New York was, and still is, the city that never sleeps.

By necessity, a stop in the port for any ocean-going ship involved interaction with New York's legendary harbour pilots. These men worked as freelancers, on a fee-for-service basis, and they expected a generous tip. With that in mind, their appearance was an integral aspect of the service they provided. New York harbour pilots took pride in their work, and they dressed accordingly. The pilot who was on board the *Mont-Blanc* on this Saturday night—like the one who had guided the ship into the harbour three weeks earlier—was smartly attired in a black frock coat, matching silk hat, and white gloves; he would not have looked out of place in the ballroom at one of the city's many posh hotels.

Aimé Le Médec might well have smiled at the absurdities of the situation had there not been more pressing matters on his mind. He knew just enough *anglais* to grasp the essence of what the harbour pilot was telling him in that distinctive New York honk. Once he had deciphered the man's words, Le Médec relayed their essence to his second officer. Joseph Leveque stood with his gloved hand resting on the handle of the ship's telegraph, the device that relays a captain's orders from the bridge to the engine room, down in the ship's clattering, sweaty bowels.

Inside the *Mont-Blanc's* wheelhouse, helmsman Alphonse Serré strained to see in the darkness; a tiny light that glowed dimly illuminated the ship's compass in its brass housing. Serré peered out the wheelhouse window. To his eyes, Captain Le Médec, Leveque, and the New York harbour pilot were shadowy figures; all three men stood with their backs to him. Periodically, Le Médec reacted to the pilot's instructions by turning to peer into the wheelhouse window. He barked his instructions, emphasizing them with nods of his head or hand gestures that underscored the direction in which Serré should steer the ship.

Captain Le Médec, who had been in command of the *Mont-Blanc* for less than two months, had gotten off to a rough start with the ship's officers and crew by insisting on tight discipline and doing things "by the book." However, Le Médec had earned the crew's begrudging respect, and they had come to trust him. Alphonse Serré listened carefully and followed his captain's orders to the letter.

AS GRAVESEND BAY receded in the *Mont-Blanc*'s foamy wake, off to the ship's starboard side, Aimé Le Médec and his crew could see the glow from the lights of New York; the big city was fourteen miles northwest as the gull flies. There was no wartime blackout in effect there.

To the *Mont-Blanc*'s port side was the beam issuing from Norton's Point light, perched on the western tip of Coney Island. Responding to the harbour pilot's directions, Le Médec ordered Serré to starboard the *Mont-Blanc*'s helm, turning the ship south into the deeper waters of Ambrose Channel, the main shipping lane into and out of the ports of New York and New Jersey.[10]

The air temperature on this December night was a few degrees above freezing. Le Médec turned up the collar of his greatcoat and pulled his captain's hat snug atop his head. A westerly wind that was blowing out from the New Jersey shore sharpened the nip of a raw wintery chill in the air. Frothy swells were rolling eastward across the waters of Lower New York Bay, out toward the black expanse of the open ocean. This same atmospheric turbulence had scattered lead-coloured clouds that for much of the day had pelted the city with icy rain.

Once the New York harbour pilot had collected his fee—and his tip— he shook Captain Le Médec's hand and wished him good luck before he disembarked at the Ambrose Channel lightship. The *Mont-Blanc* then continued seaward under a night sky that was infinitely vast, clear, and black, save for the canopy of stars. The heavens were almost as deep and unfathomable as Aimé Le Médec's mood on this night.

As he contemplated the voyage ahead, the captain craved a cigarette. However, he dared not light one, not tonight and not tomorrow. Never on this voyage. The pungent, toxic odour emanating from the barrels of benzol that were stacked two deep on the deck served as a constant reminder of the hazardous cargo the *Mont-Blanc* was carrying.

Le Médec thrust his hands even deeper into his coat pockets. Beneath his feet, the thrumming of the *Mont-Blanc*'s engines was strong and steady. It was familiar and it was comforting. Staring into the darkness ahead there was nothing for the captain to see, nothing other than the cold, merciless expanse of the Atlantic Ocean. The first leg of the *Mont-Blanc*'s homeward voyage to Bordeaux was the passage to Halifax, a port the captain had never visited but was now most eager to reach.

Ordinarily, he'd have charted a course that would have kept his ship well clear of Cape Cod. In peacetime, the *Mont-Blanc* would have proceeded northeast by east, at about seventy-five degrees magnetic, before making the necessary turn northward toward Halifax. However, with his ship riding low in the water, down to her Plimsoll line—the mark painted on the hull to indicate the maximum depth to which the vessel can be safely immersed when carrying a full load of cargo—Le Médec was uneasy. He feared bad weather lay ahead. The New York harbour pilot had cautioned him as much, and his own mariner's instincts told him this was indeed the case. Not wanting to take any chances, given the nature of the ship's cargo and her slow speed, Le Médec intended to play it safe.

Hoping to avoid heavy seas and any prowling German U-boats, he reasoned it would be prudent to hug the coastline from Newport, Rhode Island, north to Bar Harbor, Maine. From there, Le Médec knew he had no option but to cross the 100 miles of ocean at the mouth of the Bay of Fundy. Once the *Mont-Blanc* reached the southern tip of Nova Scotia, it was only a half day's sailing to Halifax, with its deep, safe harbour. Once there, Le Médec desperately hoped the *Mont-Blanc* would succeed in qualifying to join an Allied convoy for what, one way or another, promised to be a perilous trans-Atlantic voyage home.

CHAPTER 3

WARDEN OF THE NORTH

Halifax, Nova Scotia, December 3, 1917

The SS *Mont-Blanc* battled heavy seas and gale-force winds on her 850-mile journey northward to Halifax. Meanwhile, the weather was fair and the temperatures mild as the Norwegian-registered ship SS *Imo* was arriving in the Nova Scotian port city.

Captain Haakon From of the *Imo* and Aimé Le Médec of the *Mont-Blanc* had never met and were utterly unaware of each other's existence. It is unlikely that their paths would ever have crossed, even in peaceful times.

As the *Imo* steamed into the Halifax harbour and dropped anchor on the west side of Bedford Basin, never in his wildest dreams—or nightmares—could Captain Haakon From have envisioned what fate held in store for him and his thirty-nine crewmen; the captain had other matters on his mind on this day. Time was of the essence to him. Bound for New York City from the Dutch port of Rotterdam, From and his ship were making a hasty stop in Halifax.

This historic Nova Scotia seaport, established by the British in 1749 and named in honour of the second Earl of Halifax, had provided a counterbalance to the influence and military power of the French fort at nearby Louisbourg. The Royal Navy officers who chose the site of the Halifax settlement chose well. The harbour is renowned as being one of the world's finest. On a map, it resembles "a lopsided keyhole,"[1] the bottom of which, the harbour's entrance, emerged eons ago when the massive forces that heaved the Earth's tectonic plates threw up that knobby chunk of land that is Halifax Peninsula, five miles long and two miles across at its widest point. Those same forces of nature created McNabs Island, a rocky drumlin at the harbour entrance that was destined to serve as the anchor for a network of forts and gun emplacements. The British erected these fortifications to safeguard the eleven-mile channel that leads to Halifax's inner harbour. That passageway, situated on a southeast-to-northwest axis, passes through a bottleneck called the Narrows. At its most constricted, the gap here is less than 600 yards wide. The city of Halifax—the "Warden of the North," as historian Thomas Raddall dubbed it—grew up on the western side of the Narrows.[2] To the east is the neighbouring city of Dartmouth, smaller and less populated.

The Halifax Peninsula's gently rising hills surround the port's sheltered inner harbour; the Bedford Basin anchorage area is five miles long, three miles wide. Halifax Peninsula is an appendage of the larger Chebucto Peninsula, and in the tongue of the Mi'kmaq people, who inhabited this area for thousands of years before the arrival of Europeans, it is called Chebucto or *Jipugtug*, "the big harbour." Similarly, the French dubbed it *La Baie Saine*, "the Safe Bay."

The *Imo* had already visited Halifax twice in 1917. On this third call, Captain From planned to take on food and fuel while checking in with the British naval officials. Examining officers from the Royal Canadian Navy and Canadian customs agents in Halifax inspected ships from all neutral countries—the Norwegian-registered *Imo* being one of them—that carried cargoes into or out of the European war zone. Until 1916, in keeping with the British naval blockade that was starving the German enemy into submission, the Royal Navy inspected neutral ships at British ports; however, with Germany's U-boat campaign intensifying, the North Sea had become an increasingly dangerous place for ships of all nations. By 1917, the Kaiser's submarines were sinking three merchant marine vessels each day on average, and so the captains of vessels from most non-combatant countries refused to enter the submarine danger zone around the British Isles. Examining officers began doing their inspections on the other side of the Atlantic, in the port of Halifax.

MOST OF THE *IMO*'s crew were Norwegians; a few Swedes and some Danes completed its complement. That being so, while the ship was docked in Halifax, the men—being citizens of "non-combatant nations"— were forbidden from leaving their ship or even communicating with people on shore. There was one small compensation: harbour regulations allowed alcohol on the ships of neutral nations. However, drinking, playing cards, and carving scrimshaw can only hold a sailor's attention for so long. The temptation was strong to break the rules and sneak ashore for a few hours of libidinous adventures. The wartime economic boom that brought prosperity to Halifax also spawned a brisk market for vices and pleasures of the flesh.

A well-intentioned but ineffectual provincial law that had come into effect on July 1, 1916, banned the sale of alcohol in Halifax. Despite this, back-alley speakeasies—and their low-class cousins, the "blind pigs"— were a popular attraction for thirsty locals and for the throngs of visiting sailors who came ashore looking for a good time. Located on the waterfront streets between the harbour and Citadel Hill, the 200-foot rise atop which sits Fort George, the port's original fortifications, these establishments did a roaring business. Business was no less brisk at Halifax's many houses of ill repute. "Brothels blossomed through the old quarter and along Water Street [near the harbour]," one observer noted, "like buds in spring."[3]

Despite the chafing restrictions that hung over them, the men of the *Imo*'s crew welcomed any respite they could enjoy in Halifax. The twelve-day crossing from Europe had been onerous; being on the North Atlantic in late autumn is always a challenge, and no more so than when a ship is sailing in ballast, as the *Imo* had done on this voyage. Adding to the crew's unease was the knowledge that Haakon From was not a patient man. Mind you, on this voyage—like others he had made in recent months—the captain had good reason to be in a rush. People were depending on him, and many lives hung in the balance.

The Commission for Relief in Belgium (CRB), an American-driven philanthropic agency that was doing vital humanitarian work, had chartered the *Imo* to deliver emergency shipments of food to war-ravaged Belgium and northern France. The British naval blockade that had put a chokehold on the German enemy was having an unintended and unexpected impact. With food in desperately short supply back home, the million-man German army was feeding itself by confiscating essentials from the people in occupied lands. This made for especially bleak conditions in Belgium.

Walter Hines Page, the American ambassador to Great Britain, sprang to the rescue, convincing both sides in the war to allow monthly essential food shipments into Belgium. The CRB, headed by Iowa-born mining-engineer-turned-philanthropist Herbert Hoover, began overseeing the food deliveries. The man who was destined to become the thirty-first president of the United States was a Quaker by faith, a born organizer by temperament, and a staunch American patriot by conviction. His involvement in the Belgian relief effort would prove life-altering for Hoover; it marked the end of his engineering career by starting him on what he described as "the slippery road of public life."[4] That same road would lead him to pursue a political career that culminated in his 1928 election to the White House.

Finding the $11 million per month it took to pay for food shipments was a daunting challenge for Hoover; starving Belgians were devouring 78,000 tons of wheat, rice, corn, and peas each month. Most of the money for relief shipments came from friendly neutral governments, philanthropic agencies, and a few wealthy individuals; Hoover personally underwrote some of the costs.

No less a problem was the logistics of arranging deliveries of the food shipments to the CRB's Belgian partner, the Comité National de Secours et d'Alimentation. The British would allow only vessels from neutral nations to penetrate their naval blockade. That was why the CRB chartered a dozen ships; one of them was the *Imo*, which was part of the Norway-based South Pacific Whaling Company's fleet. The *Imo*'s forty-seven-year-old Norwegian-born master, Haakon From, was an experienced sea captain and a man of steely Nordic determination who never backed down from a challenge.

THE FROM FAMILY ORIGINALLY were farmers. In Viking times—in the ninth and tenth centuries—they lived in a settlement called Fraun; the place name means "fertile" in Old Norse. Over time, Fraun morphed into "From" (which rhymes with "roam"). It was from this place that the Froms derived their surname. Fraun (or From) is not to be found on any map of modern Norway; the settlement has long since been subsumed as part of the history-laden town of Sandefjord. Located seventy miles south of Oslo, at the southwestern entrance to the Oslofjord inlet, Sandefjord is renowned for its Viking heritage, the popularity of its sulphur springs health spa, and its ties to the whaling industry. In the last half of the nineteenth century and early decades of the twentieth, the whaling revenue made Sandefjord the richest city in Norway.

It was in Sandefjord that Haakon From was born on July 16, 1870. He was the third of eight children—and the second of three sons—born to Anna Barthea (Schrøder) and Hans Kristian Kristofferson From.[5] Anna, the daughter of a ship owner and sea captain, was a homemaker, while Hans was a middle school teacher. Staunchly religious and an avowed teetotaller, he also served as the sexton of the local Lutheran church and was prominent in his community.[6] The Froms were aristocratic in temperament and lifestyle; books, music, and art filled the family home. Indeed, Hans Kristian From's erudition was reflected in the names he and his wife, Anna, chose for their sons. In celebration of their Nordic heritage, the Froms named their eldest boy Ragnvald, after the legendary king of Vestfold, the area in which Sandefjord is located. Their youngest son—who would become a celebrated professional artist—was named Einar, after the undying warriors of Norse mythology. Haakon was a favoured name of Norwegian kings from the thirteenth century onward.

While the details of young Haakon's early life are unclear, we do know he followed a predictable career path. Sandefjord being one of Norway's busiest seaports, there were always jobs for able-bodied young men in the whaling industry or in the merchant marine. Haakon From was able-bodied, and he was bright and determined to succeed in life. In March 1888, he signed on as a crew member of the Sandefjord-based bark *Craigotton*. Four months shy of his eighteenth birthday, Haakon From sailed out of Sandefjord on his first of many trans-Atlantic voyages.[7]

The young man's rise through the ranks of the merchant marine was steady. In 1894 he won appointment as a first mate, and the following year he became captain of the bark *Vidfarne*, an aging wind-powered cargo ship. It was a respectable position for a thirty-four-year-old mariner, one that From could have settled into. However, in the autumn of 1896, he changed tack in his career, signing on as the second mate aboard the steam-powered Danish cargo ship SS *Botnia*. Career-wise it was a step backward, but From had evidently decided that steam-powered ships were the way of the future. If appearances are any indication, it is also clear that he was convinced his maritime career was on an upward trajectory.

A STUDIO PHOTOGRAPH of Haakon From and his two brothers, probably taken in the early years of the last century, depicts three stylishly—and formally—dressed young Norwegian gentlemen. All three are clean-shaven and all display the same prominent nose and protruding ears as their father does in photographs. The From brothers' lips are full—like their mother's. Their eyes are attentive and focused.

Eldest brother Ragnvald wears a top hat and greatcoat. He stands stiff and proud as a mannequin, his right hand tucked inside the breast of his coat, à la Napoleon Bonaparte.

Einar, the youngest of the From brothers, sports morning garb—a snappy double-breasted greatcoat and striped trousers; a bowler hat is perched atop his head, and on his hands are black kid-leather gloves.

Haakon, of slighter build than his brothers, seats himself on the end of an ornate deacon's bench. Smartly outfitted in his merchant marine uniform, he sports a white dress tie. A peaked mate's cap rests at a jaunty angle. Haakon gazes directly at the camera lens. He is the very picture of a young man filled with self-confidence and youthful swagger.

By the time he was twenty-nine, From felt his prospects were sufficiently bright for him to take on the responsibilities of married life. In 1899, he wed twenty-three-year-old Bertha Finsen, the daughter of a sea captain—"Kitty" to her family and friends. The following February, the first of the couple's two daughters, Gudrun, was born; a second, Magnhild, would follow a year later, in 1901.[8]

From's maritime service record during this period includes a four-year gap, from 1905 to 1909. During this time, both his father and brother Ragnvald died, and it seems that Haakon remained at home in Sandefjord. His occupation during this period is not known. However, while From was not wealthy enough to purchase his own home—census records show that he and his family lived in a rented flat[9]—he and his wife employed a young woman as a servant.

THE FROM BROTHERS—RAGNVALD AT BACK, EINAR ON THE RIGHT, HAAKON ON THE LEFT—POSED FOR THIS STUDIO PHOTO CIRCA 1900. (COURTESY OF ARNE FROM)

From resumed his nautical career in 1910, and for the next seven years he served as captain of various Norwegian cargo and whaling ships that sailed the seven seas. Like Aimé Le Médec, Haakon From went wherever the next assignment took him. Such was the life of a captain in the merchant marine of the day.

IN MAY 1914 HAAKON FROM became master of the SS *Imo*, 430 feet long, 5,043 gross register tons (GRT). Powered by a triple-expansion steam engine, the *Imo* could travel at a top speed of twelve knots, roughly fourteen miles per hour.[10] The ship's original owners, the White Star Line, christened her the SS *Runic* when the Harland and Wolff shipyards in Belfast built her in 1889. That same shipyard had built the RMS *Titanic*, although this was not the *Runic*'s only historical tie to that legendary passenger liner. Captain Edward Smith, who in April 1912 was in command of the *Titanic* on her ill-fated maiden trans-Atlantic voyage, served as captain of the *Runic* for a few months in early 1891.

Smith was long gone from the ship by 1895, the year she was sold to the West India and Pacific Steam Ship Company and renamed the *Tampican*. Fast-forward two more owners and seventeen years to 1912,

THE SS *IMO*, CIRCA 1915. (COURTESY OF THE VESTFOLDMUSEENE IKS)

when the South Pacific Whaling Company purchased the ship for use as a whaling supply vessel and renamed her the *Imo*. And as mentioned earlier, she was one of the ships the Commission for Relief in Belgium hired in 1917 to deliver emergency food shipments to Belgium. It was in hopes of protecting the *Imo* from U-boat attack that the ship's crewmen painted the words "Belgian Relief" on each side of her hull in ten-foot-tall red letters on a white background.

The logbooks show that in 1917 the *Imo* made a couple of voyages, carrying shipments of grain from New York to ports in Europe. One of these trips in particular stands out, for it offers insights into Haakon From's personality and his at times feisty manner. Patience was not one of his virtues. The captain had strong opinions that he was not shy about voicing, and he could be a demanding taskmaster. In August 1917, nine of the *Imo*'s crew jumped ship in New York harbour. It seems that From's temper sometimes got him into trouble. That was certainly the case in Philadelphia during the first week of October 1917.

The *Imo* was visiting the City of Brotherly Love when Captain From had some repairs done on the ship's engine and boiler. The tab for this work, carried out over a ten-day period by Schmaal Engineering Works, came to $9,221. For reasons unknown, Haakon From refused to pay the bill. He was adamant about it when Gustav Schmaal and his lawyer, Willard M. Harris, boarded the ship to demand the money. Captain From repeated his refusal to pay and demanded that his unwanted visitors leave the ship. Frustrated by his recalcitrance, attorney Harris went ashore to file a statement of claim—"a libel and complaint" notice—at the local court office. In the attorney's absence, From invited the unsuspecting Schmaal into his captain's cabin for a chat; like many Norwegians, Haakon From spoke excellent English. However, at that moment, he was in no mood for conversation.

With no witnesses on hand, the captain pounced. "[He] acted like a maniac," the shipyard owner would recall. "[From] glared at me like a man out of his mind and snarled like a beast. Raising his big fists, he brought them down on my head, knocking me to the floor. Then, cursing horribly, he picked me up bodily and hurled me through the door of the cabin. As soon as I regained my feet, I ran for my life."[11]

Schmaal having fled, From promptly set sail. However, the *Imo* did not get far. Thirty miles down the Delaware River, attorney Willard Harris and a United States marshal were lying in wait for the *Imo* at the town of New Castle. When From ignored the marshal's demand to stop, Harris and the officer gave chase in a tugboat. With help from a Coast Guard patrol vessel, the two men boarded the *Imo* and served Captain From with legal papers ordering him to return to nearby Wilmington. The *Imo* remained tied up there—paying a $2,000 per day berthing fee— while lawyers tried to sort out the dispute over the Schmaal repair bill.

When the matter came before a judge of the U.S. District Court, the South Pacific Whaling Company was obliged to post an $11,000 bond before the *Imo* could leave Wilmington. Harris and the attorney representing the *Imo*'s owner eventually reached an out-of-court settlement; the details of the deal were not included in the documents Willard Harris filed with the court on May 4, 1918, to end the legal action against the *Imo*.[12]

There is no way to know what prompted Haakon From's refusal to pay the *Imo*'s repair bill or why he reacted so aggressively toward Gustav Schmaal. It may have been that the captain disputed the quality or the cost of the work. Or it may have been that From had taken a personal dislike to Schmaal, who was of German heritage. One of the attorneys who had represented From and the *Imo* in U.S. District Court told a journalist that the "*Imo*'s captain was intensely anti-German."[13] If that were so, there is a plausible reason for his refusal to pay his bill and for his antipathy to Schmaal. From may have felt his behaviour was "payback" for German wrongs done to Norway, especially the shipping industry. Norwegian sailors were proud to sail under their country's national flag.

Norway, a proud seafaring nation, remained neutral during the Great War. Yet in the first three years of the conflict, the country lost more ships to German mines and torpedoes than did any other non-combatant. If the data recorded by the British military are correct, between August 8, 1914, and April 26, 1917, German U-boats and mines sank 436 Norwegian merchant marine vessels, resulting in the deaths of more than 1,100 Norwegian sailors.[14] "The magnitude of the injustice paralyzes the judgment," a British observer noted. Indeed, that seems to have been the case. It was also likely that at least a few of the Norwegian ships that had fallen victim to German attacks belonged to the South Pacific Whaling Company, the *Imo*'s owner. No less likely is that Haakon From personally knew—and had friends among—many of the men who had gone down with their ships. If so, that may well have helped fuel his antipathy to Germans and eagerness to get on with the work of delivering emergency food shipments to the hungry people of Belgium and France. There can be no doubt that the captain was impatient to do so. From's hastiness was in some measure responsible for the tragedy that would play itself out and cost so many lives in Halifax.

CHAPTER 4

Halifax, Nova Scotia, December 5, 1917, Late Afternoon

The *Imo*'s crew members were rested and ready to sail for New York after their Halifax layover. Fresh supplies were on board, and Captain Haakon From was impatient to be on his way. However, two small tasks remained before the *Imo* could depart: the ship needed to receive the mandatory clearances from naval and customs officials, and she would have to take on fifty tons of steam coal to fuel her boilers for the passage to New York.

It was a few minutes after noon on a bright sun-splashed Wednesday as the tugboat chartered by George Smith from Pickford & Black, the South Pacific Whaling Company's local agent, pulled alongside the *Imo*. Smith was there to ferry Haakon From over to the Canadian warship HMCS *Niobe*. There the Norwegian master could pick up the official papers he needed before he could leave Halifax.

With the weather being fair and unseasonably mild, conditions on the water were almost ideal for this time of year. As a result, the harbour was abuzz with traffic. The area around *Niobe* was thick with boats coming and going, tooting and whistling. Because time was money to a busy shipping agent, George Smith frowned at the prospect of the anticipated delay in dropping off Captain From at *Niobe*. Smith had pressing business to deal with, and so to save time, he went to the Pickford & Black wharf, while the *Imo*'s captain cabbed it over to *Niobe*'s berth at Pier 4 in the north end of the Naval Dockyard.

The British government had presented the aging 11,000-ton, 450-foot battle cruiser to Canada as a gift. *Niobe* was the second ship in the fledgling Naval Service of Canada when in August 1911 it officially became the Royal Canadian Navy (RCN). Mind you, *Niobe* was no great prize.

By the time the war began in Europe, *Niobe* was outdated, prohibitively expensive to operate, and no longer seaworthy. On September 6, 1915, the ship was "paid off"—the naval term for being decommissioned. However, rather than heading to the scrapyard, she was permanently moored at the Naval Dockyard in Halifax. There she served as a training and depot ship. Acting Commander Percy F. Newcombe, the veteran Royal Navy officer who was in charge, was a "handsome, athletic, low-forehead type, champion boxer in the army and navy."[1] He had lost a foot in the fighting on V Beach in the 1915 battle at Gallipoli.

Now—like many of his Royal Navy (RN) brethren—Newcombe was "on loan" to the fledgling RCN, which had a dire need for experienced officers. Despite the circumstances, or perhaps because of them, Newcombe insisted on maintaining strict naval discipline aboard *Niobe*. Historian John Griffith Armstrong notes that, "As one old hand remembered, the same routine, rules and regulations, and discipline were maintained . . . just as if she were on active service at sea."[2]

When the RCN was born in 1910, Canada had been a nation for only forty-three years and had a population of just seven million. Regardless—and perhaps because of this—the Liberal government of Wilfrid Laurier, nationalist in its outlook, championed the creation of a Canadian navy that would help promote national sovereignty. In time of crisis, the service would accede to British command, but otherwise it would be under Canadian direction and control. Not surprisingly, the legislation advancing this initiative was as contentious as it was divisive. The Liberals used their parliamentary majority in 1910 to pass the government's Naval Services Bill despite furious opposition from an unlikely alliance of pro–British Empire Conservatives and Quebec nationalists.

When on August 29, 1911, King George V gave the bill royal assent, Conservative leader Robert Borden was perturbed. Only begrudgingly did he accept the fact that Canada now had its own navy. Borden represented Halifax in the House of Commons, and like many residents of the city, he had a deep and abiding affinity for the Royal Navy and the British monarchy.[3] For many years, even after the RN withdrew from Halifax, the British fleet sometimes visited the city during the summer months. Support for a continuation of Canada's reliance on the RN remained strong in Halifax, even if locals endured a love–hate relationship with haughty British officers who had been stationed there. Borden may have been similarly ambivalent, yet he remained intent on scuttling plans for the creation of the RCN. With that in mind, when Borden made the future of the fledgling service a pivotal campaign issue in the hard-fought October 1911 general election, the Conservatives prevailed.

Buoyed by his electoral win, Prime Minister Borden travelled to London to confer with Winston Churchill, First Lord of the Admiralty. Afterward, Borden pledged that Canada would contribute $35 million toward the cost of building three new Royal Navy dreadnoughts. The money was included in a piece of legislation known as the Naval Aid Bill. The Liberal opposition fought tooth and nail to prevent its passage, until finally, on May 15, 1913, the Conservatives made history when they invoked closure. This was the first time in Canadian parliamentary history that a governing party had ended debate and forced a vote to affirm a piece of legislation. However, this was not the end of the matter, or of the controversy.

Two weeks later, the Liberal-controlled Senate sparked a full-blown constitutional crisis when it rejected the Naval Aid Bill. The move called into question the roles of the upper chamber and of Parliament itself in the legislative process. Borden was livid. But what could he do? He was still trying to decide when war broke out in Europe a year later. Borden had no choice but to suddenly shelve all questions about the future of the RCN.

IN THE SUMMER OF 1914, even as war was erupting in Europe, the RCN was a victim of benign neglect on the part of the Borden government; three years after its birth, the fledgling service remained a skeleton force with fewer than 350 men in uniform, and experienced officers were in short supply.

Halifax was the home of the new Royal Naval College of Canada, which opened its doors in January 1911 to a class of twenty-one cadets. However, when the first graduates emerged after their two years of training, there were no Canadian ships on which to serve, and so each new officer served a one-year nautical apprenticeship aboard a Royal Navy ship before looking to the service for career opportunities. Such was the dearth of RCN activity that Halifax-based United States Coast Guard ships carried out the east coast iceberg patrols, which began in the aftermath of the 1912 *Titanic* disaster.

By necessity, the ranks of the RCN swelled once the Great War began. "The role of the Royal Canadian Navy operating out of Halifax was the rugged if ignominious one of patrolling the Nova Scotia coast and keeping the Halifax harbour approaches mine-swept every day," historian Thomas Raddall would write.[4]

The British government mobilized 30,000 Royal Navy Reserve officers and men, and scores of officers—including those Canadians who were graduates of the Royal Naval College of Canada—were "loaned" to the RCN.

In August 1914, HMCS *Niobe* had no ammunition for its guns, while a four-person caretaker crew that consisted of a petty officer, a gunner, a carpenter, and one sailor maintained the vessel. By 1917, *Niobe* was the ersatz home of more than 1,000 RCN officers and sailors. Many of these men bunked in temporary wooden structures that stood on the deck of the "Hotel *Niobe*," as sailors jokingly dubbed her. In addition, the ship fulfilled another vital function; when the government repurposed her, she became the RCN's east coast administrative headquarters. Stationed on board were the offices of naval control, naval intelligence, and the port of Halifax's chief examining officer (CXO), the naval officer who served as the wartime harbourmaster. In December 1917, the CXO for Halifax harbour was Acting Commander Frederick Evan Wyatt, a disgruntled forty-year-old Englishman (more about him presently).

HMCS *NIOBE*, THE ROYAL CANADIAN NAVY'S DEPOT SHIP. (ROYAL CANADIAN NAVY)

IT WOULD BE an understatement to say that Halifax was a busy wartime port. In addition to the fishing boats and innumerable local cargo haulers engaged in cabotage—that is, carrying goods and passengers in area waters—that routinely called at Halifax, more than 2,000 cargo ships passed in and out of the harbour in 1917. And Halifax had become the main embarkation point for the 250,000 Canadian troops who would depart for the war in Europe.

Whenever a civilian ship arrived in the harbour, naval regulations enacted in 1914 dictated that an RCN naval patrol boat under the CXO's command should meet the vessel at the examination anchorage, just outside the harbour entrance at McNabs Island. There the CXO's representative boarded each ship to inspect it and examine its cargo manifests. Similarly, the captains of all outbound ships were required to alert the CXO's office when they were departing and to provide details of their intended destination and sailing route. This was Haakon From's purpose for visiting *Niobe* on the afternoon of December 5.

After finishing his business there, the captain returned to the Pickford & Black office on Upper Water Street. By now, it was about 2:30 p.m. Veteran harbour pilot William Hayes was waiting at the shipping agent's office. Captain From recognized Hayes as being the same pilot who had guided the *Imo* into Bedford Basin on December 3. Agent Smith advised From that Hayes would be guiding the ship out to sea again when she sailed for New York.

Hayes, five foot ten and heavyset, was forty-three years old and had worked at his trade for more than two decades. The scion of a seafaring family and son of a harbour pilot, Hayes hailed from Herring Cove, a fishing village located on the eastern shore of the Chebucto Peninsula, ten miles south of Halifax. He was a soft-spoken man, but people listened when he talked. This was not something Hayes did a lot.

That was fine with Haakon From. The *Imo*'s captain had little time for small talk; he was eager to get going. However, Smith advised him that his ship's departure might be delayed past its scheduled three o'clock time. With the war in Europe into its fourth calendar year and Nova Scotian coal being in short supply, the Pickford & Black agent was having trouble arranging a delivery for the *Imo*; his regular supplier was unavailable, and so he had called another firm. "The coal tender will be here by 3:00 p.m., at the latest," Smith assured From.

Accepting that news, the captain and Hayes made their way to the *Imo*. There they waited for the coal delivery. With every passing minute, Captain From's patience grew shorter. By the time the coal delivery tender finally appeared, From was fuming. He was still grumbling when customs officer Arthur Lovett stopped by to deliver the cocket—the government customs document with its official seal—that From needed to have in hand before his ship could leave Halifax.

Lovett, Hayes, and Captain From conferred while the work of filling the ship's coal bunkers continued apace. Nonetheless, it gradually became evident there was no way the *Imo* would be leaving port that day, and there was nothing Haakon From could do about it. The imperatives of the navy's wartime protocols—or was it fate?—had dictated as much.

THE THREAT POSED by the appearance of German U-boats in the waters off Canada's east coast by early 1915 had prompted Allied military authorities to invoke a series of countermeasures. For one thing, they imposed a nighttime blackout. Regulations dictated that each evening at sunset, all lights in Halifax and Dartmouth be shaded. For another, in June the RCN installed a curtain of anti-submarine nets at the mouth of Halifax harbour. The move closed off access to the port from either side of Georges Island. In addition, with the U-boat threat at its peak by mid-1917, the RCN deployed a fleet of ten minesweepers that kept the waters off the Chebucto Peninsula free of enemy mines. Meanwhile, navy personnel had installed a second set of anti-submarine nets farther south on the harbour channel that led to the inner harbour.[5] Guard ships opened both anti-submarine gateways at first light each morning and closed them each evening at sunset.

Halifax being north of the forty-fourth parallel, the sun sinks below the western horizon early each afternoon when it is a fortnight before winter solstice; nightfall arrives around 4:30 p.m. So it was that on the afternoon of December 5 with less than an hour of daylight remaining, harbour pilot William Hayes and customs agent Arthur Lovett were both eager to get away after concluding their business on board the *Imo*. Lovett had matters to tend to back at his office; Hayes wanted to get home after another long day on the job.

"Captain From, by the time your coal is loaded, the anti-submarine nets will be closed," Hayes advised the *Imo*'s master. "I'm going home for the night, but I'll be back first thing tomorrow morning. We'll get under way then."

Haakon From was not happy about the demurrage. He had no patience for delays of any sort, and so he cussed roundly even though he knew he really had no choice but to agree to Hayes' plan. When From nodded his grudging acceptance, his two visitors departed. The *Imo*'s captain then retreated to the privacy of his cabin, his pet dog trailing at his heels.

AFTER LEAVING THE *IMO*, William Hayes planned to return to the Pickford & Black office; he had one quick detour to make first. He dropped by the harbour pilots' office on Bedford Row to report that the Norwegian ship would not be leaving for New York until early next morning. Fifteen-year-old office clerk Edward Beazley, who was on the job owing to the wartime labour shortage, recorded the information. It was Beazley's duty to keep track of the comings and goings of ships in Halifax harbour and to assign the pilots who guided vessels into and out of the port. He also posted the details on a big blackboard on the wall of the pilots' office.

With the *Imo*'s scheduled departure delayed, the names "*Imo*" and "William Hayes" remained on the chalkboard. Beazley planned to erase the words in the morning, after the Norwegian ship left for New York.

It was dark by the time Hayes arrived back at the Pickford & Black office. He wanted to let George Smith know he intended to return the next morning at 7:30 to guide the *Imo* out of the harbour.

"I'll have a boat here to take you to the steamer," said Smith. "See you then, Bill. Have a good night."[6]

Hayes, his wife, Gertrude, and their three children lived in nearby Herring Cove most of the year, but in the winter, they rented a house in Halifax's North End. That is where Hayes headed now. When he had gone, Smith telephoned the customs office. He wanted to ensure that Arthur Lovett knew the *Imo* remained anchored in Bedford Basin and would not be leaving Halifax until next morning. The customs officer, having been aboard the *Imo*, already knew this, of course.

Had Smith or Lovett been a tad more conscientious, one of them might have reported to naval officials that the *Imo* was still in port and would not be leaving Halifax until first light next day. All it would have taken was a quick phone call to the CXO's office or to the duty officer aboard HMCS *Acadia*, the RCN patrol boat that on this day was safeguarding the harbour entrance and serving as a nautical traffic cop. The information about the *Imo*'s new schedule might have made a crucial difference the next day; perhaps it even would have altered the course of events and prevented the tragedy that was about to occur. We will never know.

For his part, customs officer Lovett did not bother to share any of this information with his naval contacts. Apparently, he did not feel it was very important. After all, ships occasionally missed their departure times; the *Imo* would be on her way to New York bright and early Thursday morning. Regardless, Lovett reasoned, he was a busy man; it was not his job to inform others that a particular ship had or had not sailed. If the "navy boys" were on the ball, the CXO and his staff would know that the *Imo* was still in port. "We never stopped at the guard ship on the way back [home]," Lovett would later explain. "Our only purpose is to inform [navy officials] what ships we were going to clear"—that is, to leave the harbour.[7]

George Smith had his own excuse for not ringing the CXO's office or the guard ship *Acadia* to report that the *Imo* remained anchored in Bedford Basin on that Wednesday night. When asked about this later, he would explain that for a time he had made it a practice to call *Niobe* on behalf of the pilots who were guiding Pickford & Black ships into and out of the port. However, Smith had stopped doing this after one of Commander Wyatt's staff had called to let him know it was no longer necessary for him to report in; the pilots themselves were supplying the information to the CXO on their comings and goings.[8] However, as would become shockingly clear, that was not necessarily so.

CHAPTER 5

SOMEBODY WAS GOING TO "BE MADE A GOAT FOR THIS"
Halifax Harbour, December 5, 1917

It is no exaggeration to say that relations between the Halifax harbour pilots and the port's naval officials in 1917 were muddled and dysfunctional. To some extent, the problems were rooted in the personalities of the individuals involved. At the same time, the differences were also related to the history of the Halifax pilotage system and of the port itself.

The first Europeans to visit the Chebucto Peninsula had hired members of the Mi'kmaq First Nation to guide their ships. However, when in 1749 Lord Edward Cornwallis arrived with 2,576 Protestant settlers in tow to establish the British settlement that would become known as Halifax, he had a problem: the Mi'kmaq, who were allied with the French, were hostile to the British.

Cornwallis, unwilling to risk trying to make it into Bedford Basin on his own, waited a week for the arrival of another British ship that he knew would have a pilot on board. Instead of making peace with the Mi'kmaq, Cornwallis issued an infamous order that historians came to refer to as "the Scalping Proclamation." He offered a bounty to anyone who killed a Mi'kmaq, adult or child, and produced proof.

Once Cornwallis had established the Halifax settlement, it was not long before local fishermen and mariners were offering piloting services to visiting ships. By 1826, the House of Assembly—Canada's oldest legislature, which began its sittings in 1758—moved to regulate pilotage services in Halifax and to require pilots to pass licensing exams. The rules the Assembly ratified stood for almost half a century. With Confederation in 1867, pilotage became a federal responsibility. And in 1874, Parliament passed a bill that imposed further restrictions on the qualifications and activities of Halifax's harbour pilots.

A newly created Halifax Pilotage Commission, made up of seven commissioners and the secretary-treasurer, assumed responsibility for selecting, licensing, and supervising the port's harbour pilots. Staff in the pilotage office assigned pilots to incoming and outgoing ships. The commission also kept track of all vessels over 120 tons that called at the port, and in doing so helped determine the federal customs duties imposed on cargoes those ships carried. The money was a vital source of government revenue. By 1910, for the first time ever, federal income topped $100 million; the lion's share came from just two sources: customs duties and taxes on alcohol and tobacco. (Income tax, a "temporary" wartime measure that would be imposed by the Borden government in 1917, was still ten years in the future.)

Regulations for Halifax harbour allowed a maximum of twenty-five pilots and six apprentices, although there was seldom a full complement of pilots on the active roll. Being self-employed "entrepreneurs," they competed for pilotage assignments on the inbound and outbound ship traffic. The payment of pilotage tariffs was obligatory at the time, but having a pilot on board was not; most incoming ships engaged one anyway. Why not? The fee had to be paid, and pilotage certificates were required for customs purposes.

Halifax's harbour pilots jointly owned and operated a couple of pilot-age boats. The schooners *America* and *Columbia*, which initially cost $5,000 each, took up positions just outside the harbour entrance, alternating a week on duty with a week off. "One of these pilot boats would be continually sailing around the approaches to Chebucto Head with a full roster of pilots and pilot boat crew, waiting to hail or flag vessels requiring a pilot."[1] Apprentice pilots, a cook, and other crew, as needed, kept things running smoothly on the pilot boats and operated the tenders that ferried pilots to arriving and departing ships.

It was customary for the fourteen shipping agents who carried on business in Halifax in 1917 to alert the pilotage office whenever a ship they represented was due to arrive or depart. However, the notification system was imprecise and weather-dependent; when an agent failed to convey information by dropping by the pilotage office in person or by calling on the telephone, signals were relayed ship-to-shore and vice versa by tooting steam whistles or by showing flags, flashing lights, or giving hand signals. Marine radio—"wireless telegraphy," as it was then known—was still in its infancy in 1917. Most mariners regarded Italian inventor Guglielmo Marconi's wondrous invention as a novelty; the captains of passenger ships saw it as a device that enabled them to send or receive passenger telegrams. ("Dear mother, having a grand time. See you soon!") Some ships had wireless sets; others did not. Even for those vessels that did, radio operations were haphazard at best. Initially, there was nothing in law that set out standardized hours during which the wireless operator turned on the ship's apparatus or even monitored it, and the spectrum for radio signals was unregulated. Frequencies often overlapped, and messages sometimes drowned each other out. The *Titanic* disaster in April 1912 had led to standardization of radio equipment, hours of operation, and distress frequencies. However, in 1917, although a growing number of ships were equipped with wireless sets, the technology was still not universally available or understood. Nor was it routinely in use in most ports—Halifax among them.

FROM ITS VERY BEGINNINGS as a garrison town and a Royal Navy naval base, Halifax's fortunes and prosperity were inexorably tied to the sea. The city's chief asset has always been its deep, secure harbour. The French explorer and navigator Samuel de Champlain made note of both qualities in his logbook when he visited in 1604. However, what historians have aptly described as the "tyranny of location" has always offset Halifax's geographical recommendations. The port sits on the periphery of the Canadian, North American, and North Atlantic trade routes. For two centuries, Halifax's fortunes surged or ebbed on the tides of war. Thus, in the late eighteenth and early nineteenth centuries, when a seemingly endless succession of conflicts reshaped North America's political map, Halifax-based privateers made their fortunes by capturing and looting French, Spanish, and American ships.

Despite the recurring tensions between the United States and Great Britain, Halifax merchants cultivated trade ties with the West Indies and with American ports along the eastern seaboard, Boston in particular. In their formative years, the populations of Halifax and Boston were thick with immigrants of English, Irish, and Scottish heritage. The flow of people and commerce between the two cities was steady.

More than 30,000 United Empire Loyalists, including freed black slaves, moved north to British North America in the wake of the American Revolution; many of these migrants resettled in the Halifax area. In the late 1860s, in the years immediately after the Civil War, the population flow reversed. The Boston area became home to the largest community of Nova Scotians outside the province. Once Canada became an independent country in 1867, relations between Washington and Ottawa were sometimes frosty. The already extensive social, economic, and blood ties between Nova Scotia and New England remained vibrant, but even they were not enough to keep Halifax's economic prospects from fading as the nineteenth century ended. With the city's link to the Canadian hinterland being a single railway line, Halifax's importance as a port, commercial hub, and garrison town ebbed. That was especially true in the lean years of the crippling depression that gripped North America in the mid-1890s. Halifax was a hostage to circumstances, even when the economy began to improve in neighbouring New England and in the rest of Canada.

These were peak decades for immigration; millions of Europeans crossed the Atlantic in pursuit of "the American dream." The majority of these newcomers gravitated to New York or Boston, at least initially. Those immigrants who settled in Canada—and the number who did so was far smaller than the number who flocked to the United States—tended to bypass the Maritime provinces. In 1913, more than 96,000 European immigrants landed in Halifax; almost all of them moved on to settle in Montreal, Toronto, or southern Ontario, or else they answered the siren call of free farmland in the Canadian West.

FOR THE FIRST 150 YEARS of its history, Halifax was a vital Royal Navy port in North America. However, after the Crimean War (1853–1856) there were persistent signs that change was in the wind. Britannia still ruled the waves, and the Royal Navy remained supreme, but the United States was emerging as a global power, while in Europe the ambitions of Germany, France, Italy, and Belgium were growing.

In the midst of the headlong rush by these nations to establish colonial empires in Africa and Asia and to challenge British control on the seas, it was becoming obvious that the imperial economic model was unsustainable. Empire building is an expensive proposition; ruling the world costs a lot of money. In the nineteenth century, the RN had squadrons in the West Indies and North America. There were also British ships stationed in the waters off China, in the Indian Ocean, and in the Mediterranean.

All that changed when British forces began retreating from the Empire's far-flung colonies. Concentrating the kingdom's strength at home was the best use of resources, the admirals and generals in London reasoned. Once Canada became a self-governing country, it was inevitable that the British would begin pressuring the new Dominion to take on responsibility for its own defence. After all, the threat of an American invasion was abating. Mind you, not that it much mattered. If the United States military had decided to invade Canada, the British knew there was little they could do to resist. As a result, in the summer of 1871, most of the British soldiers and sailors who were still in Canada went home. The only exceptions were small contingents of RN officers who remained in Halifax and in Esquimalt, on Canada's west coast. The reprieve proved to be only temporary.

As the twentieth century dawned, Great Britain and Germany were vying for naval supremacy. It was a competition destined to end badly for both sides. Likewise for the city of Halifax. When the headstrong John ("Jackie") Arbuthnot Fisher became First Sea Lord of the Royal Navy, one of his priorities was to cut costs by further reducing the size of the North American squadron.

The last of the Royal Navy's men in Canada packed up their kit bags and sailed away on November 15, 1905. The move devastated Halifax economically; local merchants and businesses suffered as the once-bustling Naval Dockyard became a place of "rust and ghosts." The Royal Navy shuttered Admiralty House and sold off its furnishings, and the British army mothballed its fortifications. The city that author Rudyard Kipling—and echoed by Thomas Raddall—had dubbed "the Warden of the Honour of the North,"[2] was left as high and dry—and sober—as a shipwrecked sailor.

At the time, Canada had no navy of its own and a tiny army that consisted mostly of militia. The federal government in distant Ottawa had little interest in the military or in the city of Halifax. The denizens of central Canada were equally indifferent. News of the withdrawal of the last of the

British forces from Halifax—after more than 150 years—went all but unreported in Canadian newspapers. Nova Scotia seemed to be a long way from the major population centres of Toronto and Montreal. "Haligonians ... although steadfastly refusing to admit it even to themselves, were the lethargic and anemic citizens of a stagnant backwater," as one observer would later put it.[3]

By default, control over the port of Halifax now fell under civilian authority. A chief official in the new administrative scheme was harbourmaster Francis Rudolf, whose powers and responsibilities were set out in an 1896 Order-in-Council issued by the federal government.[4] All the interested parties had regarded the work of harbour pilots, while integral to the orderly and safe operation of the port of Halifax, as being primarily a local matter. It had been this way since long before Confederation.[5] All that changed when the war began in the summer of 1914. Halifax— "the Empire Port," as the jingoistic *Halifax Herald* dubbed the city— became Canada's most important Atlantic gateway. Traffic in the harbour now came under naval regulations that governed signalling, examining, and the comings and goings of ships; however, who exactly had the authority to enforce these dictates and who had the final say over operations—senior officers of the fledgling Royal Canadian Navy or their counterparts in the venerable Royal Navy who returned and again were based here—was not entirely clear. To many British eyes, the upstart Canadian navy—with its "fleet" of two warships and handful of support vessels—was a "tin pot navy" that was unworthy of respect. At the same time, the haughty British tended to look down their imperial noses at "colonials." Given Halifax's importance to the Allied war effort, such an attitude proved to be problematic.

A similar lack of respect led to troubled dealings between Acting Commander Evan Wyatt, who was the naval chief examining officer, the civilian harbourmaster Rudolf, and the civilian harbour pilots who guided ships into and out of the port. At times, relations between Wyatt and these civilians were tense, even hostile.

DECISION MAKERS AT the British Admiralty in London had deemed the job of organizing the trans-Atlantic convoys that kept open the shipping routes to the British Isles and France as being too vital to entrust to the untested and undermanned RCN. That responsibility instead remained in the hands of Halifax-based Royal Navy officers. Although their commander, Rear Admiral Bertram M. Chambers, was experienced and competent, the fact that he was the highest-ranking naval officer in Halifax was a source of much irritation to RCN officers and their boss in Ottawa.

That man was Admiral Charles E. Kingsmill, born in Guelph and educated at Upper Canada College. Kingsmill himself had enjoyed a thirty-seven-year career in the Royal Navy; however, his service in His Majesty's Navy had ended on a sour note. When a new RN battleship captained by Kingsmill ran aground off New Brunswick one summer day in 1907, the captain faced a court martial. The accident really was not his fault—Kingsmill was eating dinner in his cabin when the ship ran aground, damaging the hull along two-thirds of its length—but as master of the ship, he was ultimately accountable. The resulting blot on his service record effectively ended Kingsmill's RN career. He retired, returned home to Canada, and in 1908 used his political connections with the Liberal government of Wilfrid Laurier to wrangle a new job for himself. Kingsmill became head of the Fishery Protection Service in the Department of Marine and Fisheries. Then when the Naval Service of Canada was born in 1910 and was included within the same ministry, he became the service's first director.

Kingsmill's past as a Royal Navy officer did not deter him from carping about the naval command situation in wartime Halifax. "It is most undesirable to have an Officer coming from England to take charge over the heads of our officers who have been in Halifax and on the Coast since the War and are cognizant of all local conditions," he complained in November 1917.[6]

Kingsmill's political masters in Ottawa evidently agreed with his comments, for the minister in charge echoed the same arguments in his appeal to British politicians and Admiralty officials. Not that such a plea was all that effective, mind you. In the end, Admiralty officials responded to the Canadian concerns in a perfunctory way, although Chambers got a new job title: Port Convoy Officer and Senior Officer of Escorts, Halifax. The conciliatory verbiage changed nothing; Chambers continued to do pretty much as he pleased. That meant RCN officers in Halifax were left to handle only mundane administrative matters and tend to anti-submarine defences and patrols in the waters around the mouth of the harbour and along Canada's east coast.

EDWARD BEAZLEY HELD a crucial job in the port of Halifax. Whenever the teenaged clerk in the pilotage office learned from a shipping agent that a ship was arriving or departing, it was his responsibility to assign a pilot to serve as its guide. The use of harbour pilots had become standard practice in Halifax and in most other seaports. It was not compulsory in Halifax, but the masters of almost all visiting ships anted up.

While the harbour pilots waited for arriving ships, they whiled away the hours aboard the pilotage ship doing what mariners have always been wont to do. In the wake of a June 30, 1916, plebiscite, the city and the port were officially "dry." However, a politically motivated 1918 Royal Commission report that delved into the activities of Halifax pilots alleged that "intoxicating liquor was being permitted to be taken on board the pilot schooners." Occasionally, or so it was charged, some pilots overindulged.[7]

The Royal Commission went on to suggest that drunkenness was not the only mischief afoot. Its report stated some pilots were in cahoots with sea captains to defraud the government; it was said that complicit masters pocketed payments in return for signing papers that attested pilots had provided services they had not actually provided. In addition, because the records of the Halifax Pilotage Commission were poorly kept and incomplete, it was impossible for auditors to figure out after the fact who had performed what services or when.

The Royal Commission report did not stop there. It went on to state that the pilotage office was not observing the 1896 regulations that governed the training of apprentices; when a pilot retired, moved away, or died, as often as not, he was not replaced, at least not in a timely manner. The upshot was that in December of 1917, by the Halifax Pilotage Commission's own count, the roll of active harbour pilots included the names of just fourteen men—eleven short of a full complement. On average, the pilots were thirty-seven years of age and each had fourteen years' job experience. At a time when a typical Canadian factory worker was fortunate to earn $1,200 per year,[8] Halifax harbour pilots were doing very well indeed. Given the "shortage" of qualified pilots in the port, those who were working typically earned more than $5,000 annually, and it was rumoured that some were taking home as much as $1,000 per month when all sources of income—including tips—were taken into account. CXO Evan Wyatt was well aware of all this.

The number of ships visiting Halifax and the volume of cargo passing through the port had increased dramatically as the fighting in Europe intensified. By 1917, Halifax was handling more than seventeen million tons of cargo per year—about eight times its pre-war volume. On occasion, the increase in traffic led to unacceptable wait times for arriving ships. However, when Commander Wyatt asked officials of the Halifax Pilotage Commission—of which civilian harbourmaster Francis Rudolf was a board member—to increase the number of pilots, his pleas went unheeded; there was no love lost between Wyatt and Rudolf. Understandably so. Wyatt was an outsider who had usurped Rudolf's authority and slighted him. "I know more about positioning and berthing [ships] than he ever would in the whole of his life," the commander asserted.[9]

Adding insult to injury, Wyatt refused to provide Rudolf with a boat that he needed to get around the harbour. Mind you, this was not the only cause of friction between the CXO and the locals. Wyatt also waged a spirited war with the harbour pilots and their administrative body.

COMMANDER F. EVAN WYATT, CIRCA 1920. (COURTESY OF JOEL ZEMEL)

As the King's harbourmaster, the commander supposedly held sway over the harbour pilots and all other aspects of harbour operations. However, because the pilots were civilians, he had no recourse when they failed to follow his orders or provide him with information on ship traffic. "There never seemed to be any way of punishing pilots for violations of this kind," Wyatt complained.[10]

THERE WAS YET another source of friction between Wyatt and the harbour pilots. Wyatt knew that Edward Beazley, the clerk in the office of the Halifax Pilotage Commission, routinely gathered all the information Wyatt needed to do his job. That being so, it seemed logical to him that young Beazley should share it with the CXO's office. In May 1917, Wyatt fired off a memo to James Creighton, the Secretary of the Halifax Pilotage Commission, instructing him to see to it that Wyatt received information on all ship traffic into and out of the harbour. Creighton dutifully conveyed this request to the pilots and posted his memo on the bulletin board in his office.

Initially, Beazley was amenable to doing as Wyatt had asked. However, after several weeks of dutifully telephoning the CXO's office several times each day, the teenager began to feel he was wasting his time. Unless he spoke to Wyatt personally, Beazley surmised that the staff in the CXO's office were not bothering to record the information he was reporting. What's more, Beazley felt the navy men sometimes made fun of him. Wyatt's staff denied this; if Beazley felt that way, they insisted, it was because he talked like a meek child. Regardless, Beazley made the unilateral decision to stop calling the CXO's office to report on ship traffic.

The commander was irate when he eventually learned this. For reasons only Wyatt could explain, instead of questioning his own staff about what was going on, calling Beazley himself, or complaining to Secretary Creighton, Wyatt tried to obtain the information in a roundabout way. He asked the shipping agents to provide him with daily updates on the vessels in the harbour. This approach worked fine for a few months; however, like pilots, the agents were busy with their own duties, and they were under no legal obligation to comply with Wyatt's request. Inevitably, it was not long before some of them began neglecting to call the CXO's office with their reports. Others simply passed the buck; they asked the pilots themselves to call in reports on ship traffic.

Wyatt was exasperated. He still was not getting information on harbour traffic on a timely or regular basis. In frustration, on three occasions he wrote to his commanding officer, Captain Edward H. Martin. "Reports [come] in very occasionally & spasmodically, & making it difficult to trace shipping movements in the port & impossible to regulate sailings," Wyatt complained in a June 21, 1917, missive.[11]

Wyatt, being an experienced naval officer, knew the ropes. He understood how things worked in the navy. He also was savvy enough to know he would be wise to create a paper trail showing he had been doing his job. "For months and months, I saw an accident or collision was coming," he would later say. "I could see there was somebody going to be made the goat for this, and I did not wish to be made the goat. You can call it intuition or what you like, but that was my idea."[12]

CHAPTER 6

Clear and Present Danger

Halifax, Nova Scotia, December 5, 1917, Late Afternoon

The *Mont-Blanc*'s engines were labouring hard as she lumbered past Sambro Island, twenty miles south of the mouth of Halifax harbour. The lighthouse that came into view off the starboard bow—North America's oldest navigational beacon—had been a guide and a comfort for mariners since 1759. Whenever a ship's lookout sighted that light, he knew the passage to Halifax was nearing its end.

After having battled heavy seas and blustery west winds for three long days and three long nights on the voyage from New York, Captain Aimé Le Médec and his men were eager to reach port. Any doubts about whether or not their aging ship could maintain a speed of eight knots had proved to be well founded; fully loaded, as she was with a belly full of high explosives, the *Mont-Blanc* had struggled, lumbering along at the glacial pace of seven knots. Now having almost reached the end of the first leg of their journey home to France, the ship's crew members breathed a huge collective sigh of relief.

A few minutes after they had passed Sambro Island, the mood of everyone on board lightened still further when the lookout spied yet another welcome sight. A few miles ahead, just off the port bow, was Chebucto Head lighthouse, white and stark atop a grey granite outcropping that is the most easterly point of Chebucto Peninsula. The lighthouse is fifteen miles from Halifax as the gull flies.

Standing on the *Mont-Blanc*'s open-air bridge a half-hour later, Captain Le Médec and First Officer Glotin caught sight of the guns and fortifications at the mouth of Halifax harbour. The wind had slackened, and the sea in the examining anchorage off McNabs Island was calm.

"*Très bien. Halifax,*" said Le Médec. He nodded and smiled. "*Nous sommes ici.*"

"*Oui,*" Glotin replied.

Le Médec was relieved they had completed the first leg of their journey home. *Jusqu'ici tout va bien,* he thought. *So far, so good.* Now they had only to wait for the armed RCN tugboat to deliver a naval examining officer who would come aboard to review the ship's cargo manifest and issue permission to enter the secure inner harbour, Bedford Basin. There the *Mont-Blanc* could drop anchor in the convoy-marshalling area. The crew were looking forward to doing so and to the respite, even if it was only for twenty-four hours. Captain Le Médec had told his crew that the *Mont-Blanc* would be joining a convoy scheduled to sail to Europe on Friday.

The captain prayed that his wait for the naval examining officer would not be a long one; the afternoon was fast disappearing, and he was keen to get to the anchorage area. The captain was eyeing his pocket watch when Glotin called out, "*Voici un bateau!*"

Le Médec trained his binoculars on the approaching craft. The skiff knifing its way toward them was not a naval vessel but rather a Halifax Pilotage Commission boat. On board was the pilot who would guide the *Mont-Blanc* into the harbour. That man, Le Médec was about to learn, was

Francis ("Frank") Mackey, a veteran harbour pilot. Mackey was in a hurry, for he knew the RCN would soon raise into place for the night the anti-submarine nets at the mouth of Halifax harbour. Once that happened, the *Mont-Blanc* would be going nowhere, not until morning.

Francis Mackey waved in greeting as one of the *Mont-Blanc* crewmen lowered a Jacob's ladder over the side of the ship, which was still coasting toward the examining area. Although he was just a hair over five foot five with a thick chest and heavy build, Mackey climbed quickly and easily. He had scrambled up such rope-boarding ladders countless times in his quarter century as a harbour pilot; Mackey's grip was strong and sure. At the top of his climb, he took hold of the *Mont-Blanc*'s bulwark with both hands. Then, stepping through the open passenger gate, he landed with feet squarely on the deck of the French ship. There to greet him was Captain Le Médec. The Frenchman smiled and extended his hand. As Francis Mackey seized it with a firm grip, Le Médec sized him up. The first thing the captain noted was that although the pilot sported a bow tie and was neatly dressed, unlike his counterparts in New York, he did not dress for show.

Mackey's demeanour and appearance bespoke a quiet self-confidence that sprang from a lifetime spent working on the water. Ruddy faced, with a receding hairline, bushy eyebrows, and a walrus moustache, he was a native of nearby Ketch Harbour. That 200-year-old fishing village is located seven miles south of Herring Cove, the Chebucto Peninsula home of Mackey's fellow pilot William Hayes. The two men were fast friends, for they had been cut from much the same bolt of sailcloth.

Mackey, who was born in 1872, had spent most of his forty-five years of life on and around ships. He had gone to sea at age twelve, serving as a cabin boy on vessels that plied the waters of the St. Lawrence River. He had then worked alongside his father, fishing for cod on the Grand Banks. Mackey was just twenty-one when he became an apprentice pilot; although he had little formal schooling in his youth, he was fond of memorizing and reciting poetry, and he was a gifted storyteller. Mackey was also a quick study. In 1895, after just two years of apprenticeship, he passed his licensing examinations to become a pilot, second class. He achieved his first-class designation in 1898, and the following year got his master's certificate for coastal trade. At the time, he was the Halifax Pilotage Commission's most qualified pilot, and his services were in high demand.

By 1900, Mackey was doing so well for himself that he married, taking as his bride red-haired Lillian Wrayton. Four years his junior and the daughter of a prominent local sea captain, Lillian had been born and raised in Halifax's affluent South End. Marrying her affirmed and ensured Mackey's upwardly mobile social standing in the community.

By 1917, Mackey had been guiding ships into and out of port for twenty-four years. He had never had an accident, not one; and he took great pride in his unblemished record. On this Wednesday afternoon, Mackey had just finished guiding another ship out to sea, and

PILOT FRANCIS MACKEY WAS ALWAYS STYLISHLY DRESSED. (DIGITALLY ENHANCED BY JOEL ZEMEL. COURTESY OF JANET MAYBEE/THE MACKEY FAMILY)

after disembarking, he had made his way over to the *Mont-Blanc*, his final charge of the day.

Captain Aimé Le Médec was eager to talk with Mackey, but the Frenchman's command of English was poor. The truth was—as he would later admit—he felt embarrassed whenever he tried to speak the language. Similarly, Mackey's grasp of French was spotty. The two men immediately sensed and accepted that any dialogue between them would be rudimentary, and it would be limited. Not that it mattered much.

Francis Mackey was confident that he and the captain would be able to make do. "I just know a few words, but the captain could understand. I knew port and starboard. I knew full speed, half-speed, and stop in French."[1]

SUNSET IN HALIFAX on the evening of December 5, 1917, came at exactly 4:19 p.m. The *Mont-Blanc* had arrived in the examining area just as darkness was falling like a stage curtain over the blacked-out city. As if on cue, just as the last streaks of the setting sun, trailing long and red, faded from the western sky, McNabs Island lighthouse woke from its diurnal slumbers. The lamp snapped to life. Every minute or so, the shaft of light it cast swept out over the sea and then traced the shoreline before arcing across the harbour entrance.

The daylight having disappeared, the colours of the water and surrounding lands also faded to black. As they did so, the unseasonal warmth that had been in the air that afternoon slipped away. The temperature was dropping. Feeling the chill, Captain Le Médec suggested to pilot Mackey that they retreat to the warmth of the captain's cabin. There, beneath the ship's bridge, the two men could sit comfortably while they waited for the arrival of the navy examining officer.

Mackey was not surprised to see that Le Médec's mahogany-panelled cabin was neither grand nor spacious; the space was not much larger than ten feet by ten feet. The austere furnishings, *de rigeur* in 1899 when the ship was new, were typical of the master's quarters on a tramp steamer of the day. The brightworks, while still polished to near new-brass shininess, had seen better days. So had the small, sturdy table that sat in the middle of the floor, where bolts secured it so it would not jump around in a heavy sea. The captain's bunk and the upright wardrobe that completed the cabin's minimalist decor were similarly anchored in place. The cabin was neither cheerful nor homey; the riveted plates of bulkhead metal that were the walls of Le Médec's quarters bore the same joyless wartime grey colour as the rest of the *Mont-Blanc's* rusting hull.

When the captain and pilot had taken seats, Mackey began trying to question the Frenchman on the details of the cargo his ship was carrying; the pilot had noticed that the *Mont-Blanc* was riding low in the water. He could not have missed it. Captain Le Médec struggled to explain in broken English that his ship was carrying munitions. Mackey nodded, but he offered no comment; there really was nothing for him to say. He figured he had grasped the essence of Le Médec's reply, at least enough to realize the one point that really mattered: the *Mont-Blanc* was a floating bomb.

The conversation between harbour pilot and captain moved on to the likelihood that the port's anti-submarine nets would soon be closing for the night. Anchored to the seabed by concrete weights, the nets were raised into a defensive position each night, and they were reopened each morning at first light. Similarly, the naval gatekeepers opened and closed the nets intermittently during the day to allow ship traffic to pass. A varied schedule lessened the chance of any lurking German U-boat slipping into the harbour.

Mackey was still attempting to explain all of this to Le Médec when there arrived at the cabin door Mate Terrance Freeman of the Royal Canadian Naval Volunteer Reserve, one of the port's examining officers. Freeman apologized for his tardiness. He had been busy inspecting another ship that had arrived in the examination area a few minutes before the *Mont-Blanc*. The mate nodded to Mackey, whom he recognized. Mackey excused himself from the conversation while Freeman introduced himself to Le Médec.

"Captain, may I see the papers for your ship—the cargo manifest and the orders the convoy officer in New York had issued?" said Freeman.

Le Médec grinned sheepishly as he handed over his documents. "We're all explosives," he blurted in his broken English.

Freeman's eyebrows arched. He glanced first at Le Médec, then over at Mackey. The captain's revelation had come as a surprise to Freeman. Not many munitions ships stopped in Halifax harbour, certainly not many that were as slow and as heavily laden as the *Mont-Blanc*. What's more, Freeman had no idea that CXO Commander Wyatt and his staff had been watching for the *Mont-Blanc*'s arrival or that they had received word of a December 2 cable from Commodore E.J. Wells, the senior port convoy officer in New York. That message, which was addressed to Rear Admiral Bertram M. Chambers, RN, the port of Halifax's convoy officer, had included the names of the *Mont-Blanc* and a couple of other Allied cargo ships that were en route to Halifax. Wells asked to have these vessels included in a convoy that was scheduled to leave Halifax for Europe on Friday, December 7. Wells had sent this message twice.

On the first go-round, he had neglected to include the information that the *Mont-Blanc* was carrying almost 3,000 tons of munitions and high-octane fuel. Such a cargo was not unusual in itself. What *was* unusual was the fact that the *Mont-Blanc* was carrying nothing but French munitions and that she was much slower than most munitions ships. Wells evidently had deemed it to be of sufficient importance that he underscored both points; he had sent Halifax a "corrected copy" of his original message.[2]

Commander Wyatt had received a copy of the Wells cable, but it is unclear if any other naval officials in Halifax did as well—most notably Wyatt's superior and acting superintendent of the Naval Dockyard, Captain Frederick C.C. Pasco. The former RN officer was filling in for Captain Edward H. Martin, who was away for a month, attending meetings at the Admiralty Office in London. Martin was the principal delegate in a Canadian mission charged with the task of negotiating with British officials in an effort to reduce tensions between senior officers in the Royal Navy and its Canadian offshoot.

Martin's absence had little impact on the day-to-day operations of the port or on the examination process. Terrance Freeman had processed other munitions ships, a few of them anyway, and he had a passing familiarity with the regulations that governed movement of munitions ships into and out of Halifax harbour. However, Freeman would later admit that he really did not know "the nature of [explosives] very much." The examining officer grasped only that the ship's cargo "was something that would do some damage."[3] The pungent smell emanating from the drums of benzol sitting on the *Mont-Blanc*'s deck underscored that notion for it was a palpable reminder of how volatile the ship's cargo was.

Despite the clear and present danger, the *Mont-Blanc* was flying no flags that would have alerted other ships that she was carrying munitions; international shipping laws did not require Captain Le Médec to do so. No matter. He was not eager to broadcast the news that his ship was carrying such a dangerous cargo. To do so, he reasoned, was suicidal; it would have alerted the captain of any U-boat that spotted the *Mont-Blanc* that here was a ship that was a prime target.

Francis Mackey understood all these concerns, but he was also wary of the need to comply with any naval regulations governing the transport of munitions. Ever prudent, he asked Mate Freeman to check with the CXO's office whether he should take any extra or special precautions while guiding the ship into the inner harbour. The *Mont-Blanc*'s cargo was an oddity, and Mackey did not want to take any chances.[4] Freeman nodded when Mackey mentioned this, and he assured the pilot he would look into the matter. However, if he did so, the mate neglected to tell Mackey what he had learned. The pilot would never hear back from him.

The details of the *Mont-Blanc*'s cargo were only of passing interest to Mate Terrance Freeman. There really were no prohibitions on the movement of munitions ships into or out of the harbour, although there had been before the outbreak of the war; civilian harbourmaster Francis Rudolf had routinely denied such vessels access to Halifax harbour on the rare occasions when they appeared. That all changed in 1914 when the navy took control of operations of the port. What was peculiar about this—in retrospect, maddeningly and inexplicably so—is the fact there *were* restrictions on munitions ships entering ports in the United Kingdom and most ports in the United States, including New York. The *Mont-Blanc* never should have been allowed into Halifax harbour; however, no one with the authority to draft and implement similar safety regulations—in the Royal Navy, the Royal Canadian Navy, or the Canadian government—had bothered to prohibit munitions ships from entering the port of Halifax. This grave oversight was destined to cost many innocent people their lives.

AFTER FINISHING HIS REVIEW of the *Mont-Blanc*'s papers, Mate Freeman returned the documents to Captain Le Médec. "Unless you hear from me to the contrary, you may proceed up harbour on a signal from [the examining officer's] ship, which will be given as soon as it is light enough for good navigation," he said.

The captain was uncertain of the meaning of Freeman's words, but when he glanced over at Mackey, he grasped that the examining officer had just confirmed that the *Mont-Blanc* would have to remain anchored in the examination area off McNabs Island until first light on Thursday morning.

After double-checking to ensure that Mackey had heard and understood his instructions, Freeman tipped his cap to Captain Le Médec and Mackey and then departed. It was now 5:30 p.m. Back on his boat, Freeman signalled HMCS *Niobe* to let the naval control office and the CXO know that the French cargo ship SS *Mont-Blanc* was among the ships that had arrived at the harbour entrance, and she would be spending the night there. Freeman also reported that the ship was carrying a cargo that consisted solely of explosives, and that he issued her captain permission to enter the harbour at first light on Thursday morning.

It was with that awareness in mind that Captain Le Médec invited pilot Mackey to spend the night on board the *Mont-Blanc*. Mackey could easily have gone home and returned to the *Mont-Blanc* early the next morning. He, his wife, Lillian, and their five children—with a sixth on the way—lived in a handsome four-bedroom frame house at 382 Robie Street in Halifax. Located in the city's residential South End, the dwelling was across the street from Camp Hill, which was the site of a new war veterans' convalescent hospital.

Mackey decided it was easier for him if he stayed on the ship overnight, and so he accepted Captain Le Médec's invitation. That decided, he sat down to dinner with the captain and his senior officers, First Officer Jean-Baptiste Glotin and Second Officer Joseph Leveque. The foursome met in Le Médec's cabin for their meal. Afterward, they passed the evening attempting to chat, although Mackey, who spoke only a few words of French, found it a chore to join in or even to follow the conversation. The Frenchmen spoke quickly, and Mackey's problems were compounded by the fact that alcohol, the great facilitator of conversation, was not permitted on board French ships in wartime. Thus, the men had only coffee to sip after their meal. However, as they were relaxing, Mackey reached into his jacket pocket and brought out some cigars. When he offered them around, Le Médec's eyes grew as big as saucers. Although the captain wanted a cigar, he shook his head and smiled sheepishly. "*Non! Il est interdit de fumer,*" he said apologetically. "No smoking on the ship."[5]

CHAPTER 7

As darkness settled over the city of Halifax, residents were making their way home after another working day or from their day's outings. For so many of them, tonight would be their last on this earth. Of that, they were of course blissfully unaware. If this night was memorable in any way, it was that it was so very ordinary. Except for the weather. It was unseasonably mild; with less than three weeks until Christmas, there still was not a flake of snow on the ground.

The bloodletting in Europe, now into its fourth calendar year, dominated the headlines. In Canada, news about the federal election that loomed twelve days hence appeared on page one of the five Halifax newspapers. On the inside pages, those same newspapers were chock full of advertisements for holiday gift-giving ideas. Local shops had "on offer" quantities of Prince Edward Island potatoes, kid gloves ("Always applauded as gifts"), furnace coal, and Victrola record players (at prices from $27.50 to $520, "easy payments arranged, if desired"). The Francis A. Gillis Building

Supplies Yard had asbestos wallboard in stock and ready for quick installation; this wondrous material, an advertisement announced, was "cheaper and better than plaster for immediate use."

There were also advertisements about the latest "moving picture entertainments" that were being screened in downtown theatres, notices of vaudeville performers who were appearing in Halifax's music halls, and a reminder about a lecture by one Dr. Adam, "personal friend of Premier Lloyd George [of the U.K.]." This member of the Imperial Munitions Board was "one of England's greatest orators," and, the notice reminded readers, Adam had "a message for YOU—the mothers, wives, sisters, and daughters of the soldiers at the front."

Haligonians were avid consumers of the latest war news, for they were keen supporters of Canada's involvement in the Great War. In the words of the *New York Times*, Halifax was "the most British city in [North] America."[1] The affinity that residents felt for all things British reflected itself in their manners, speech, and social divisions.

"Halifax society was conditioned by the presence of generations of well-born, sometimes aristocratic, British officers, and showed it. The higher up the social pecking order in that small but cosmopolitan seaport town, the more people identified with England."[2] That had always been true. After all, it was the British who founded Halifax, and it is a time zone closer to the United Kingdom than any other mainland city in North America.

Not surprisingly, Halifax's military enlistment rate during World War I was one of the highest in Canada. In addition, the port was the main jumping-off point for Canadian troops who were bound for the battlefields of Europe, and Halifax was the home of Prime Minister Robert Borden, who had served as the local Member of Parliament for nine years. Borden, a staunch imperialist, fretted that as the fighting in Europe dragged on, it was becoming ever more difficult for the government to recruit enough men to keep pace with battlefield losses. As a result, in

August 1917, he introduced conscription, a move that Liberal leader Sir Wilfrid Laurier and most French-speaking Quebeckers bitterly opposed. The ensuing quarrel split the country along linguistic fault lines and divided both the ruling Conservatives and the opposition Liberals.

Apart from their city's ties to Great Britain, Haligonians were keen supporters of the war in Europe for another reason, one that was less patriotic than it was mercenary. The conflict was a major boon for the local economy. Halifax was Canada's most important Atlantic seaport and a vital player in the Allied war effort. The economic benefits that flowed out of both developments were welcome in a city that had seen some lean times in recent years.

The 1872 opening of the Intercolonial Railway (ICR) that linked Halifax to the rest of Canada and to the northeastern United States had failed to generate the economic boom its backers anticipated or touted. Halifax's distance from the central Canadian heartland proved decisive in that regard. Businesses in Toronto and Montreal continued moving their goods for export by rail to Boston or other American ports. Halifax business interests were further frustrated when efforts to attract or build the

THE HALIFAX RAILWAY LINES, LOOKING NORTH FROM NORTH STREET STATION, CIRCA 1900. (NOVA SCOTIA ARCHIVES)

large-scale port facilities their city needed to compete proved fruitless. The 1914 outbreak of war in Europe changed all that, raising Halifax's profile and ensuring the port was vital to Canada's war effort.

IF ON THE AFTERNOON of December 5, 1917, you had stood atop Fort Needham hill and looked eastward, you would have enjoyed a bird's-eye view of Halifax harbour on the eve of destruction; this was the proverbial calm before the storm. The port spread out below, with its forty-nine wharves, was a going and vital concern. All the major Canadian, British, and American shipping lines—White Star, Cunard, and CGT included— had offices or agents in town. Thousands of workers toiled in waterfront industries or those with nautical concerns. All type and manner of commercial vessels, Allied warships, cabotage craft that carried cargo and passengers, and fishing boats all routinely visited Halifax. On this particular day, there were thirty-one ships at anchor in Halifax harbour; the naval examining officer had cleared another ten—the French munitions ship *Mont-Blanc* among them—to enter the port next day. All of these vessels had dropped anchor off McNabs Island as they awaited their turn to proceed to the inner harbour at Bedford Basin.

On the western side of the kidney-shapped Halifax Peninsula is a narrow inlet called the Northwest Arm. If you had been looking down from Fort Needham on December 5, 1917, you would not have seen the Northwest Arm, but you could have surveyed Halifax's bustling North End with its Richmond neighbourhood—so called because textile mills located here had used cotton fibres imported from the southern United States, presumably from the area of Richmond, Virginia. Most Halifax industries were located along the waterfront and in the city's North End.

As Hugh MacLennan observed in his classic novel *Barometer Rising*, Halifax has always had "a genius for looking old and for acting as though nothing could possibly happen to surprise it,"[3] and that definitely was the

case in Richmond. Many of the two- and three-storey wood-frame structures here—multi-generational family homes, boarding houses, churches,
schools, shops, pubs, and small businesses of all types—were dilapidated
and cried out for paint or repairs. Often for both.

Similarly, many Halifax streets were in poor shape, being unpaved, save
for the space between the rails of the city's antiquated tramcar network.
"The [downtown] business section and some of the residential streets [in
Halifax] had flagstone or concrete sidewalks and the old genteel south end of
Barrington ('Pleasant') Street . . . had its worn red-brick walks and cobbled
gutters; but everywhere else the townsfolk strolled on paths of household
cinders dumped by the city's collection wagons and casually raked level."[4]

Spring and autumn were seasons of driving rains in Halifax. When
the skies opened, the city's dirt streets grew ankle-deep in mud. In the heat
of summer, the horse-drawn carts and slovens—the low-slung wagons
with high driver's seats that hauled heavy loads in Halifax and other port
cities—and the newfangled "horseless carriages" that were still a novelty in
Halifax, kicked up swirling clouds of dust.

North End residents watched their steps while navigating the streets,
whatever the season. The gutters were filthy and hazardous to the health.
Garbage collection was haphazard at best. The draft horses that hauled
delivery wagons, not being much for social niceties, routinely left their
malodourous calling cards.

Such were the realities of everyday life in Halifax's bustling North
End. So, too, was the daily commute to and from waterfront workplaces.
The din of industry was the neighbourhood soundtrack—the tooting of
the steam whistles on ships in the harbour, and the thunderous chugging
and coupling sounds of the passenger and freight trains as they went
about their business.

The railway tracks that skirted the Richmond neighbourhood ran
through the heart of the ramshackle community of Africville, perched at

the north end of the Halifax Peninsula on a rise overlooking Bedford Basin. Africville was home to poor black families, most of whom were descendants of slaves who had fled north to Canada from the United States in the wakes of the American Revolution and the War of 1812. For most intents and purposes, slavery had ended in Nova Scotia in 1801, but discrimination lingered on like a chronic illness.

Most Africville residents earned their living by farming, fishing, or working as labourers. The city collected property taxes in Africville, but residents never got proper public utilities or health services. Adding insult to injury, because the community's residents had no political clout or ability to resist, the city of Halifax located its least desirable facilities here—a prison, an infectious diseases hospital, a slaughterhouse, and even a fecal waste depository. In 1915, Halifax city council declared that Africville would always be "an industrial district." Despite all this, Africville was a vibrant and proud little community that by 1917 was home to about 400 residents.

South of Africville, the railway ran along the Halifax waterfront. Spur lines served the thriving industries here, among them the Halifax Dockyard, the Nova Scotia Cotton Company, the Acadia Sugar Refinery, and the Hillis and Sons Foundry.

Many of the workers who toiled in these establishments lived nearby. The North End was unabashedly working class, but not exclusively so. For convenience sake, some business owners chose to live near their factories and workshops, and these outliers built grand homes. "North of North Street, Admiralty House acted as a magnet for prestigious estates that came to occupy Gottingen Street and farmland to the west."[5]

However, most of Halifax's social, economic, and political elite—merchants, professionals, bureaucrats, senior military officials, and academics—lived in the city's "upper crust" South End. The fashionable streets around Dalhousie University campus and the 150-acre greenspace that is Point Pleasant Park were desired locations. According to writer

Robert MacNeil, "cultured" Haligonians who resided in the city's relatively affluent South End had their own distinctive dialect. "The lilt and
music of the speech—its rise and fall and its rhythms—were English."[6]

The South End was a place of leafy streets and spacious homes. In
some, servants scurried about dusting the crystal chandeliers, cleaning
stained glass, polishing the brass fixtures and the silverware, and serving
five o'clock tea that the hostess offered along with "muffin and gossip." As
one American visitor observed, "Dirty the town certainly is on the outside . . . [it] is only necessary to see the inside of a Halifax drawing room to
know no matter how far off England is geographically, practically one is in
that pleasant land."[7]

ACCORDING TO GOVERNMENT census data, Halifax's population in
1917 was about 50,000; the actual head count may well have been double
that. People from small towns, villages, and farms all over Nova Scotia
and the neighbouring Maritime provinces flocked to Halifax in search of
work and other opportunities.

While the majority of Haligonians hailed from the United Kingdom,
there was also a significant number of people of German heritage, as well
as a small Jewish population and blacks, many of whom resided in the
aforementioned Africville. Many of the males of Anglo-Saxon lineage
were former soldiers and sailors who had stayed put after completing their
stints in the British military. Thousands more were dirt poor, desperate
Irish immigrants; a large number of them were members of the Irish dias-
pora, having crossed the sea to escape the ravages of the potato famine
that claimed more than a million Irish lives in the years 1845–1851.

Across the harbour in neighbouring Dartmouth, the ethnic mix was
similar to that in Halifax, minus the Jewish and black components. But
Dartmouth also had one demographic element that Halifax did not: a
small Mi'kmaq presence. These descendants of the Chebucto Peninsula's

first inhabitants could trace their roots back thousands of years, yet these few dozen Mi'kmaqs now found themselves reduced to squatting on a rocky eleven-acre parcel of land on the shore of Tufts Cove. The makeshift Mi'kmaq community of Turtle Grove, in the shadow of the Oland Brewery, was a place of abject poverty and hardship. The housing there was rude shacks and tents, and apart from a makeshift school, there were no public services. Living on the margins of white society, the Mi'kmaq people had little interest in events that happened in Halifax. Sadly, this ignorance would not be blissful.

ECHOES OF THE CONFLICT in Europe, half a world away, reverberated loudly in Halifax and Dartmouth and affected daily life in both communities. On the evening of December 5, 1917, residents shuttered their blinds and drew their drapes just as they did each evening at sunset in compliance with the military blackout that was in effect. That reality, along with the presence of warships in the harbour, Royal Navy officers in the Naval Dockyard, thousands of troops passing through the port, hospital ships arriving from Europe laden with wounded warriors, and the port's robust role in Canada's war effort all served to create a sense that the front was close by and that the attendant dangers were very real. Almost every family in Halifax seemed to have at least one man in uniform or know someone who was. At the same time, residents talked about—and dreaded—the possibility that German naval vessels or zeppelins might bombard the city. Despite such fears and even with all the turmoil and uncertainty all around them, the mood of the people in Halifax and neighbouring Dartmouth was surprisingly upbeat. The war had brought uncertainty and death, but it had also brought economic prosperity and a renewed sense of purpose.

HALIFAX'S CONCERNS WERE of no importance to Aimé Le Médec. He had never been to Halifax before, and he had no interest in remaining here any longer than necessary. The captain of the *Mont-Blanc* was intent on just one thing: joining a convoy and getting home to France as quickly as possible. On the evening of December 5, Le Médec was in his cabin having dinner with harbour pilot Francis Mackey and his senior officers and counting the hours until daylight, when Mackey would guide the *Mont-Blanc* into Halifax's inner harbour at Bedford Basin.

Meanwhile, six miles to the northwest, in the same anchorage area that Aimé Le Médec was so eager to reach, Captain Haakon From sat stewing in his cabin aboard the war-relief ship *Imo*; he could barely wait to leave Bedford Basin. By this time, the Norwegian ship had finally finished taking on the load of steam coal she needed to continue her voyage. If From had had any say in the matter, by now he and his ship would have been at sea, two hours out of Halifax and bound for New York City. The captain was still unhappy to be spending another night in port. No matter, he had no choice but to grin and bear it.

CHAPTER 8

On the Eve of Disaster

Halifax, December 5, Early Evening

The hands of the clock on the bulkhead of the chief examiner's office aboard HMCS *Niobe* read 17:30 hours—5:30 p.m. in civilian parlance. It was quitting time for workers at His Majesty's Naval Dockyard and in factories, offices, and shops all across the city. Commander Evan Wyatt, the forty-year-old CXO for the port of Halifax, glanced at his watch. He and his wife, Dorothy, had a social engagement, and the commander was planning to leave work early. It was never easy for him to do so. Wyatt had quickly discovered after his September 1915 appointment that working long hours was expected—and even demanded—of him.

As the CXO, Wyatt was on call seven days a week, year round— Christmas and other holidays included; after all, as his fellow officers were quick to remind him, "There's a war on." When Wyatt was not on duty, he was supposed to be reachable by telephone. Always.

The long workdays and hectic schedule were irksome, but the aggravation they caused was nothing when compared with the frustrations of the commander's ongoing differences with his naval colleagues and with civilian officials, whom he had assumed—at least when he was still new to his job—would support his efforts to make the port run smoothly and safely. Patience not being one of Wyatt's virtues, he could be dismissive or even condescending when dealing with subordinates or others for whom he had no respect. That included the port's civilian harbourmaster, the members of the Halifax Pilotage Commission, and many of the pilots themselves. In Wyatt's mind, dealing with them was akin to—as the saying goes—"trying to herd cats." The pilots had been doing things their own way for many years; they were not about to change because some snooty Englishman told them to do so. He had no authority to punish them if they ignored his directives.

Wyatt's fellow naval officers were equally disrespectful. Technically, although he was "on loan" to Canada's fledgling navy and his monthly paycheques came from Ottawa, Wyatt was officially still a member of the Royal Naval Reserve (RNR).[1] Despite this, the lack of respect the Royal Navy officers in Halifax accorded the RCN and anything to do with this "tin pot navy"—including Wyatt's role in it—only compounded the irritations of his job.

None of this was what Wyatt had signed on for when he became the CXO. Nor could this have been the career arc he dreamed of as a young man growing up in England. In those days, all indications were that Frederick Evan Wyatt might well be destined for great things.

English born, Wyatt—whom family and friends knew by his middle name, Evan—was a bright lad. In 1890, at the age of twelve, he was one of just eight students in the kingdom to win a prestigious Queen's Scholarship. Initiated by Queen Elizabeth I in 1560, the prizes enabled winners to attend the Royal College of St. Peter—better known as Westminster School, owing to its affiliation with storied Westminster Abbey in London. The school, with its roots dating back to the twelfth century, has long been a training ground for the sons of some of England's most prominent families.

The Westminster School records indicate that Wyatt was a "competent student" who also played cricket and football "without any great distinction."[2] An 1893 class photo depicts fifteen-year-old Evan Wyatt as looking every inch the archetypal young academic and so "veddy British." Clean-cut, square-jawed, dark-haired, and resolute, he appears in the photo attired in suitably tweedy garb. He wears an academic robe over his dark-brown suit. A matching waistcoat, an Eton collar, and a watch fob that is draped across a pudgy girth complete his scholarly mien.

UPON LEAVING WESTMINSTER in the summer of 1894 *sans* diploma, Wyatt followed his father's career path when he volunteered for duty in the Royal Navy Reserve. By 1905, young Wyatt had risen to become a lieutenant and had earned a master's designation, meaning he was qualified to captain a ship. Despite this, the realization that it was difficult to make ends meet on what a naval officer earned tempered any sense of accomplishment Evan Wyatt may have felt.

Low wages were an ongoing source of irritation for the men of the RN and RNR— officers, ratings, and ordinary seamen alike.

YOUNG EVAN WYATT IN 1893.
(WESTMINSTER SCHOOL)

Most ranks had not seen a pay raise in half a century. "So far as his pay is concerned, no officer under a captain's rank can really afford to marry. . . . The lieutenant can barely live on his pay," one outspoken admiral complained in a letter to the editor of the *Times of London*.[3]

In 1905, Wyatt and other lieutenants in His Majesty's Royal Navy Reserve took home sixteen shillings per day, which totalled £292 per year. Given that in England at the time, a skilled industrial worker earned about £110 annually and a teacher £176,[4] naval officers earned a living wage, but not much more. And after years of economic stagnancy, the cost of living was beginning a slow, steady rise. Compounding the woes of reserve officers—for lieutenants and those above—non-active service meant reduced wages, or "half-pay." The RNR meted out these reduced wages quarterly, a maximum of seven shillings per day.

Hard pressed to pay his bills, Wyatt signed on as a quartermaster with the Peninsular and Oriental Steam Navigation Company, a well-known British line that carried cargo, mail, and passengers worldwide. In 1907, Wyatt had an even better job offer in the United States, and so he retired from the RNR[5] and took a job with the United Fruit Company, serving as captain of a banana boat.

With Wyatt's career prospects looking up, in January 1909, at age thirty-one, he married. His bride, twenty-eight-year-old Madeline Flora Izod, came from a well-to-do family. Her father, a pioneer in the corset industry, squeezed out a good living as the owner of a factory that manufactured the then-fashionable ladies' undergarments.[6]

Wyatt and his new wife took up residence in London, where she gave birth to a son in 1910. However, the Wyatts separated not long afterward. Evan Wyatt worked overseas and sent monthly support payments home to his wife and son. He was back on the United Fruit Company payroll when war broke out in Europe in the summer of 1914 and the British government mobilized 30,000 RNR officers and men. Wyatt was among them. His orders were to report to Halifax.

After doing so, it didn't take Wyatt long to realize he could not pay his bills on his RN salary. That was the case even after he received a promotion to lieutenant commander on January 15, 1915. The preferment, while welcome, brought only a nominal pay increase. Wyatt, who was nothing if not ambitious, was eager to find a way to make more money.

Having learned that the RCN paid its officers more than did the RN, in April 1915 Wyatt sent a job application letter to Admiral Charles Kingsmill, the director of the Naval Service of Canada. In his query, Wyatt touted his skills and asked Kingsmill to consider him "for any position that you may have now, or after the war."[7] Among his qualifications, Wyatt listed his experience as a "master of mail and passenger steamers," his training as a navigator and pilot, his business acumen, and his fluency in French.[8]

Wyatt's timing was perfect. With war raging in Europe, the five-year-old RCN was in dire need of experienced officers. Thus, when in response to Kingsmill's inquiries, Captain R.G. Corbett, HMCS *Niobe*'s commanding officer, recommended Wyatt as "a most trustworthy and capable Officer,"[9] Wyatt won another promotion. Captain Edward Martin, the superintendent of the Halifax Naval Dockyard, announced on September 15, 1915, that Wyatt was the port of Halifax's new chief examining officer (CXO). In addition to being responsible for overseeing all traffic entering and leaving the harbour, Wyatt was also now in charge of anti-submarine defences. As he was about to discover, he had taken on a big job.

Wyatt was pleased with his promotion and with a pay raise that lifted his annual salary to about £340. His career fortunes and his finances were looking up. Or so he thought. However, an unexpected development was about to complicate his life anew.

IN MARCH 1916, Evan Wyatt's estranged wife in England petitioned for and won a divorce. She took sole custody of the couple's five-year-old son, and the court ordered Wyatt to pay £12 per month in maintenance on the first day of each month.[10] When Wyatt fell behind in his support payments, word of it reached Ottawa. Admiral Charles Kingsmill was outraged; a "gentleman" in 1917 did not get divorced. Although Kingsmill was the head of the Canadian navy, he really had no authority to reprimand Wyatt for matters in his personal life; however, that did not stop the admiral from firing off a letter in which he chided Wyatt and demanded that the commander explain his behaviour.[11]

Wyatt responded to Kingsmill's letter by insisting that the whole situation was the result of "a misunderstanding." He pledged that he would immediately send a cheque to his wife to cover any arrears in support payments and that he would make all future payments on time. That did not happen. There were more problems, most of which were not Wyatt's fault. Regardless, his naval career had hit the wall.

EVAN WYATT DIDN'T CARE for navy life in Halifax, but he had a diversion. Wyatt had fallen in love with a local girl: Dorothy Manners Brookfield was a Halifax socialite. Twenty-eight years old, she was the fourth of five children of Edith and Walter Brookfield, a lumber baron. The extended Brookfield family were prominent in Halifax and had extensive business interests throughout Nova Scotia.

After Evan Wyatt and Dorothy Brookfield married on February 1, 1917, they settled into their life together in a house on Vernon Street in the city's fashionable South End. Wyatt's nascent ties to the Brookfield family were his entrée to the Halifax society. It was a genteel milieu in which he felt very much at home.

To Edith and Walter Brookfield, the commander seemed a suitable match for their youngest daughter, Dorothy. Although he was a portly, forty-year-old divorcé, at a shade over six feet tall, he still cut an impressive figure in his naval uniform. Wyatt was also well mannered, a "gentleman" who spoke with an accent that to a Nova Scotian ear seemed refined but "not plum in your mouth," as the English say. ("Pohts-muth," he would utter, *not* "Ports-mowth.")

Not surprisingly, Dorothy and Evan Wyatt were a popular couple in South End drawing rooms and at social events. On the evening of December 5, the Wyatts planned to attend a wedding party. The commander had donned his overcoat and cap and was about to leave his desk when Mate Roland Iceton, one of his assistants, approached him.

"Sir, Mate Freeman just called the naval control office with his evening report," Iceton reported. "That French munitions ship, the *Mont-Blanc*, has arrived from New York. But the net's in place for the night, so it's too late for her to enter the harbour today. Freeman has ordered the ship to lay over for the night in the examination area. Francis Mackey will guide her into port first thing tomorrow."

Having duly received that information, Wyatt nodded. Then, with a tip of his cap, he hurried out into the darkness. The commander was in a rush to get home and freshen up, for he was looking forward to his evening off. He would worry tomorrow about the *Mont-Blanc* and all the other ships and the nettlesome daily business of the CXO's office. Little did Wyatt know that the next morning he would have a lot more to worry about than he could have ever imagined. Or feared. The CXO's world—like that of everyone in Halifax—was about to change forever.

CHAPTER 9

THE DAY BEGINS

Richmond Area, Halifax, December 6, 1917, 6:00 a.m.

This day that would forever change—and cut short—the lives of so many innocent men, women, and children began inauspiciously. At six o'clock, an hour and twenty minutes before the sun was scheduled to rise on this Thursday morning, the blacked-out city remained cloaked in darkness. In the southwest sky, the crescent moon floated against a cloudless, star-flecked backdrop.

Those who were up and about early would recall that the weather was mild, benignly so for early December and with just nineteen more days until Christmas. This was unusual, but not unheard of, for Halifax. What little breeze there was, as gentle and unhurried as a newborn baby's breath, barely ruffled the Union Jack atop the flagpole at His Majesty's Naval Dockyard.

In areas of the harbour, a wispy haze lingered low over the water. The crews of scows, tugboats, skiffs, ferries, and naval vessels that did the daily tasks that kept the port running smoothly were still gearing up, getting ready for another day. Not Commander Evan Wyatt. Most days, the CXO of the port of Halifax was still at home at 6:00 a.m. His routine was to be on duty by 7:30 a.m. By then, many other navy men aboard the depot ship HMCS *Niobe* were already on the job. Able Seaman Lambert ("Bert") Griffith was among them.

Griffith and his shipmates rose each morning at six bells. That gave them enough time for "stowing of hammocks, hands [then] down to the galley for cocoa at 6:20 [a.m.]. Day men fall-in [at] the front battery for scrubbing down and brass polishing and cleaning of steel stanchions. . . . Whilst the activities were in progress two hands were preparing breakfast."[1]

Griffith, a resident of Red Deer, Alberta, had joined the RCN the previous year. English born, he had immigrated to Canada in 1906. When the war broke out in 1914, his younger brother joined the Canadian army. Although Bert Griffith was thirty-four and a family man, he also wanted to do so. The wartime RCN was in dire need of men—especially older men who were willing to serve on the home front—and so Griffith signed up "to fight for King and Country." Posted to Halifax, he was assigned to work— two weeks on, two weeks off—as a member of the boom crew that each day raised and lowered the port's anti-submarine nets. When he was not on the water, he returned to HMCS *Niobe* to work at general naval duties.

LIKE BERT GRIFFITH and the sailors aboard HMCS *Niobe*, by 6:00 a.m. the crew of the Norwegian relief ship *Imo* and the other vessels anchored in Bedford Basin were starting their daily routines. In the naval examination area outside the entrance to Halifax harbour, so too was the crew of the French munitions ship *Mont-Blanc*. Another busy day in Halifax harbour was beginning.

Most day-shift factory workers punched in at seven o'clock. All across the city, thousands of men and women were getting ready for work. "It was the habit of workers' wives to give their husbands breakfast and return to bed," one observer noted, "and it was rare to see a prosperous man in his office before nine."[2]

Those who lingered over breakfast or who commuted to work on foot could hear resonating in the distance the chimes of the Citadel Hill clock. The familiar ding-dong sound had echoed over the city for more than a century. It was Prince Edward, the Duke of Kent and commander-in-chief of all British military forces in North America, who had ordered the installation of a clock on Citadel Hill. He had hoped it would improve the punctuality of soldiers in the local garrison. It did not, but in the years that followed its 1803 installation, that sonorous sound became part of life in downtown Halifax and much of the city's genteel South End. The clock's chimes were less audible on the streets of the North End. There, the shrieking of factory whistles marked the start and end of the workday. People set their watches not by the chimes of the Citadel Hill clock but rather by the sound of a field gun atop Citadel Hill, which boomed at noon each day and again at 9:30 p.m.

MARY EUGENIA ("JEAN") HINCH was too busy to worry about the time. She had more pressing and vital concerns. When you are the mother of ten children ages two to nineteen, that was to be expected. There are always household chores to do, meals to make, and a child—or two—who needs some attention, a hug, or perhaps a scolding.

Life was not easy for Mary Jean and her husband Joe, although they had been happily married for twenty-four years. She kept the home fires burning; Joe, age fifty, worked the graveyard shift at the busy Naval Dockyard graving dock, which in 1917 was the largest on Canada's east coast. The fifteen dollars that Joe Hinch brought home each week was not a lot of money, but it was enough to put food on the table, and the family made do. "Bricks and mortar make a house," the Irish proverb advises, "but the laughter of children makes a home." Mary Jean Hinch evidently believed that with all her heart, for she never complained. She was accustomed to doing much with little.

Mary Jean herself came from a large family. Halifax born, she was the eldest daughter of Elizabeth (Halloran) and James Jackson. The Jacksons and their nine children—three others had died young—were Irish Catholics, as were many of their neighbours and friends. Life for one and all centred around the focal points of St. Joseph's Church and the adjacent church-run school on Gottingen Street.

In December 1917, Halifax's North End was home to sixty-eight members of the extended Jackson clan. Elizabeth Jackson, the family matriarch, had been a widow for sixteen years. She now lived, along with two of her sons, their wives, and two grandchildren, in the family's long-time home at 1 Roome Street. The rest of the Jacksons along with their spouses and children lived within easy walking distance. The city directory for 1917 showed Jacksons residing at seven North End addresses. Members of the extended family routinely got together or shared meals. They celebrated special occasions, and they supported each other when times were tough. All the Jackson children, like many of the offspring of other families in Halifax's closely knit North End, had big families. Mary Jean and Joe certainly did.

By age forty, Mary Jean had given birth to fourteen children, four of whom had died—two on the same dark day in the spring of 1917—after falling victim to scarlet fever. In the early decades of the twentieth century, scarlet fever (a product of the same bacteria that causes strep throat) was one of the leading killers of Canadian children. Such were the grim realities of life in an era when one youngster in six died before age one.

Despite the painful losses she had endured, Mary Jean never wavered in her religious faith, her zest for life, or her "can-do" spirit. Mentally and physically, she was remarkably robust. She had also managed to retain her good looks; she was still an attractive woman. "Her long auburn hair framed a heart-shaped face with delicate, even features and a clear, almost translucent complexion."[3] Mary Jean took pride in her appearance and her dress—so much so that her sister Ada, a year younger, had affectionately dubbed her "Dude." Although the masculine nickname did not quite fit such a grand lady, the sartorial sentiment did.

ON THE MORNING of December 6, Mary Jean Hinch was out of bed early, as was her habit. It was still dark outside as she sat sipping a cup of tea and gazing out the kitchen window of the family's big, old two-and-a-half-storey frame home. Located at 66 Veith Street, the rental dwelling was perched on the hillside overlooking the Narrows. For Joe Hinch, it was a short walk to the graving dock where he worked the night shift.

The Hinch home was maybe 100 yards west of the water, no farther. Four doors to the north of the house was Richmond Street, a thoroughfare that ran down the hillside to Pier 6, one of the busiest of Halifax's forty-nine commercial wharves.

This morning, with all ten of her children still snuggled in their beds, Mary Jean was savouring the early-morning solitude and quiet—both were rarities in her busy days. Seated at her kitchen table, she hummed to herself as she waited for water to boil in the two huge pots that sat on the two stoves in the house, one in the kitchen, the other in the hallway. With any luck, Mary Jean would get some laundry done before Joe came home from work or the children began to stir. Once the daily rush began, it would be a scramble to prepare Joe's breakfast and get the kids dressed, fed, and off to school.

The wash water was still simmering when nine-year-old Joe Jr. padded into the kitchen, sleepy-eyed and with hair dishevelled. "Mama, I got a sore throat," he whispered, his voice raspy and hoarse. "I don't feel good. Can I please stay home with you today?"

Kids were always looking for excuses to stay home; Mary Jean knew that. Her two eldest girls, nineteen-year-old Clara and seventeen-year-old Helena, were staying home. Both were battling colds; a bad one was going around. Mary Jean felt Joe Jr.'s forehead.

"Yes, you can stay home, Joe. But let's get something into you for that cold, and then it's back to bed with you."

The rest would cure whatever ailed little Joe, or so his mother hoped.

CHAPTER 10

RENDEZVOUS WITH DESTINY

Halifax Harbour, December 6, 1917, 7:00 a.m.

It was still dark when Aimé Le Médec rose from his bunk on this quiet Thursday morning. Sleep had not come easily to the captain of the *Mont-Blanc*. After taking his Wednesday evening meal with harbour pilot Francis Mackey and two of his senior officers, Le Médec and his guests had sat in his cabin talking until bedtime. When the others had gone, the captain was alone with his thoughts.

When finally he extinguished the light and climbed into his bunk, Le Médec contemplated what lay ahead for him and his ship. As he lay there in the darkness, the light beam from the McNabs Island lighthouse that periodically swept across the water and illuminated the *Mont-Blanc* reminded Le Médec that the ship had completed the first leg of her homeward voyage. So far, so good. And in the morning the ship would find sanctuary for a day or two in Halifax's inner harbour. It was the trans-Atlantic crossing that Le Médec dreaded. He had been musing about that when he drifted off to sleep and he still was when he rose from his bunk next morning.

Le Médec's pocket watch advised him it was a few minutes after seven o'clock as he dressed. The eastern sky was growing light when the captain peered out the porthole of his cabin. Beneath his feet, he felt the familiar thrum of the ship's engine; it was already idling at the ready. First Officer Jean Glotin would be waiting for the order to weigh anchor and get under way. Le Médec knew it was time to go to the bridge.

Mackey, the harbour pilot, had advised the captain and his officers that the *Mont-Blanc* would be moving at about four knots on its way into Bedford Basin, and so it would take the ship ninety minutes to reach the anchorage area. In preparation for the time he knew he would spend on the bridge's weather deck, Le Médec wore his navy-blue single-breasted pea jacket. This heavy wool garment, with its slash pockets and two cuff bands of white, gold-flecked piping, was standard attire for CGT captains. Completing his uniform, Le Médec donned his weathered captain's cap with its brass crest badge that bore his employer's lettered logo.

As he emerged from his cabin, Le Médec noted that the morning was calm. The briny air was nowhere near as cold as he had feared, although the captain could see his breath. It was a few minutes past the "nautical dawn"—that time of the morning when the sun is exactly twelve degrees below the horizon and there is just enough light for a mariner to view the sea conditions.

The moon was a silvery crescent in the southwestern sky, itself a deep purple in that soft otherworldly half-light of the predawn. To Le Médec's discerning eyes, the heavens were as clear and deep as a Brittany well. On the water this morning, a wispy layer of mist hovered; it was not thick enough to cloud the outline of McNabs Island, that brooding silhouette that loomed a half-mile off *Mont-Blanc*'s starboard bow. The beam from the island's lighthouse continued its periodic sweep across the water. A second beam, this one off to the port side, was also at work. Close by the *Mont-Blanc*, Le Médec could see other ships in the examination area; he counted *un, deux, troix . . . neuf.* There were nine other vessels waiting to enter Halifax harbour. All had clustered around the RCN gunboat that supervised the movement of ships into and out of the port. Le Médec saw there was just one vessel ahead of the *Mont-Blanc* in the morning queue of inbound traffic. The early morning silence was broken by the rumbling engines of two RCN outbound minesweepers. Le Médec watched them pass, then made his way up to the bridge.

CAPTAIN LE MÉDEC found pilot Francis Mackey, the ship's second officer Joseph Leveque, and helmsman Alphonse Serré waiting for him on the bridge. Leveque had his binoculars trained on the RCN gunboat as he watched for the signal that it was time for the *Mont-Blanc* to get under way.

Following some perfunctory smiles and a good-morning greeting—"*Bonjour à tous*"—Captain Le Médec and pilot Francis Mackey took their places. The two men stood one on each side of the whistle cord they would pull to alert other ships of their intentions as the *Mont-Blanc* steamed northward toward the harbour. Le Médec made eye contact with his second officer. "*Levez l'ancre*," he said.

Joseph Leveque responded by relaying the order to weigh anchor to First Officer Jean Glotin, down on deck. That preliminary out of the way, all eyes on the bridge turned toward the tramp steamer SS *Clara* as she steamed past.[1] The American ship had received the go-ahead to enter the anti-submarine gates ahead of the *Mont-Blanc*. Francis Mackey knew the pilot who was guiding the *Clara*; twenty-nine-year-old Edward Renner had been a harbour pilot for six years. According to the records of the Pilotage Commission, he had a good record.[2] But like his colleagues, Renner was accustomed to doing things his own way, and when he did, it sometimes brought him into conflict with the CXO; Evan Wyatt had occasionally complained about Renner's job performance. In the wake of what was about to happen on this fateful morning, Wyatt's concerns in that regard would become a major point of contention. Not just yet, however. No one was thinking about this as Renner set about guiding the *Clara* into port.

The moment the frothy whiteness of the ship's backwash came into view, the officer of the watch aboard the RCN gunboat that was acting as gatekeeper that morning flashed the sign the men on the bridge of the *Mont-Blanc* were waiting for. It was Francis Mackey who deciphered the flickering message: "*Mont-Blanc*. Hoist identification. Proceed Bedford Basin to await further orders."[3]

Le Médec understood. He nodded and then handed to Leveque a slip of paper upon which RCN examining officer Terrance Freeman had written the code number that was the *Mont-Blanc*'s ticket to gain admittance to the harbour. "*Vérifiez ce numéro*"—"Have this number run up," Le Médec instructed.

"*Et le drapeau rouge pour les explosifs, capitaine?*" asked Leveque.

"*Non*," came the reply. "*Ce n'est pas nécessaire.*" Not necessary. The captain felt there was no need to hoist a red flag, which was the internationally recognized nautical symbol to indicate a ship had explosives on board. Le Médec was correct. Technically, at least. A red flag was required only when stevedores or crew aboard a ship were loading or unloading explosives. No one aboard the *Mont-Blanc* was doing either, not on this morning.

Leveque shrugged and did as ordered. And when the appropriate flags were fluttering on the yardarm, Leveque reported this and announced that the ship's anchor had been raised and secured in place. The *Mont-Blanc* now being ready to go, Le Médec nodded to Mackey. Although the pilot well knew the mandated speed limit in the harbour was five knots, he was acutely aware of the volatility of the *Mont-Blanc*'s cargo. As a result, he was intent on proceeding even slower and with the utmost caution. "Half-speed," said the pilot. "*Demi-vitesse.*"

"*Allez-y, à demi-vitesse*," echoed the captain.[4]

Leveque responded promptly. His gloved hand slid the handle of the telegraph to the appropriate setting. Half-speed. Down below, in the *Mont-Blanc*'s engine room, Third Engineer Louis Brun heard the jangling of the telegraph's bell over the incessant pounding of the ship's engine.

Shouting through the speaking tube, he confirmed that he had received the captain's order. "*Très bien. Demi-vitesse!*" he cried.

Brun called out the order to his companions. Their shirtless torsos were already sooty and glistening with sweat as they set about shovelling more coal into the firebox of the ship's boilers. Satisfied that everything was in order, Brun dutifully scribed the order he had received on the engine room chalkboard. As he was doing so, the rhythmic pounding of the *Mont-Blanc*'s engine grew ever louder. Astern, the ship's single propeller began churning the icy water. As the *Mont-Blanc* edged forward, the red, white, and blue tricolour flag, mounted aft, waved lazily in the cool morning air. It was a few minutes after eight o'clock, and the *Mont-Blanc* was on her way to her rendezvous with destiny.

AT ALMOST THE SAME MOMENT the *Mont-Blanc* was entering Halifax's outer harbour, twelve miles to the north, there was a similar flurry of nautical activity in Bedford Basin. Bjarne Birkland, third officer of the *Imo*, was weighing anchor in advance of the ship's departure for New York. Captain Haakon From was impatient to get going. Like Aimé Le Médec, his counterpart aboard the *Mont-Blanc*, From had slept fitfully. Unlike Le Médec, who dreaded his departure from Halifax, From could not get away fast enough.

Later, some people would speculate that alone in his cabin on the night of December 5, the feisty Norwegian had eased his frustrations by uncorking a bottle of liquid relief. There were no wartime prohibitions on consuming alcohol on board neutral ships—who would or *could* have enforced them even if there had been?—and there were rumours that From enjoyed a drink, or two, now and then. The truth was, the captain had grown up in a family of teetotallers, and he was not known to drink. Yet Haakon From's behaviour on that fateful morning would raise questions.

The *Imo*'s captain made no secret of the fact he was angry that Wednesday's unexpected coaling delay meant his ship had to stay another

PRIOR TO THE OUTBREAK OF THE WAR, THE CIVILIAN HARBOURMASTER
WOULD HAVE DENIED A MUNITIONS SHIP SUCH AS THE *MONT-BLANC* PERMISSION
TO ENTER HALIFAX HARBOUR. (NOVA SCOTIA ARCHIVES)

night in Halifax. The RCN examining officer having cleared the ship to leave the port, From was now intent on leaving post-haste. Keen to make up for lost time, he repeatedly eyed his pocket watch over breakfast. Where, he wondered, was the harbour pilot, this Hayes fellow, who had guided the *Imo* into port and would guide her out again?

William Hayes had spent the night at home with his wife, Gertrude, and their three children. As he hurried down Fort Needham hill this morning, he had a good view of the harbour, which was still quiet. Hayes could see the cargo vessels that waited at the deep water piers on both sides of the Narrows. At Pier 4 in the Naval Dockyard, the familiar silhouette of the depot ship HMCS *Niobe* loomed large. Several smaller Canadian patrol boats, some American naval vessels, and two Royal Navy armed merchant cruisers had dropped anchor nearby. Three Royal Navy warships, HMS *Knight Templar*, HMS *Changuinola*, and HMS *Highflyer*, were in port waiting to serve as escorts for Europe-bound convoys.

Highflyer, in particular, was attracting attention. The light cruiser was anchored toward the Dartmouth side, a few hundred yards south of the Naval Dockyard. The warship, which had arrived in port five days earlier, was now refuelled and ready for a scheduled Friday departure. After nineteen years at sea, *Highflyer* was starting to show her age. However, at

375 feet long she was still an imposing presence. Grey and solid, her reputation preceded her. *Highflyer* had seen action on several occasions during the war, most notably when she sank the much-larger German armed merchant cruiser *Kaiser Wilhelm der Grosse* in a battle off the coast of Spanish Sahara. And so *Highflyer* was the object of curiosity in Halifax harbour. Hayes, like many mariners, had taken note of her presence.

By the time he arrived at the pilotage office on Bedford Row in downtown Halifax, it was almost eight o'clock. Two miles to the south, the *Mont-Blanc* was steaming northward at a leisurely pace, easing her way toward Bedford Basin. The flock of gulls trailing in the ship's wake swooped and dived, stark slashes of white against the cloudless blue sky. Off to the east, the horizon flared with the dawn. "The rays of light, first red, then orange, then shining gold like the heart of a fire, poured from the seaward horizon in the harbour and lit up the mist which lay like a liquid over the flat water. The drops of moisture flashed like quicksilver."[5]

At the pilotage office, Hayes found tugboat captain George Fenton waiting for him. With no time to waste, the two promptly set off for the *Imo*. They made just one quick stop on the way. Hayes checked in at HMCS *Acadia*, the naval control vessel that had stood watch at the entrance to Bedford Basin. As was his habit, the pilot alerted the duty officer that his charge this morning—the Norwegian relief vessel *Imo*—would be leaving port as soon as possible. Hayes' gesture was a courtesy rather than a procedural necessity. The officer with whom the pilot spoke, Lieutenant Arthur Adams, Royal Navy Volunteer Reserve (RNVR), did not bother to relay news of Hayes' visit to the CXO's office aboard HMCS *Niobe* or to the navy men on HMCS *Gulnare*, a converted fishing trawler that on this day was serving as the port's guard ship. In Adams' mind, the news that the *Imo* was departing for New York was not important. She was the only vessel leaving Bedford Basin that morning, and she had received clearance to go the previous day. "I sent no message, as it was not customary [to do so]," Adams would later explain.[6] Instead, the lieutenant sat down to his breakfast.

GEORGE FENTON'S TUGBOAT pulled alongside the *Imo* just as Bjarne Birkland and a couple of other crewmen were weighing anchor in preparation for their ship's departure from Halifax. Second Officer Peter B'Jönnas waved to Hayes as he came aboard the *Imo*. B'Jönnas, like Captain From, First Officer Ingvald Iverson, and various members of the ship's Norwegian crew, spoke fluent English.

"Good morning, sir. We're all ready to go," called B'Jönnas, shouting to make himself heard over the clanking of the anchor chain as it retreated through the hawsehole. Nodding toward the *Imo*'s bridge, which was amidships, he added, "Captain From is waiting for you."

Hayes found the captain and First Officer Iverson on the open-air area of the bridge. From, as impatient as a landlord on rent day, stood with his hands thrust into the pockets of his greatcoat and shifted his weight back and forth from one foot to the other. In the wheelhouse, Johan Johansen, the *Imo*'s twenty-year-old helmsman, was at the ready.

From greeted Hayes with a perfunctory handshake and a hasty "Good morning." The captain had little time for pleasantries today. He wanted to get away as quickly as possible, and the ship was ready, and conditions on the water were ideal. The morning weather was fair, the wind light. The wispy haze that had been hanging over the harbour was beginning to clear as the sun rose and the air grew warm. Little did anyone in Halifax know that this would be "the last day of fine weather for more than a week," as one observer would recall.[7]

"Shall we get going, Mister Hayes?" said Captain From.

Hayes nodded. Then, turning to First Officer Iverson, he intoned, "Ahead slow, please. Steady as she goes."

Iverson shifted the handle of the ship's brass telegraph to the "ahead slow" position and then relayed the same instructions to the engine room via the speaking tube. Satisfied with this, William Hayes turned and peered through the open wheelhouse window at the *Imo*'s youthful helmsman. "Steady as she goes, Mr. Helmsman," Hayes sang out. Johan Johansen nodded.

Down below, in the heat and noise of the cramped confines of the *Imo*'s engine room, Chief Engineer George Louis Skarre was in charge. The *Imo*'s second engineer oversaw operations as the engine room crew summoned to life the ship's 424-horsepower engine. The fourth engineer recorded in a logbook the orders that came down from the bridge, while a "donkeyman"—an all-purpose helper—confirmed those orders, echoing them back to First Officer Iverson on the bridge. All was running smoothly and normally. As the *Imo* began to move, she slowly knifed her way through the tranquil waters of Bedford Basin; she was travelling at a leisurely two knots. This made the helmsman's job easy, and that was a good thing, for there were more than thirty other ships anchored on the western side of the Basin that morning; many of them were scheduled to join the *Mont-Blanc* in a Europe-bound convoy that was due to leave next day. At the *Imo*'s helm, Johan Johansen steered a zigzag through the nautical maze. When finally the *Imo* was clear, Johansen headed the ship toward the Narrows, the quarter-mile-wide entrance to Bedford Basin. William Hayes, like Captain From, smiled in silent approval. Turning back to First Officer Iverson, he advised, "Full ahead."

When that order was conveyed to the engine room, the pounding noise of the *Imo*'s engine grew louder. For the first time in two days, Captain From's mood brightened. His ship was picking up speed, moving at about six knots—roughly seven miles per hour—and above the harbour speed limit. The *Imo* would soon leave Halifax behind. Then it would be full speed ahead to New York. Once he was in the open sea, Haakon From intended to do his best to make up for lost time.

CHAPTER 11

En route to Bedford Basin, the *Mont-Blanc* continued to make slow but steady progress. Pilot Francis Mackey briefly brought the ship to a halt below Citadel Hill, pausing to allow the early morning passenger ferry to cross between Dartmouth and Halifax.

By 8:15 a.m. the *Mont-Blanc* was under way again and was passing the Naval Dockyard, where all was still relatively quiet. Few of the navy men who were already at work took much notice of the *Mont-Blanc*; Captain John L. Makiny aboard the RCN-chartered armed tugboat *Nereid* was an exception. Makiny and his crew were getting ready for another day of patrolling Halifax's anti-submarine net defences. This morning, *Nereid* was anchored near Pier 4, at the north end of the dockyard, not far from the depot ship HMCS *Niobe*. Makiny, as was his habit, was watching the early morning harbour traffic, "looking to see what was going out or coming in," he would later recall. "I took my little glasses and I seen [*sic*] this loaded ship coming in. . . . She was, I should positively swear, not [going] four knots; very slow."[1]

On the *Mont-Blanc*'s bridge, pilot Mackey, Captain Aimé Le Médec, and First Officer Jean Glotin were unaware that the *Nereid*'s captain was watching their ship. All eyes on the *Mont-Blanc* were focused on HMS *Highflyer*. Spotlighted by the morning sun, the big ship was an impressive sight, what with her three huge smokestacks, two masts, and a deck that bristled with guns. The outgoing tide had "chafed the stern and swung her bow toward the north. She lay there lean and grey and cruel, and pointing straight at the Narrows."[2]

Pilot Mackey gave *Highflyer* a wide berth. He advised Captain Le Médec to order helmsman Alphonse Serré to bear slightly right, to starboard. This path took the *Mont-Blanc* east, toward the Dartmouth side of the harbour. As the French ship passed *Highflyer*, Mackey advised the Frenchmen that *Highflyer* would be serving as the naval escort for the convoy the *Mont-Blanc* hoped to join for the voyage to France. Le Medec nodded. Then, in a gesture of respect, he ordered that the *Mont-Blanc*'s colours be dipped. Lowering and raising the flag was the customary nautical salute when a merchant ship passed close to a warship.

Highflyer's officer on watch, Lieutenant Richard Woolams, RNR, had just come on deck. He was still getting his bearings when he spotted the *Mont-Blanc* passing 100 yards to *Highflyer*'s starboard side. Woolams waved and returned Le Médec's greeting, ordering the flagman to dip the warship's white ensign in a reciprocal show of good etiquette. Having done this, Woolams peered through his binoculars at the *Mont-Blanc*. She was out of Marseille, or so the words painted on her escutcheon indicated. Like others who saw the ship in the harbour on this day, Woolams wondered what cargo she was carrying. He could see the *Mont-Blanc* was travelling at a snail's pace and riding low in the water with her head slightly down. The lieutenant studied the metal drums on the *Mont-Blanc*'s deck. This curious load, which was surrounded by a jerry-built wooden matrix, looked to be held in place with guy ropes. Even at this distance, Woolams could smell a faint gasoline-like odour.

"Fuel oil, or perhaps petrol," *Highflyer*'s officer on watch muttered to no one in particular. "Whatever it is, she's damned sloppily loaded. No speed either. The convoy admiral won't be very happy about that one."[3]

TWO MILES NORTH of *Highflyer*, the *Imo* was threading her way through the maze of ships anchored in Bedford Basin. On a chart of the Halifax harbour where north is at the top, the Norwegian ship was steaming left to right on a short dogleg arc. Once the ship entered the Narrows, pilot William Hayes intended to keep the *Imo* in mid-channel until she passed HMS *Highflyer*, the Naval Dockyard, and HMCS *Niobe*. Then, with the harbour's anti-submarine gates, Georges Island, and McNabs Island in the *Imo*'s wake, she would be on her way to New York. That could not happen a moment too soon for Haakon From. Thus, down in the *Imo*'s engine room, Chief Engineer George Louis Skarre, following the orders that came from the bridge, was running the engines all out. The *Imo* was gaining speed as she turned south and entered the nautical bottleneck that is the Halifax Narrows.

THE WIPSY MIST that had cloaked parts of the harbour in the pre-dawn darkness still lingered in stretches of the channel between McNabs Island in the south and the Narrows in the north. On the *Imo*'s bridge, pilot Hayes and Captain From were squinting into the morning sun. Following Hayes' directions, helmsman Johan Johansen turned the ship southeast. On a previous visit to Halifax, he recalled veering to starboard as the *Imo* entered the Narrows. Doing so, he had oriented himself by sighting various buildings in the Halifax skyline—in particular, the towering silos of the Acadia Sugar Refinery, twelve storeys high. Today, the *Imo* was taking a different route. Johansen knew this, but he did not question it. The man providing directions was a local harbour pilot who knew these waters.

Captain From was of the same mind, and so he busied himself with plans for all he needed to do in New York. Meanwhile, most of the *Imo*'s thirty-nine-man crew were eating breakfast in the galley. All was going smoothly. Or it was until William Hayes sighted an approaching ship far in the distance. At first glance, the vessel appeared to be in the same lane in which the *Imo* was travelling.

Hayes had spotted the American freighter SS *Clara*, which had preceded the *Mont-Blanc* through Halifax harbour's anti-submarine gates. Aboard the *Clara*, pilot Edward Renner had the ship on a path that saw her steaming along on the Halifax side of the main channel. As a result, when she veered slightly to port, the *Clara* would pass the southbound *Imo* on the Norwegian ship's starboard side. This manoeuvre was more than an "excuse me" breach of nautical etiquette.

The rules of navigation for ships as they pass in a harbour or a narrow channel dictate that each vessel bear to the right, passing on the other ship's port side. If, for any reason, there is confusion or doubt, standard procedure is for the ship's pilot or captain to signal his or her intentions audibly—that is, with a horn, a siren, or a whistle. This protocol is as straightforward as it is simple: one quick burst of sound indicates the intention to pass on the right. Two bursts, on the left. Three bursts is a signal that the ship is about to reverse her engines.

Halifax harbour pilots knew the nautical "rules of the road," which were second nature to all mariners. That was as true for William Hayes on the bridge of the *Imo* as it was true for Francis Mackey aboard the *Mont-Blanc*. Both men were veteran pilots; Hayes had twenty-four years' experience, Mackey nineteen years. Edward Renner, the man piloting the *Clara*, was a relative newcomer to pilotage, with just six years on the job. Regardless, he, too, knew and understood his responsibilities; however, as the Greek fabulist Aesop noted, "Familiarity breeds contempt."

Renner and the other Halifax harbour pilots sometimes did things "their own way," ignoring or bending the rules. When they did so, it angered naval officials—port CXO Commander Wyatt, in particular. Wyatt insisted on doing things "by the book." But that did not always happen, and it certainly did not happen on the morning of December 6, 1917, in Halifax harbour. The consequences would be grave. Renner's casual approach to his job was about to set in motion a Rube Goldberg-like chain of consequences that proved disastrous in ways that no one could possibly have foreseen or even imagined.

THE *IMO* WAS SLIGHTLY on the Dartmouth side of the Narrows as she and the *Clara* drew near each other. William Hayes, having no idea who was piloting the *Clara*, found the exchange of whistle signals unusual. However, because he was in a hurry, he was willing to ignore protocol. "[Hayes] blew one, and I answered with two [toots]," Renner would say. "He answered me with two . . . he wanted to go to starboard."[4]

Hayes did as he had signalled. The *Imo* and the *Clara* passed starboard to starboard; the ships were close enough that Renner could call out to Hayes. In the days before radio came into widespread nautical use, ships communicated using flags, lights, and megaphones. Renner used a megaphone to hail the *Imo*. As a courtesy, he wanted to alert the ship's pilot to the weather conditions between McNabs Island and Pier 9 on the Halifax side of the harbour. Renner suspected that if it chanced to thicken, the hazy mist that was lingering there in spots could pose a navigational hazard for southbound ships.

"I hollered out and I told [Hayes] there was a ship coming astern," Renner would recall. "He said, 'What did you say?', and I said a ship is following right behind me."[5]

After waving to acknowledge that he understood Renner's warning, Hayes turned his binoculars southward. Doing so, he spotted the vessel Renner had referred to; she was emerging from the mist, less than a mile off the *Imo*'s starboard bow.

THE *STELLA MARIS* was a familiar sight in Halifax harbour. William Hayes immediately recognized the 125-foot former British navy gunboat and minesweeper. Captained by Horatio H. Brannen, a forty-five-year-old native of Woods Harbour, Shelburne County, and operating under charter to the RCN, the vessel served as a tugboat and salvage vessel.[6] Squat, with two masts—one fore, one aft—and painted grimy wartime grey, she was belching black smoke from her single funnel. When she was hard at work, the *Stella Maris* looked nothing like the "lady of the sea" or the "Virgin Mary" that her Latin name suggested. Today, she was playing the role of charwoman.

When Hayes sighted her, the *Stella Maris* was emerging from the south end of the graving yard. Captain Brannen and his twenty-three-man crew were towing two barges loaded with ashes from the Naval Dockyard. Ropes held the carriers together in tandem behind the tugboat. From bow to stern, the *Stella Maris* procession was 100 yards long and moving at glacial speed.

On this morning, Captain Brannen's twenty-one-year-old son was at the tugboat's wheel. Walter Brannen was the first to spot the *Imo* bearing down on them. "I couldn't see her very plainly. There was a mist. [I saw] her starboard first, her broad side. . . . We were going up, and she was coming down. She was headed more over towards Dartmouth at the time."[7]

The younger Brannen reckoned the *Imo* was travelling too fast for the harbour. Horatio Brannen also saw this and shared his son's concern. "Why in God's name is that ship traveling so fast?!" he asked.[8]

ON THE *IMO*'S BRIDGE, William Hayes and Captain From were not concerned about their ship's speed; conditions were good, and they were in a hurry. So Hayes was annoyed suddenly to see the *Stella Maris* chugging toward them mid-channel. The pilot cussed under his breath. He knew he would have to act quickly in order to avoid colliding with the

Stella Maris or one of those damned barges she was pulling. A ship needs room to manoeuvre; it cannot stop or turn on a dime. That is especially true if a ship is sailing in ballast, as the *Imo* was on this day.

Hayes was still puzzling over what the *Stella Maris* was doing in midchannel when in the distance he spotted another ship emerging from behind the profile of HMS *Highflyer*. Through the morning haze, this newcomer looked to be maybe a half mile off. Backlit by the rising sun, the vessel was a silhouette. However, to Hayes' discerning eyes, she was riding low in the sparkling water, and the way white foam was curling away from her bow suggested she was moving slowly.

Hayes' gut told him this ship—*not* the *Stella Maris*—was the subject of Edward Renner's cautionary message. With that in mind, Hayes advised Captain From to sound the *Imo*'s whistle. A moment later, a shrill and demanding toot shattered the morning's tranquility. As the sound echoed across Halifax harbour, it drew curious glances from people on shore and on vessels around the harbour.

"Steady on, a little port!" Hayes called to Johan Johansen at the *Imo*'s wheel.

The pilot's direction to shift the rudder slightly to the left moved the ship in his field of vision a few degrees in the opposite direction, to starboard. Hayes wanted to be closer to the Dartmouth side of the Narrows. Doing so, he reasoned, would eliminate any chance of a collision with both the *Stella Maris* and that approaching northbound cargo ship. Hayes was familiar with the Dartmouth side of the harbour. The water here was shallower than it was out in the main channel, but at a depth of almost fifty feet, it was deep enough for safe navigation. Hayes was also aware that because the *Imo* was sailing in ballast, she was riding higher in the water and had a shallower draft than normal. However, she also needed a bit more room to manoeuvre.

CAPTAIN HORATIO BRANNEN could see that the *Imo* had changed course. From his perspective in the wheelhouse of the *Stella Maris*, the Norwegian relief ship appeared to have "swung down channel." Even so, that single toot from her whistle continued to echo in his ears. *Something* about the situation still did not feel right. Like father, like son, Walter Brannen shared his father's concern. "I noticed the position [the *Imo*] was in, and I thought she couldn't be blowing for us. She was practically down on us then, and there was no need of her coming to starboard to get clear of us."[9]

It was only when he poked his head out the wheelhouse door and looked toward the stern of the ship that Walter Brannen realized what had prompted that toot of the *Imo*'s whistle. Brannen saw the danger Hayes had spotted: an inbound ship that was emerging from the mist. It was difficult to accurately say how far off she was. Judging distance on the open water is tricky at the best of times; objects become magnified.

Acting on his father's directions, Walter Brannen hastily steered the *Stella Maris* back toward the Halifax side of the harbour. The elder Brannen hoped they would be well out of harm's way there. Ordinarily, he would have been right about that. Not today.

When the *Imo* swept past the *Stella Maris* a minute or two later, about 150 yards of water separated the two ships. As Captain Brannen watched, he noted that the *Imo* was slightly to the Dartmouth side of the main channel.

IT WAS NOW almost 8:30 a.m., and as far as Francis Mackey and Captain Le Médec were concerned, the *Mont-Blanc*'s commute to Bedford Basin was going smoothly. The near-placid waters of Halifax harbour sparkled in the morning sunshine. With the sun in the ship's wake, the *Mont-Blanc*'s open-air bridge was in shadows, and the men standing there found the air cool. But the day had started off well and was shaping up to be a good one for Captain Le Médec and his crew. This being the *Mont-Blanc*'s first visit to Halifax, the Frenchmen were looking forward to catching their collective breath before they joined the convoy in which she would continue her trans-Atlantic passage. With any luck, the *Mont-Blanc*'s crewmen might even have a few hours to unwind, possibly even to go ashore for some fun.

Le Médec and Second Officer Joseph Leveque had been impressed and reassured by their up-close view of HMS *Highflyer*. The men were chattering away in French, sharing their impressions of the ship and discussing what they could see of Halifax. Francis Mackey continued to monitor ship traffic in the channel ahead. He remained acutely aware of the volatility of the *Mont-Blanc*'s cargo and felt uneasy about it. This was why he had advised Captain Le Médec that he intended to proceed "as slow as we possibly could." [10]

MACKEY SPOTTED THE *Stella Maris* and the *Imo* not long after the *Mont-Blanc* passed HMS *Highflyer*. Just as Hayes had done, Mackey recognized the profile of the *Stella Maris* the moment he sighted her. The feathery ribbon of black smoke streaming from her funnel reassured Mackey that Horatio Brannen's tugboat and the two scows trailing her were making for the Halifax side of the harbour. The *Stella Maris* was of little concern to him. His eyes focused on that approaching ship, which he figured was the *Imo*. "I could see the north [end] of the Narrows and . . . the sun on the light brown paint of [her] mast." [11]

Mackey was familiar with the *Imo*, having piloted her on one of her previous visits to Halifax. Mackey also knew that William Hayes had drawn the assignment to guide her into and out of port this time around. The two pilots had chatted the previous afternoon while riding together in the Pickford & Black skiff. Hayes had mentioned to Mackey that a coaling problem had delayed the *Imo*'s departure from Halifax.

Mackey had made a mental note of that information. However, he had not heard the *Imo*'s single whistle blast a few minutes earlier, nor had anyone else aboard the *Mont-Blanc*. The men on the French ship became aware of the *Imo*'s approach only when Mackey noticed her steaming south on the Dartmouth side of the channel, a half-mile distant. To Mackey's dismay, he saw the Norwegian ship was closing on them quickly; her speed and direction gave Mackey reason for concern. The *Imo* was already close enough that Mackey and Captain Le Médec could read the words "Belgian Relief," which were emblazoned on the *Imo*'s hull in ten-foot-tall red letters painted on a white background. Experience told Mackey that unless the *Imo* changed course, she was going to cut across the *Mont-Blanc*'s intended path. If that happened, the two ships might collide.

Having confirmed the *Imo*'s identity, pilot Mackey's temper flashed. William Hayes was his friend, and he was a veteran harbour pilot, but Mackey could not fathom what Hayes was up to—that is, *if* it indeed was Hayes who was piloting the *Imo*. There was no time to wonder if he was. "Looks as if that damned fool is aiming to come down in our water," Mackey snapped. "Why the devil doesn't he get over to his own side?"[12]

The *Mont-Blanc* was still proceeding at a crawl, and Mackey was confident the ship was where she was *supposed* to be, in her proper channel. She also had the right-of-way. Being confident on both counts, Mackey grabbed the *Mont-Blanc*'s whistle cord and gave a quick, sharp tug. He meant that one toot to be an attention getter and a signal. Mackey hoped that if William Hayes was piloting the *Imo* this morning, he would heed Mackey's warning that he was asserting his claim to the right-of-way. But there was a problem with Mackey's strategy. A big one.

A single toot of a ship's whistle normally indicates a vessel is changing course, veering to starboard. Mackey knew this, and so he hedged his bet, advising Captain Le Médec to reduce the *Mont-Blanc*'s speed to an absolute minimum. "Dead slow!" he said. "And take her a little to starboard."

Le Médec understood. "*Très lentement*," he called out. Then turning to Alphonse Serré at the *Mont-Blanc*'s wheel, the captain ordered him to

give the ship's wheel a half-turn to steer her to the right, a little to starboard. "*Et dirigez-la doucement à tribord.*"

Mackey nodded his approval. He wanted to put as much distance as
possible between the *Mont-Blanc* and the *Imo*. To do so, he would risk
going closer to the Dartmouth shore.

WILLIAM HAYES WAS PUZZLED by the single toot sounded by the
whistle of the approaching inbound ship that he had been watching; however, he had no choice but to believe the pilot of this other ship intended to
go to the right. Hayes advised Haakon From to answer with two quick
blasts of the *Imo*'s whistle. She would bear left, to port. This would move
the *Imo* closer to the Dartmouth shore. If he did this, Hayes reasoned, it
would ensure that both ships would have ample room to pass safely, starboard to starboard. That was how the *Imo* and the *Clara* had passed a few
minutes earlier. Hayes knew that doing this was contrary to the nautical
"rules of the road." However, this was one of those occasions when necessity seemed to trump convention.

CONFUSION, LIKE FEAR, is contagious. Francis Mackey and Aimé Le
Médec were growing more confused and fearful with each passing
moment. There was barely a quarter-mile of water now between the *Mont-
Blanc* and the *Imo*, and both pilot and captain were in a quandary. "[The
Imo] wanted to pass me on my starboard side," Mackey said.[13] He was
puzzled as to why because he instinctively knew there was not enough
room for that to happen. "What in God's name is that idiot doing?" he
shouted. "Hard aport! Stop the engines!"[14]

Now Mackey was angry. Seizing the *Mont-Blanc*'s whistle cord, he
gave another sharp pull in hopes of attracting the attention of whomever
was on the *Imo*'s bridge. The gesture was a desperate one. Mackey understood that his options were limited; the window for him to take evasive
action and avoid a collision was rapidly closing. If the *Mont-Blanc* and

the *Imo* continued on their current courses, the ships would crash, possibly head-on. If that happened, Heaven help them. They would all die. If the two ships only brushed each other as they passed, or even if they managed to miss each other entirely, Mackey feared the *Mont-Blanc* would strike bottom and run aground. "Having on a load of explosives, I didn't want to put her ashore, and if I had reversed my engines, I knew she would slew ashore." [15]

The pilot's heart was in his mouth. Sweat beaded his brow. Mackey could scarcely believe his ears when mere seconds after the sound of the *Mont-Blanc*'s whistle had died away, the *Imo* answered not with one toot, but rather with *two*. This was the last sound the men on the bridge of the *Mont-Blanc* ever expected—or wanted—to hear. "I didn't understand," Le Médec would recall. "I asked myself why the *Imo* was giving two blasts." [16]

A single toot would have indicated the pilot of the Norwegian ship had heard and understood Mackey's message and was about to veer right, taking the *Imo* out toward the main channel. Two toots meant the trespasser was intent on holding her course. Mackey was aghast. "The first thought that struck me at that time—knowing Hayes as I do—I said that could not be *your* order. . . . I didn't think Hayes would do that." [17]

By now, there was no doubt the *Imo* and the *Mont-Blanc* were on a collision course. The *Mont-Blanc*'s engines were idling; however, her momentum continued carrying her forward. The gap between the ships was shrinking rapidly: a hundred yards, seventy-five yards, fifty yards . . .

The *Mont-Blanc* and the *Imo* were now so close that the men on the bridge of each ship could see each other's faces. As yet, only those who were aboard the French ship realized the perils of the situation or the extent of the devastation that could follow any collision. In the event, even Captain Le Médec and his crew had no inkling of the scale of the death and suffering that was about to be unleashed.

CHAPTER 12

If it really is true that a person's character reveals itself in moments of high drama or danger, we know all there is to know about Aimé Le Médec. In this penultimate moment before disaster occurred, the captain of the *Mont-Blanc* leapt forward to make a last-ditch effort to avert disaster. Le Médec knew that under French law—and the rules of international maritime navigation—he was ultimately responsible for the safety of the ship and her crew. But what could he do? Even with the *Mont-Blanc*'s engines idling, with her cargo holds so fully loaded it was impossible to halt her forward momentum.

Even had it been possible to do so, dropping the ship's anchor would do no good; it was too late for that. At the same time, there was no room for him to veer closer to the Dartmouth shore. The captain's nautical instincts, honed by his more than two decades at sea, told him that in mid-channel they might have at least some opportunity to avert the crash that now seemed inevitable. The only chance was to steer the ship sharply to the left, to port. "*Venez à bâbord!*" he shouted to helmsman Alphonse Serré.

"Almost together we were of the same mind," Mackey would later say.[1]

If only there had been even a few more seconds to spare, Le Médec's gamble might have worked, for the ship responded to her rudder. In the next instant, hopes soared on the *Mont-Blanc*'s bridge; Le Médec and Mackey saw the words "Belgian Relief" on the side of the *Imo*'s hull. However, those same hopes were dashed as quickly as they arose.

STANDING ON THE BRIDGE of the *Imo*, William Hayes knew a collision was coming. Impulsively, he seized the *Imo*'s whistle cord and tugged sharply. One, two, three times. The shrill toots that echoed across Halifax harbour announced that the *Imo* was reversing her engines. A bell rang in the *Imo*'s engine room at almost the same instant that on her bridge Hayes was calling out to Jonas Johansen, the *Imo*'s helmsman, "Hard to starboard!"

Hayes' decision to reverse the *Imo*'s engine was a last-second Hail Mary gamble. Like the move by Captain Le Médec of the *Mont-Blanc* to change course abruptly, in isolation it might have succeeded in averting disaster. However, in his haste to act, the *Imo*'s pilot had overlooked one vital fact: reversing the ship's engines created what physicists call transverse thrust. It redirected the ship's bow perpendicularly: in this case, to starboard. And because she was sailing in ballast and was unusually light, the horizontal displacement was magnified. As a result, the *Imo*'s bow was now pointed dagger-like at the starboard side of the *Mont-Blanc*'s hull at almost a ninety-degree angle.[2]

IT WAS NOW 8:45 a.m. and both the *Mont-Blanc* and the *Imo* were near mid-channel but still on a collision course. *Mon Dieu!* My God! How could this possibly be happening? Le Médec wondered.

In those final few moments before the crash, perhaps twenty seconds before impact—Le Médec would later say he was unsure of how long it was—he grabbed the whistle cord one final time. The captain yanked three times, and three toots rang out over the harbour. Just as William Hayes had done aboard the *Imo*, Le Médec intended to reverse his ship's engines. Doing so, he hoped, might at least soften the impact when the *Imo*'s bow slammed into the *Mont-Blanc*. The captain also prayed that any damage to the bow of his ship would be confined to the area around the ship's number-one cargo hold. That space was packed with drums of wet picric acid, which Le Médec had been advised were relatively stable. It was the contents of the *Mont-Blanc*'s number-two hold that were most hazardous, for it was packed with crates of TNT. The captain was well aware that this yellow-coloured solid is dangerous to handle or transport; any violent or sudden shock, or even a jarring motion, could set it off.

"Agonizing seconds passed in surreal slow motion as the physical laws of impetus and thrust wielded their effect."[3] To those men aboard the *Mont-Blanc* and the *Imo*, what was happening seemed like a bad dream. However, it was all too real.

The *Imo* was now a 430-foot-long torpedo that was hurtling forward at four or five knots as it slammed into the *Mont-Blanc*. The crash produced a thud that was heard around the harbour. Heads turned, all eyes going to the two vessels that had collided. Onlookers saw that the *Imo*'s bow had plunged deep into the starboard side of the French ship. Exactly how far it went would never be determined with certainty; in fact, that question would be a matter of debate. However, witnesses would later report that the gash in the *Mont-Blanc*'s number-one cargo hold extended almost as far into the ship as her hatch combings. Even more significant, the force of the impact unseated several barrels of the benzol that were stacked on the *Mont-Blanc*'s deck. The containers broke open when they hit the deck; their volatile contents spilled out and cascaded into the gash in the

Mont-Blanc's hull, like salt being poured into a wound. "[The *Imo*] struck us so hard she slew us around and brought us in line with the south side of Pier 6 [on the Halifax side of the waterfront]," said Francis Mackey.[4]

Strangely, those who were aboard the *Imo* barely felt any shock from the crash. Second Officer Peter B'Jönnas and three of his men were on the foredeck at the moment of impact. B'Jönnas was closer to the point of impact than anyone else. Asked later to describe what he felt as the *Imo* sliced into the *Mont-Blanc*, his answer was succinct. "Very little," he would say.[5]

Even the four men on the ship's bridge, all of whom knew the collision was coming and had braced themselves for the impact, were surprised that it happened with so little effect. From his vantage point in the wheelhouse, helmsman Johan Johansen could not see the actual collision. He felt only a slight jolt. "I couldn't tell whether the [*Imo*] was going ahead or laying still," he said. "She was moving so slow I could not notice."[6]

IN THE MOMENTS immediately after the *Imo* and the *Mont-Blanc* collided, there was a lull, a pause mere heartbeats in duration. As yet, the extent of the damage to either ship was unclear.

The first sounds to emerge from the two ships were shouts of confusion, fear, and bewilderment. Shipboard bells jangled. The gulls circling above squawked in distress as an angry mechanical roar emerged from the bowels of the *Imo*. Now at a determined full throttle and tugging ferociously in reverse, the Norwegian ship's engines sent a plume of acrid smoke shooting from the ship's funnel. Her propellers churned the harbour water frantically. The flukes on the *Imo's* bow anchor had snared themselves on double-riveted steel plates deep within the hull of the French ship. "Metal rasped against metal, and the friction threw out a rain of sparks, which instantly ignited the benzol that had seeped into the hold."[7]

With a sudden start, the two ships disengaged as if the rope in a frantic tug-of-war had snapped unexpectedly. The *Imo* lurched eastward, toward

Fire at Halifax

THIS PHOTO BY LIEUTENANT VICTOR M. MAGNUS, RNVR (INSET), WHO WAS ABOARD HMS *CHANGUINOLA*, WAS TAKEN JUST MINUTES AFTER THE EXPLOSION ON DECEMBER 6. MAGNUS' CAMERA WAS POINTED NORTHWEST, TOWARD WHERE PIER 6 AND THE *MONT-BLANC* HAD BEEN. THE RICHMOND AREA OF HALIFAX IS ABLAZE IN THE DISTANCE. (COURTESY OF DAMIAN SAUNDERS/ANN FOREMAN)

the Dartmouth shore. The *Mont-Blanc* shot in the opposite direction, toward Halifax. On the French ship's crumpled foredeck, tiny wisps of fire appeared. Fed by the miasma of benzol vapours, the flickering flames, blue and gold, danced like impish sprites. But that changed in a wink. As they flared and spread, the tenor of the flames became angry and ominous.

Billowing plumes of black smoke, which are characteristic of a benzol-fuelled fire, began pouring from the gap in the *Mont-Blanc*'s hull. The flames there "became deeper, like an opaque and fulminant liquid, then swept over the canisters of benzol [on deck] and increased to a roaring tide of heat."[8]

On the Halifax side of the harbour, Lieutenant Victor M. Magnus, RNVR, and his shipmates aboard HMS *Changuinola* watched the fire aboard the *Mont-Blanc* grow in intensity. The RN warship, an armed merchant cruiser, had dropped anchor near the Naval Dockyard after arriving in port the previous day. On this morning, the ship was taking on coal, and the crew were busy making ready for Saturday departure on convoy escort duty. The mood on board *Changuinola* was relaxed, and as word spread that a ship was on fire in the harbour, crewmen stopped to watch; Lieutenant Magnus was among them. The twenty-nine-year-old native of Essex, England, an avid photographer, snapped some photos as he stood on deck this morning. He chanced to be in the right place at the right time with his primitive pocket camera. Little did Magnus know that some of the images he was taking would be historic, for they are among the very few that depict the scene in the harbour on the morning of the great Halifax explosion of 1917.

CHAPTER 13

"I Don't Like the Look of That Fire"

Halifax Harbour, December 6, 1917, 8:45 a.m.

As the two stricken ships drifted apart, the *Imo*'s second officer, Peter B'Jönnas, and third officer, Bjarne Birkland, set about assessing the damage their ship had suffered. Just above the waterline, there was a jagged three-foot-wide hole in her bow. The anchor that had snagged on the *Mont-Blanc*'s innards was still hanging by its chain but was now bent and useless. Apart from the fact that the *Imo* lay across the shipping channel, awkwardly positioned, it seemed that the ship had come through the accident relatively unscathed. The *Mont-Blanc* had not fared nearly as well.

B'Jönnas could see that the gash the *Imo*'s bow had cut into the starboard side of the French ship was "on deck, in front of the Number One hatch."[1] Flames were visible there and inside the hull, and great clouds of black smoke were rolling skyward.

"I don't like the look of that fire. What cargo do you think the French ship is carrying?" Birkland asked B'Jönnas. "God help us all if they've got explosives on board."

That thought had occurred to both men. But it was a possibility so horrid that neither of them liked or wanted to contemplate it.

"I doubt that they do," B'Jönnas replied. "If they did, they'd be flying a red swallow-tail warning flag, or they'd surely signal or call out to let us know. By the look of it, I'd say there's case oil or gasoline in those barrels piled on her deck. That could be a big problem if they don't put that fire out."

Birkland nodded in tepid agreement. He had correctly sensed that B'Jönnas really had no idea what the *Mont-Blanc* was carrying. What's more, the intensity of the fire that was raging unchecked on her foredeck suggested that whatever was burning, the situation aboard the ship was already critical. The actions of the Frenchmen underscored that notion. They were scurrying like ants and making no effort to fight the fire. Seeing this told B'Jönnas that something was amiss.

By now, a half-dozen other *Imo* crewmen had joined B'Jönnas and Birkland on the foredeck. All were wide-eyed in disbelief as they watched what was happening on the *Mont-Blanc*. "By God, the Frenchmen are taking to the lifeboats," B'Jönnas muttered.

JEAN GLOTIN, THE FIRST OFFICER of the *Mont-Blanc*, had been standing on the bridge beside Captain Le Médec and pilot Mackey when the collision with the *Imo* occurred. Immediately afterward, on Captain Le Médec's order, Glotin rushed down to the foredeck to assess the damage. "It was difficult to estimate exactly [the extent of it] on account of the smoke," Le Médec would later explain. "I thought the ship was going to blow up at once."[2]

Glotin took deep breaths. He was struggling to maintain his composure, for it was his job to reassure the crew and help keep the men calm. At age thirty-three, Glotin was an experienced mariner. He prided himself on keeping his head in a crisis. He had done so in a similar emergency nine months earlier. On March 24, Glotin had been the second officer aboard the French cargo ship SS *Montreal* when a German U-boat had torpedoed the ship in the Bay of Biscay.

Glotin knew at a glance that the *Mont-Blanc*'s predicament was dire. The flames that now engulfed the vessel from the bridge forward to the bow were shooting fifty feet into the air, and the towering pall of black smoke that was rising above the ship would be visible for miles around. Likewise, the loud whumps from the explosions that erupted periodically on the *Mont-Blanc*'s foredeck sent fireballs soaring.

Each blast ratcheted up the fear level among the members of the *Mont-Blanc*'s crew. Many of the men had clustered on the afterdeck, where they anxiously awaited the order to abandon ship. They had been ready to do so for the last five days; edgy crew members had swung the ship's lifeboats out in their davits and into launching position even before the ship left New York five days earlier.

It was as obvious to the *Mont-Blanc*'s crewmen as it was to First Officer Glotin that their ship was doomed. Underfoot, the metal deck plates were warm to the touch; before long they began to glow cherry red, kitchen-griddle hot. Even more alarming was the awareness that mere inches beneath the deck, buried in the *Mont-Blanc*'s innards, "lay leashed an incalculable energy, and the bonds which checked it were melting with every second the temperature in the ship's sealed holds was soaring ever higher."[3]

Only Heaven knew how long it would be before the flames would reach the tons of TNT stored in the ship's cargo holds. When that happened—as it inevitably would—anyone still aboard the ship or within a mile or two of the blast would die. Glotin knew this, but he still was not prepared to give the order to abandon ship. The decision to do so was for Captain Le Médec to make.

MATE HERBERT WHITEHEAD, the commander of the supply ship *CD-73*, had seen there was an emergency in the harbour. "I saw . . . a ship on fire with a crew aboard [that] needed assistance," he said.[4] It took the *CD-73* less than three minutes to speed to the side of the *Mont-Blanc*. When Whitehead arrived, he saw the gash in her hull. It extended from the deck all the way down to the waterline. "As I got alongside her, the crew of the *Mont-Blanc* was lowering their boats, and I got my megaphone and shouted through the wheelhouse window, 'Jump into my boat' . . . I'd take [the men] to Bedford Basin if there was any danger. I didn't think they understood."[5]

The men of the *Mont-Blanc*'s crew were preoccupied as they waited anxiously for the formal order to abandon ship. Still uncertain about what to do, Glotin raced back up to the bridge. "Captain, the men are on the verge of panic," the first officer said. "What are your orders?"

Given the nature of the *Mont-Blanc*'s cargo, Le Médec knew there was only one answer to Glotin's question. The fire was out of control. The searing heat combined with the blinding shroud of smoke that enveloped the deck precluded any attempt by the crew to reach the ship's firefighting equipment, which was at the bow of the ship. Even if the men had been able to break out the pump and hoses, Le Médec understood the futility of spraying water on a fuel-fed fire or of any attempt to scuttle the ship. The seacocks, the valves that could be opened in a life-and-death emergency, were in the engine room, deep within the bowels of the ship. Being new to the *Mont-Blanc*, Aimé Le Médec had no idea where the seacocks were even located. Not that it mattered much. After all, who would be crazy enough to obey an order to go below, find the seacocks, and then spend the half-hour it would take to open them? Doing so would be suicide. The *Mont-Blanc* was going to blow sky high any moment. "We stood [on the bridge] until we couldn't stand there any longer," Francis Mackey would recall.[6] "I could see the flames get bigger and the smoke [rising] higher."[7]

The pilot understood the gravity of the *Mont-Blanc*'s situation. "The only thing to do is save your crew," he advised Captain Le Médec. "Get them to the boats."

However, in the next breath, Mackey raised the idea of engaging the ship's engines and going full speed ahead. Doing so, he reasoned, might drive her forward with enough speed to flood the cargo holds. With any luck, the *Mont-Blanc* would sink quickly enough to extinguish the fire and prevent an explosion.

Le Médec shook his head. There was no time for such madness, even though two men—Chief Engineer Antoine Le Gat and Third Engineer Louis Brun had dutifully remained in the engine room waiting for final orders. Both Le Gat, age forty-five, and Brun, age thirty-seven, were old salts, dedicated and fearless. It was unbearably hot in the smoke-filled bowels of the ship, yet Le Gat and Brun remained at their posts. When finally the bell tingled and Second Officer Leveque's breathless words came down through the speaking tube, the instructions he relayed were unequivocal: Le Gat and Brun were to come topside as quickly as possible; Captain Le Médec had given the order to abandon ship. Hearing this, Antoine Le Gat hurriedly wiped the sweat from his eyes, locked the safety valve on the *Mont-Blanc*'s boilers, and waved to Brun. "*Allons-y!*" he shouted. "Let's go!"

The men grabbed their shirts and ran for their lives. On the way out of the engine room, they passed the chalkboard where "*Demi-vitesse*," half-speed, was the last recorded order.

THE MOMENT THE *MONT-BLANC*'s lifeboats hit the water, the crew began pouring over the side of the ship and into them. Mere seconds had passed since Captain Le Médec's order to abandon ship. With First Officer Glotin supervising, twenty men were off the ship in less than two minutes. "Every man took the place . . . that was assigned to him by the regulations when abandoning ship," Le Médec would recall. "Men that were on the starboard side went to the port to take their right places in their boats."[8]

Le Médec and Mackey remained on the bridge for several anxious minutes after Glotin's departure, and so they were the last to go to the lifeboats; Le Médec was loath to do so. Before sending Alphonse Serré, the helmsman, and Second Officer Leveque away, he ordered Serré "to put the helm amidships."[9] It was the captain's last-gasp effort to ensure that the stricken ship did not drift to the Halifax side of the harbour.

"[Le Médec] didn't want to leave the ship," said Jean Glotin. "I compelled him to leave her . . . I forced him, taking him by the arm to the ladder."[10]

The captain was about to take his seat in the lifeboat when he noticed that Chief Engineer Le Gat was missing. Insisting that it was his duty to go find him, Le Médec was halfway up the Jacob's ladder on his return to the ship when Le Gat suddenly appeared, having responded to Jean Glotin's frantic calls. The Chief Engineer took his spot in the lifeboat. However, even then Le Médec seemed undecided about what to do next. As much as he wanted to live, he also felt obliged to do the "honourable thing." That would be to go down with his ship. There are countless examples of captains doing this, even though there is no valid reason for it. One of the most famous is Captain Edward Smith of the RMS *Titanic*. Smith doubtless could have been among the 721 survivors of the disaster had he opted to climb into a lifeboat. He did not. Shortly before his ship sank, witnesses saw him making his way to the wheelhouse. That was the last anyone ever saw of him; Smith became one of the disaster's 1,500 victims. His fate, tragic and senseless though it was, has become part of the romance of the *Titanic* legend.

Unlike Edward Smith, Le Médec listened to reason. Once he had returned to his seat in the lifeboat, the captain looked to pilot Mackey for advice on how to proceed. "I suggested at first with a wave of my hands that we go to Dartmouth," Mackey said. "I thought that we could get there quicker, and it was the opposite way of the ship."[11]

ABLE SEAMAN GEORGE ABBOTT, the coxswain of an RCN dispatch boat, was delivering mailbags from HMCS *Acadia*, in Bedford Basin, to the depot ship HMCS *Niobe* when he and a companion came upon the *Mont-Blanc*. "The *Imo* had just stopped her engines going astern, and the *Mont-Blanc* was kind of laying cross ways across the harbour" at that moment.[12]

Abbott had an unobstructed view of the hole in the *Mont-Blanc*'s hull and of the flames on her deck. Even so, with all the smoke in the air, it was impossible to tell if the fire was also burning inside the ship. Abbott noted the forty-five-gallon drums that sat two deep on the deck of the French ship. "It's nothing more than oil," he thought. There was no cause for alarm. The pyrotechnics and the explosions would be spectacular, but there was no reason for concern. Fire crews were on the way, and they would soon have everything under control.

Abbott knew that accidents happened from time to time in Halifax harbour. In this case, a French vessel had been involved and she was now burning. To make matters worse, the Frenchmen ("Damn them!") were always running away when the going got tough. The conscription debate that had become the central issue of the federal election eleven days hence was providing conclusive proof of that. Like everyone in Halifax—which was Conservative leader Robert Borden's hometown and his former parliamentary riding—Able Seaman George Abbott knew all about the divide between Canada's two solitudes, French and English. He was also aware of the stereotype of French-speaking Quebeckers as being unpatriotic at best, cowards at worst.

The puzzling scene Abbott was witnessing only seemed to underscore the truth of those ugly accusations. In the distance, he could see the two lifeboats carrying the *Mont-Blanc* crewmen who had abandoned ship. It was obvious that the Frenchmen were intent only on saving their own necks while their burning ship was adrift in the busy harbour. Never mind that Quebeckers were not "French" or vice versa; Quebeckers spoke the language of France, and their sensibilities were undeniably Gallic. The sailors pulling at the oars of the two lifeboats Abbott could see racing toward the Dartmouth shore were rowing like men possessed. Abbott could only shake his head and mutter as he and his companion continued on their morning mail run.

THE OUTGOING TIDE was drawing the *Mont-Blanc* ever closer to Halifax. The only way to prevent the ship from reaching shore was to attach a line to her and have a tugboat tow her into the middle of the harbour. With that in mind, Captain Horatio Brannen aboard the *Stella Maris* had dropped off the two scows he had been towing a few minutes earlier and his tugboat was headed toward the *Mont-Blanc*. So, too, were boats from HMCS *Niobe* and HMS *Highflyer*. The duty officer aboard *Niobe* had dispatched the depot ship's steam pinnace and a seven-man crew "to go see what could be done" to help fight the fire aboard that French cargo ship. At the same time, Commander Thomas ("Tom") Triggs, HMS *Highflyer*'s first officer, and a six-man crew had set out in the British warship's whaler with the same mission in mind.

The rapid response to the emergency was a reflection of the fact that in 1917, fire danger was a constant concern in any busy harbour. Nowhere was that more true than in Halifax. The port had myriad wooden piers, while many of the ships that were coming and going carried hazardous goods; munitions were especially problematic. Had the *Mont-Blanc* not been carrying such a hazardous cargo, her collision with the *Imo* in all likelihood would have been of little importance. Accidents happened in busy harbours, but few were as fraught with peril as the collision of the *Mont-Blanc* and the *Imo*. It was now mere minutes before a cataclysmic explosion the likes of which the world had never seen.

CHAPTER 14

The clouds of black smoke that were billowing from the fire in the harbour were visible for miles around. Hundreds of people in the Richmond neighbourhood in the city's North End, in Dartmouth, and on vessels on the water stopped to watch; all eyes turned toward the harbour. "Men were running out of dock sheds and warehouses and offices along the entire waterfront to watch the burning ship."[1] Flames had engulfed the *Mont-Blanc*'s foredeck, and the percussive thuds that boomed across the water each time another barrel of benzol exploded drew "Ooohs!" and "Ahhs!" from onlookers.

As the outgoing tide continued to pull the burning ship ever closer to shore, the threat of a major fire breaking out on the Halifax waterfront was growing by the minute. Pier 6 was one of the port's busiest cargo terminals. And like many of the wooden wharves in Halifax harbour, it reeked of wood-tar creosote. That chemical preservative, with its distinctive smoky odour, was (and still is) used to waterproof timber; however, it is also highly flammable.

Halifax being an old port city, most of its docks and many of its commercial buildings and homes were wooden. And in an era before the advent of modern water mains, efficient pumps, and well-equipped, professional fire brigades, fire danger was a constant and very real concern.

The kitchen stoves in homes of the day burned wood year-round, and wood- or coal-fired furnaces kept homes and businesses warm during the long, cold winters. Accidental fires were part of everyday life (as were tragedies and natural disasters on a grand scale, yet no city in Canada or the United States in 1917 had a comprehensive emergency disaster relief plan at the ready). Huge fires claimed lives and property and destroyed buildings. Many Haligonians in 1917 still recalled a horrific fire that had razed part of the city's downtown business core almost six years earlier. It had taken firefighters a whole day to extinguish that January 1912 blaze, which had caused hundreds of thousands of dollars in damage and destroyed homes and thirty-seven businesses.[2]

There was little wind to fan or spread flames on the morning of December 6; however, the benign weather conditions did nothing to lessen people's fears. Firefighters rushed to the *Mont-Blanc* by land and sea.

The *Stella Maris*, the first firefighting vessel on the scene, arrived within ten minutes of the collision. By this time, the burning ship had already drifted perilously close to Pier 6, which was also ablaze. The fire had now leapt ashore. With the equipment they had available, there was nothing Captain Brannen and his men could do to fight those flames. Instead they directed the stream of seawater from the *Stella Maris'* single hose onto the flames that were engulfing the *Mont-Blanc*. Brannen had no idea of what was fuelling them; it was probably oil, he figured. What puzzled him was the fact that the water his men were throwing at the flames only seemed to be stoking them. The steel plates in the ship's foredeck, now glowing red-hot, were starting to buckle in places. Down at the waterline, the seawater that lapped against the ship's hull sizzled and hissed like an angry viper.

Oil and water really do not mix. Add water to any burning oil, and the laws of physics and chemistry dictate that the water will sink. As it does so, it becomes superheated and gives off steam. The results are dramatic. Steam, being much less dense than liquid water, rises and carries oil-fed flames with it. This adds oxygen to the flames, which then burn even hotter and more spectacularly. They are also more difficult to extinguish.

By the time additional help arrived, the raging, boiling inferno aboard the *Mont-Blanc* was beyond control.

LIEUTENANT COMMANDER TOM TRIGGS and the sailors in HMS *Highflyer*'s whaler were the first to join the *Stella Maris*' crew in their firefighting efforts. Minutes later, Acting Boatswain Albert Mattison and a half-dozen men in HMCS *Niobe*'s steam pinnace joined the fray.

Triggs, the senior navy man present, had known from the start that firefighters would never be able to extinguish the fire aboard the *Mont-Blanc* before it spread to Pier 6. He and Captain Brannen agreed that the only course of action open to them was to attach a line to the ship and tow her out to mid-channel. There firefighters might stand a better chance of dousing the flames. At the same time, this would allow crews from the Halifax fire department to battle the fire that was now threatening to destroy Pier 6 and surrounding structures. The plan Triggs and Brannen had settled on was sensible, and ordinarily it might have worked. However, the blaze aboard the *Mont-Blanc* was no ordinary fire. Neither Brannen nor Triggs had any idea of what they were dealing with—or of how little time they and their men had to live.

MATE HERBERT WHITEHEAD aboard the drifter *CD-73* was one of the first would-be rescuers to reach the *Mont-Blanc* after her collision with the *Imo*. When Whitehead called out using a megaphone, he got no response. The Frenchmen were already abandoning ship. And once they had done so, they looked hell-bent on just one thing: reaching the Dartmouth shore 400 yards to the east as quickly as possible.

The *Mont-Blanc*'s lifeboats passed within mere yards of the *CD-73*; Whitehead watched in disbelief and wondered why the Frenchmen were in such a rush. "There was some talking and commotion in both boats," he observed, "but as to giving [a] warning, I heard none."[3]

Later, there would be much speculation and finger pointing about possible reasons for the perceived failure on the part of the *Mont-Blanc*'s crew and of pilot Francis Mackey to let others—would-be rescuers, firefighters, and people on shore—know of the dangers posed by the cargo aboard the burning French ship. "It is impossible not to speculate on what lives might have been saved had the *Mont-Blanc* sailors managed to convey warnings to Whitehead's vessel," military historian John Griffith Armstrong has written.[4]

Mackey, Le Médec, and members of the *Mont-Blanc*'s crew would insist they had done their best to alert others that the *Mont-Blanc* was packed with explosives. Alphonse Serré, the *Mont-Blanc*'s helmsman, would claim he had "made signs to all the boats in the vicinity to go away . . . but no one seemed to understand [us]."[5]

Leading Seaman T.N. Davis from HMS *Highflyer*, riding in the ship's whaler when it raced toward the *Mont-Blanc*, would be one of the few witnesses to confirm the Frenchmen's claim. "As we approached the two ships in collision, we saw [two] small boats pulling for the shore, the men waving, shouting 'powder' and warning us to keep clear."[6]

Francis Mackey recounted a similar story. "There was a navy tug going past us and we [also] hailed him. . . . 'Take us in tow,' [I] hollered, but you might as well holler at a post. Nobody could hear, too much racket."[7]

The tug Mackey had spotted was the *Hilford*. Under lease to the RCN, on the morning of December 6 she was under the command of Lieutenant James Murray, RNVR. A former captain of the passenger liner RMS *Empress of Britain*, Murray was serving as the port of Halifax's sea transport officer and as an assistant to convoy officer Rear Admiral Bertram Chambers. Murray's job was to liaise with harbour pilots and the captains of the merchant ships that came to Halifax to join trans-Atlantic convoys. Murray, ever personable, was well-suited for his job, and he and Francis Mackey were friends.

The pilot was distressed to see Murray on the deck of the *Hilford*. Mackey had no way of knowing it was purely by chance that the Englishman was on the water so early that morning. He had paid a social call, visiting the master of a British cargo ship who, as a favour, had given him some kippers.[8] Murray intended to surprise his wife by serving the herring to her at breakfast. His plan was to check in at his office on Pier 9 at the Naval Dockyard and then rush home. However, when he saw two ships collide in the Narrows and one of them catch fire, he went to investigate and to see if he could be of any help.

As the *Hilford* approached, Francis Mackey stood tall in the lifeboat in which he was riding. He waved his arms and shouted, but the vastness of Halifax harbour swallowed his words. Murray did not see or hear Mackey. The lieutenant was preoccupied with the sight of the burning ship that had drifted up against Pier 6. Murray was horrified, for he was one of the handful of navy officials in Halifax who were privy to the secret that the *Mont-Blanc* was due in port today carrying a load of almost 3,000 tons of munitions. The sight of the ship on fire, abandoned, and adrift in the Narrows left Murray feeling stunned and afraid. Very afraid. He understood that any efforts to extinguish a fire aboard the ship were a waste of time, and time was of the essence. There was not even time to warn the men who were out on the water attempting to fight the fire. Instead, Murray ordered the captain of the *Hilford* to drop one of his men ashore so he could sound the alarm while the boat raced back to Pier 9. With hundreds—perhaps even thousands—of lives at stake, Murray was desperate to get to his office telephone and alert his superiors, Halifax firefighters, and local officials. All along the shoreline on both sides of the harbour, crowds of people had gathered to watch the drama playing out on the water. Lieutenant Murray knew that if the *Mont-Blanc* exploded, all of those people would die.

OUT ON THE WATER, two sailors from HMCS *Niobe* had managed to scramble aboard the *Mont-Blanc* and secure a tow line at the stern of the ship. However, when Captain Brannen edged the *Stella Maris* forward and pulled the line taut, the *Mont-Blanc* refused to budge. The five-inch hawser was too small for the job. Their many years of nautical experience told Triggs and Brannen that if the *Stella Maris* continued to pull, the tow line would snap.

"We'll have to use a ten-inch hawser. That should do it," said Brannen.[9]

Triggs agreed. He left Brannen to it while he set off in *Highflyer*'s whaler. He was intent on seeing if he could do anything to help the crew of the *Imo*. There were few signs of activity aboard the Norwegian ship. Captain From and pilot Hayes were stunned by the collision, and they were struggling to get the *Imo* turned around so she could head back to Bedford Basin.

FROM HIS VANTAGE POINT 200 yards distant, Mate Herbert Whitehead aboard the drifter *CD-73* had watched the flurry of activity around the *Mont-Blanc*. Efforts to fight the fire were quite a show. Despite the sound and fury unleashed each time a barrel of benzol exploded, Whitehead figured that firefighters would soon have things under control. "[The explosions] appeared to me to come out of the fore hatch. I came to the conclusion from the dense black smoke that was sent up by three explosions [that] the vessel was loaded with oil, and I thought I'd better get out of the way."

CHARLES MAYERS, the twenty-two-year-old third officer of the British cargo ship SS *Middleham Castle*, was another of the interested spectators who had watched in disbelief as the *Mont-Blanc* and the *Imo* collided. Mayers had been on a mission; in his pocket was a wad of money that he was on his way to delivering to the ship's captain, who had gone ashore on business. Now he was observing the fire aboard the *Mont-Blanc*, which was nestled against Pier 6 on the Halifax shore. The burning ship was less than 100 yards from where Mayers stood, close enough that he could feel heat from the flames. Something else about this fire was different. "[It] was too high, too queer, with strange colours and flame balls," he would recall. "She was shooting those flame balls of smoke up in the air and then the jetty was partly on fire, too."[10]

Mayers had a premonition something very bad was about to happen. His errand forgotten, he ran back to the *Middleham Castle* as fast as his feet would carry him.

CAPTAIN LE MÉDEC and his forty-man crew were far away from their burning ship by the time the efforts to haul her away from Pier 6 began. It would take the *Mont-Blanc*'s lifeboats less than ten minutes to travel the half-mile to Tufts Cove on the Dartmouth shore. Francis Mackey had directed them here because the inlet, home to the small Mi'kmaq settlement known as Turtle Grove, was also the site of a ferry wharf. The lifeboats could dock there, and the men could take cover in nearby woods; Mackey hoped the trees would offer shelter from the blast he knew was coming.

The moment the lifeboats reached Dartmouth, the *Mont-Blanc* crewmen jumped ashore and ran for it. A small crowd of curious locals who had gathered to watch the fire in the harbour stood with mouths agape as the crazy Frenchmen raced past them. "Shouts of terror and streams of French curses and half-prayers came in a gabble. One of [the men] cried out a French phrase over and over. Others attempting the English for powder shouted: '*Pou-dar! Pou-dar!*'" [11]

Surprisingly, despite their fear, the *Mont-Blanc* crewmen obeyed when Captain Le Médec demanded they stop for a roll call. First Officer Jean Glotin's quick head count revealed that all were present, save one man who had run ahead and was already hiding out among the spruce trees.

The roll call completed, the race to the woods resumed. As it did so, Francis Mackey joined the Frenchmen in shouting warnings to everyone he saw. A young Mi'kmaq woman named Aggie March, who stood on her front porch with her baby daughter cradled in her arms, stared at Mackey and the other men who went running past. Why, she wondered, were those crazy French sailors so agitated? She was still puzzling about that when one of the men leapt onto the porch, snatched Aggie March's baby, and ran off with the child. Aggie took off after him, catching a handful of his coat just as he made it into the woods. The man cried, "*Non!*" He grabbed hold of Aggie with his free arm, and the two of them tumbled to the bare ground with the baby between them.

CHAPTER 15

Halifax Harbour, December 6, 1917, 9:00 a.m.

The spectacular fire engulfing the *Mont-Blanc* was growing in intensity with each passing moment. The firefighters who were trying in
vain to battle the flames had no idea how perilous their situation was.
Their only thoughts were of how to gain control of the flames and keep
them from destroying Pier 6 and nearby wooden structures. "Launches
from the harbour fire department surrounded [the *Mont-Blanc*] like
midges, and the water from their hoses arched up with infinite delicacy as
they curved into the rolling smoke."[1]

Few people in Halifax were privy to the terrible truth about what was
in the cargo holds of the burning French ship. "The science of high explosives [being] a relatively young field at the time,"[2] it is unlikely that even
those navy officers who knew the *Mont-Blanc* was packed with explosives
understood that it was not fire per se that posed such a grave hazard. Heat
from a fire is generally not enough to cause TNT to explode. A detonating
agent is required, usually a volatile gas or fulminate. In the case of the

Mont-Blanc, the benzol that had spilled across the decks and fed the flames acted as the needed oxidizing agent.

The benzol-fuelled flames that were shooting 150 feet into the air were giving off ominous rolling clouds of black smoke. The *Mont-Blanc* was a gigantic powder keg. The fuse was burning, and there was no way to stop it. The crisis had passed the point of no return.

This Thursday seemed like an ordinary workday, yet every tick of the clock brought Halifax another second closer to the abyss. Mary Jean Hinch, like her family and their neighbours, knew nothing of the fire in the harbour.

Sitting in the kitchen of her home at 66 Veith Street, she was pre-occupied with her own troubles. She had an ailing child, nine-year-old Joe. Having already lost four children to illness, she was taking no chances. Better safe than sorry. Mary Jean gave little Joe a bit of breakfast and a hug before sending him and his raspy throat back to bed. No school for the lad today. Joe could stay home with her and with his older sisters Clara and Lena, both of whom were also ailing.

After soothing little Joe's hurts, Mary Jean began making breakfast for her twins. Margaret and Annie had padded into the kitchen in their pajamas. The girls, five years old, bright-eyed, and full of giggly fun and love, were the apples of their dad's eye. Today, as they did each morning when he came home from his overnight shift at the graving dock, the twins made a beeline for him.

"Mornin', Dude!" Joe called to Mary Jean. He always affectionately referred to his wife by the pet name her sister Ada had hung on her.

"You're home late this morning."

Joe explained he had been watching some excitement down in the harbour. Two ships had collided, and one of them was on fire. Mary Jean had made Joe's breakfast, and a fresh pot of tea was brewing on the stove, so she decided to get some fresh air and see the fire that Joe had told her about. After donning her snow boots and new winter coat, Mary Jean paused before the hall mirror while she preened. "Dude" was fastidious and took pride in her appearance. It was not always easy for a mother of ten to look good, but after twenty-four years of marriage and even with another child on the way—she was five months pregnant—Mary Jean did her best.

It was with her husband's caution about not getting too close to the fire in the harbour in mind that Mary Jean stepped out the front door and turned left, north toward Richmond Street. The day being unseasonably mild, Veith Street's dirt surface was not yet frozen. As yet, there was no sign of winter snow. The sun in a crisp, cloudless blue sky was casting long shadows. This seemed more like an October day than one just nineteen days before Christmas.

The back wall of the Hillis iron foundry, across the street from the Hinches' house, obscured Mary Jean's view of the harbour. The sprawling T-shaped building took up most of the block bounded by Veith Street on the west, Campbell Road on the east, Hanover Street on the south, and Richmond Street on the north; Pier 6, a block distant, lay at the foot of Richmond Street.

In the sky above the Hillis foundry, Mary Jean could see the towering clouds of black smoke. The clanging of fire bells, distant but growing louder by the second, confirmed that the fire in the harbour was big. Mary Jean was eager to see it. She quickened her steps as she beetled across the street and headed toward the weed-covered vacant lot that lay between the Hillis foundry and the Matthews house at 71 Veith Street. She knew this vantage point would offer a clear view of all the excitement.

A crowd of foundry workers and several of the Hinches' neighbours had gathered in the vacant lot. Like moths drawn to a flame, all eyes were staring down the hillside toward the spectacular fire burning at Pier 6.

MOTORIZED VEHICLES WERE still a rarity on the streets of Halifax in 1917. Only government agencies and those citizens with deep pockets could afford to purchase a car or truck. A new McLaughlin-Buick—Toronto-made and advertised as being "Canada's Standard Car"—cost about $1,400. That was a hefty price tag, and purchasers who wanted to add an "option" to their horseless carriages were obliged to shell out an extra $100 for a top to shield them from the sun or rain; adding a windscreen cost another $50.

Although Chief Edward Condon of the Halifax Fire Department was age sixty, he embraced new technology—motorized vehicles in particular.[3] The chief of Canada's oldest fire department was one of the privileged few in Halifax who owned a motor car. His spiffy 1911 McLaughlin-Buick roadster was a vehicle that befitted a man of his stature. Naturally, the chief had ordered it equipped with the optional top and windscreen. He also employed a driver. Nineteen-year-old firefighter Claude Wells took great pride in his job, almost as much as he delighted in the competition he waged with his older brother. The Wells brothers competed to see who could be first to arrive at fires. However, December 6 was Claude Wells' day off, and so Deputy Chief William Brunt was behind the wheel of the chief's McLaughlin-Buick roadster.

FIRE CHIEF CONDON (AT WHEEL) AND HALIFAX'S CITY COMPTROLLER IN THE CHIEF'S 1911 MCLAUGHLIN-BUICK. (HALIFAX FIREFIGHTERS MONUMENT COMMITTEE)

Thirty-six-year-old William ("Billy") Wells, who was also a city fire-fighter, drove the department's new motorized pumper truck, another Condon purchase. *Patricia*, as the firefighters had dubbed her, was the city's frontline weapon against fire. The 1913 American LaFrance fire engine—with its six-cylinder engine and 800-imperial-gallon-per-minute water pump—was one of the first motorized fire trucks in Canada. As such, it was the pride of the Halifax Fire Department's thirty-six full-time firefighters (and 122 part-time volunteers) as well as a source of much curiosity for Halifax residents.[4] The right-hand-drive vehicle was twenty-five feet of gleaming red metal and polished brass. Equipped with ladders, lanterns, and other firefighting gear, *Patricia* was a sight to behold whenever she sped along city streets with rotary fire bell clanging. The truck's six-person crew held on for dear life as they clung to their precarious perches.

The moment the alarm sounded at the West Street fire hall, the part-time firemen who were on duty leapt into action and raced to their places on the *Patricia*. The men were familiar with the sound of Box 83. With the danger of fire at Pier 6 and other wooden piers on Halifax's waterfront being so great, workers there routinely pulled that alarm. They did so no matter how inconsequential the initial threat may have seemed. Better safe than sorry, the thinking went.

The bell for waterfront fire alarms sounded at West Street Station almost every day. When someone down at the docks triggered the alarm on the morning of December 6, the firefighters assumed it was just another routine call.[5]

IT WAS CONSTANT UPHAM, the owner of the general store located on Campbell Road, near the Acadia Sugar Refinery, who had sounded the alarm for the fire at Pier 6. Upham's General Store was within 150 yards of the pier, so close that those customers who had gathered outside the store to watch the fire smelled benzol and felt the searing heat.

"Looks like a bad one, Connie. Maybe you should call the fire department," someone had suggested. Upham was one of the few people in the neighbourhood with a home telephone.

Constant Upham had rushed to his telephone to make several calls, sounding multiple alarms. Firefighters from four fire halls sprang into action.

At the West Street Station, a half-mile away, the *Patricia*'s crew—the "Patsys," as they called themselves—scrambled to get out the door. One of the regulars, who had come into work that morning despite being ill with flu, was in the washroom when the alarm sounded. Fire Captain William Broderick had hammered on the door. "Damn it, hurry up!" he shouted. However, when the man failed to appear, Broderick became angry. "I'll deal with you when I get back," he warned.

THE *PATRICIA* AND CREW OUTSIDE THE WEST STREET FIRE STATION IN HALIFAX. (COURTESY OF JEFF FRYMAN/HALIFAX FIRE HISTORICAL SOCIETY)

There was no time for bickering or to waste. The *Patricia* burst out the big door of the fire hall with fire gong clanging. All along the fire truck's route to the harbour, young and old alike stopped to watch. They stood with mouths agape. Children on their way to school shrieked with glee and waved as the big red fire truck swept past, barrelling down the left side of the streets—until April 1923, Nova Scotia observed British rules of the road. One woman who lived on Artz Street would recount in a letter she wrote to a friend: "I remember hearing the *Patricia* [and] the rest of the fire department go past the corner [and] they were flying, so I said to myself, 'Gee Whizz, there must be a big fire near us'"[6]

Fifty-three-year-old Albert Brunt also heard the clanging of the *Patricia*'s bell. Brunt, who earned his living as a house painter but also worked part time as a fireman, was pushing his paint cart along Gerrish Street when the *Patricia* came hurtling toward him. The sight of his forty-one-year-old younger brother, Deputy Chief William Brunt, behind the wheel of the chief's car was enough to prompt Albert to try to jump aboard the fire truck when it slowed to make a turn onto Gottingen Street; however, the elder Brunt slipped off and went sprawling. He tumbled onto the dirt roadway, scraping his knees and hands. The firemen on the truck hooted and called out, but the *Patricia* did not slow, not for a second. There was no time to stop for Albert Brunt. His pride had suffered more hurt than his body. At that moment, he had no idea how fortunate he was to have fallen off that speeding firetruck.

CAPTAIN FREDERICK C.C. PASCO, the acting superintendent of the Naval Dockyard on December 6, was an experienced, no-nonsense career navy man. He looked every bit the part. A photograph of Pasco taken around this time depicts a bearded figure standing ramrod straight and proud in his double-breasted Royal Navy uniform, four gold bars with loops on each sleeve. A captain's cap with more gold braid is perched atop his head. In his hands, folded neatly in front of him, is a pair of ceremonial white gloves.

A native of Australia, Pasco had joined the Royal Navy in 1878 as a fifteen-year-old midshipman.[7] He sailed the seven seas for the next thirty-seven years, until he retired from the RN in April 1915 at the age of fifty-two. He then signed on with the RCN, which had a dire shortage of experienced naval officers and paid better than did the RN.

Pasco took command of the naval facilities in Sydney, Nova Scotia. For the first three years of the Great War, the port served as a small outstation of Halifax. That all changed in 1917 as deadly German U-boat attacks on merchant shipping forced the British to group cargo vessels from North America into convoys. Sydney, with its large harbour, abundant coal supplies, and strategic location, emerged as one of the assembly ports for United Kingdom– or Europe-bound vessels.[8]

By all accounts, Pasco's superiors regarded him as a competent officer. As a result, on November 30 he began filling in for Captain Edward H. Martin, RCN, as superintendent of the Naval Dockyard in Halifax. Martin, on orders from Admiral Charles Kingsmill, the head of the RCN, had gone to London for talks with British naval officials.

Pasco was staying in Martin's house. He was eating breakfast there on the morning of December 6 when he glanced out the window just as the northbound *Mont-Blanc* was steaming past Pier 4 at the Naval Dockyard. Pasco, his mouth full of poached eggs and toast, noticed the ship because it was riding low in the water, but he thought nothing more of it.

The office of the superintendent of the Naval Dockyard had received word of a December 2 telegram sent by Royal Navy officials in New York to Rear Admiral Bertram Chambers, the port of Halifax's convoy officer. The message alerted Chambers that the French ship SS *Mont-Blanc*, carrying almost 3,000 tons of explosives, was one of four vessels headed to Halifax to join a Europe-bound convoy. Whether or not Pasco's staff had shared that telegram with him or whether they did and he had failed to take note of the information is unclear, although it would soon become a major issue.

At this moment, Pasco was intent only on eating his breakfast. He sipped his tea and scanned a copy of that morning's edition of the *Morning Chronicle*, which his aide had placed on a corner of the table near his plate. "Situation in Control at Cambrai" read the page one headline of the newspaper. "Grim Valor of the British Troops Has Broken Hun Offensive Move."

Pasco nodded approvingly; the war in Europe was grinding on with no end in sight, but now that the Yanks had joined the fray, the tide of battle was finally turning in the Allies' favour. But when would the fighting end? Pasco could only wonder as he glanced at the mantel clock. It was 8:50 a.m. He had just ten minutes to get to the office.

The captain was dabbing his lips with his napkin and brushing toast crumbs from his beard when he heard the jangle of a ringing telephone. A moment later, Pasco's aide entered the breakfast room to let him know an officer from HMS *Highflyer* was calling to alert the dockyard commander that "a situation" was developing in the harbour.

"Sir, there's a French ship on fire," the caller told Pasco. "The crew have abandoned her, and she's drifting toward Pier 6."

After asking a few quick questions and issuing orders, Pasco hung up the phone and went to look out the dining room window. To his dismay, the Acadia Sugar Refinery building blocked the view north toward Pier 6. Pasco could see only a towering column of black smoke that was rising high into the air. He did not like the look of it.

Intent now on learning more about what was happening, the captain told his aide to call the Naval Dockyard. When he did, there was no answer; the office there did not open until nine o'clock, when Pasco and other officers usually began their workday. Likewise, the aide had no luck reaching any of the other senior naval officials in Halifax. Pasco scratched his beard and muttered to himself.

Where in Heaven's name was Commander Evan Wyatt, Pasco wondered? He understood that the CXO was at his desk aboard HMCS *Niobe* by this time each morning. If not, he was supposed to be reachable by telephone. It was Wyatt's job to be on top of emergencies such as this one.

Pasco's concern was rising, as was his agitation. He was impatient to know more about the fire in the harbour. When his aide managed to reach the captain of the naval motorboat *W.H. Lee*, which was equipped with a pump and hoses, Pasco ordered the boat to go help fight the fire. He then instructed his aide to continue trying to reach the port convoy officer, Rear Admiral Bertram Chambers, while he went upstairs to the second floor. Pasco hoped the north-facing bedroom window there would afford him a better view of the harbour.

To his continuing dismay, the captain still could not see the burning ship that was near Pier 6. What he could see was a group of a dozen or so people atop the Acadia Sugar Refinery, just north of the Naval Dockyard. The twelve-storey building, bathed in morning sunlight, was one of the tallest on the Halifax waterfront. Its rooftop afforded those curious souls who climbed up there an unobstructed view of the harbour. Pasco scanned the sliver of water that was visible to him. "I saw the *Imo* motionless apparently, across the harbour. I didn't see the other vessel, [but] the *Imo* had apparently a certain amount of smoke coming from the fiddleys."[9]

He was still staring out the window when the phone rang again. The caller, an officer from the Naval Dockyard, had more information to share. After listening carefully, Pasco ordered his caller to send all available boats with firefighting equipment out to fight the fire. Captain Pasco still had no idea that the burning vessel was a munitions ship.

CHAPTER 16

"Good-Bye, Boys"

Halifax, Nova Scotia, December 6, 1917, 9:02 a.m.

Able Seaman Bert Griffith and his HMCS *Niobe* shipmates, having finished breakfast, still had a few minutes to spare until their workday began at nine o'clock. A buzz ran through the ship as word spread that the French vessel involved in a collision a few minutes earlier was on fire. Having been abandoned by her crew, she had drifted ashore, coming to rest against Pier 6, a half-mile to the north. When it looked as if the fire could spread from the ship to the shore, Acting Boatswain Albert Mattison and a six-man detail of men had set off in *Niobe*'s steam pinnace to see if they could be of any help to the firefighters who were battling the blaze. "A lot of us boys went up on deck to see the sight," Griffith would report in a letter home. "It didn't look very bad. There were three pretty loud explosions [and] everyone just imagined that it was oil blowing up."[1]

Not everyone aboard HMCS *Niobe* was watching the show in the harbour. Some members of the depot ship's crew were already at work. At the stern of the ship, an eight-man crew under the direction of Acting Gunner

John Gammon, a thirty-seven-year-old native of Plymouth, England, was preparing concrete foundations for the bed of a new cargo crane.

The naval diving suits the divers wore were hot and cumbersome, weighing as much as eighty pounds each. The outfit included lead boots and packs, which enabled the wearer to descend to the bottom and walk around. Hoses carried air that a manually operated pump pushed into the diver's "hard hat"—a claustrophobia-inducing metal helmet that resembled a hollowed out cannonball. Tiny portholes provided the diver with what at best was limited visibility. It took four men to power the air pump; two more men monitored the air lines to ensure there were no kinks or blockages.

By nine o'clock on the morning of December 6, two divers from *Niobe* were already in the icy water. The last thing John Gammon and his crew needed was anything that disrupted their routine. Their work was not for the faint of heart. The margin for error was razor thin. Diving accidents were common, and often they were fatal.

ABLE SEAMAN EDWARD MCCROSSAN watched the fire in the harbour from a prime vantage point at the stern of the cargo ship SS *Curaca*. The Liverpool-based *Curaca* was at Halifax's Pier 8 to take on a load of army horses. The *Mont-Blanc*, ablaze and adrift, had nudged herself against Pier 6, less than 200 yards to the south of the *Curaca*. That was so close that McCrossan could feel the searing heat. "All the crew of our ship were standing at the stern watching the fire. I counted at least seven explosions and after each one something would shoot away up in the air and burst. One piece looked to be about two feet square and whirled around as it went up. The chief engineer . . . was standing at my side and as one of the explosions took place, and whatever it was went up in the air, he said, 'That's gone a couple of thousand feet, at least.'"[2]

THE CREW MEMBERS of British cargo ship the SS *Picton* were also watching the *Mont-Blanc* burn. The *Picton* was moored next to the Acadia Sugary Refinery while a crew of about eighty longshoremen emptied her cargo holds of crates of food and explosives; the ship was about to go into dry dock for repairs. The unloading was still under way when the *Mont-Blanc* drifted ashore on the Halifax side of the harbour. When it did, the heat from the fire was so intense that Francis Carew, the sixty-year-old fore-man of the workers aboard the *Picton*, feared it could set the ship alight or ignite the explosives that were still in the holds. "That's some hot, boys. We'd better secure those hatch covers before we have a fire!" Carew shouted.

The men set about securing the ship in a race against the clock. But it was a contest they were destined to lose.

SIX-YEAR-OLD JEAN HOLDER and her sister older Doris loved school; Jean was in grade one, her sister in grade three. The two girls leapt out of bed each morning, gobbled breakfast, and dressed hurriedly. By nine o'clock, at latest, they were ready to go. It was a brisk fifteen-minute walk from their Robie Street home to Chebucto School on Chebucto Road. These days, classes began at 9:30 a.m. With coal being in short supply, owing to the war, janitors at Halifax schools were under orders to turn down furnaces at night and then to stoke them back to life in the morn-ing. Older children started school at nine o'clock when the classrooms were still chilly; younger students in the lower grades began classes a half-hour later. Regardless, the Holder girls would never have been late no matter what time classes started.

Chebucto School, with room for 700 students, was the largest and fin-est primary school in Halifax. Two storeys tall and built of sturdy red brick in the Classical Revival–style that was so popular at the time, the edifice was—and remains—a local landmark. "The swarm of people into Halifax for war work soon crowded all the schools, and at Chebucto even the great auditorium was filled with makeshift desks and screens to provide extra classes for junior grades."[3] Erected in 1910 in the emerging suburbs just west of the Richmond neighbourhood, Chebucto School met the needs of the young, upwardly mobile families who were flocking to this area of the city. George and Alice Holder were typical of them.

Thirty-year-old Alice was Irish born. Her husband, George, thirty-three and a native of Halifax, was a chartered accountant. The couple had married in 1908, and by 1917, they had six children, all of them under age eight. Despite his family responsibilities, George Holder was also a patriot and a man of principle. When the war began in 1914, he rallied to the cause, joining the army. Appointed to the rank of sergeant major, he was stationed with the 63rd Halifax Rifles on McNabs Island. Holder was obliged to sleep most weeknights in the barracks; however, the night of December 5 was an exception. "There was to be a military funeral on Thursday afternoon and Dad was in charge of the burial party," Jean Holder would recall years later. "As he had a wife and family living in Halifax, he was granted leave to sleep at home on Wednesday night."[4]

So it happened that on the morning of December 6, George Holder was at home when his daughters were getting ready for school. At nine o'clock, he accompanied the girls to the door. There they kissed their father good-bye before stepping out into the sunshine. At that moment, the Holder sisters had no idea that, like so many of their classmates, they would not attend school that day. Nor would they return to Chebucto School for many weeks.

COMMANDER EVAN WYATT, the CXO for the port of Halifax, was late for work. Most days, he was at his desk aboard HMCS *Niobe* by 7:30 a.m. Not today. Wyatt was more than an hour late, but even so, he felt chipper. Wyatt and his wife, Dorothy, had attended a wedding reception the night before. It had been an enjoyable night out. These days Wyatt welcomed any opportunity to get away from the hassles and pressure of his job, even if for only a few hours.

When he was not on duty, the CXO was perpetually on call. "My office hours are twenty-four out of twenty-four," he complained. "I'm never off the end of the telephone. I get down about 7:30 or 8 [a.m.], and [I] leave at 10 or 11 [p.m.] at night; never before 6:30 [p.m.], this is when I get off."[5] When he was not at his desk, he was at home with his wife.

As if the constant demands on Wyatt and his time were not bad enough, he was perpetually at odds with the people he had to deal with each day: Halifax's harbour pilots, his haughty erstwhile Royal Navy colleagues, and his superior officer Captain Edward Martin—whom Wyatt felt did not respect him or support him in his work. Regardless, the commander was in a buoyant mood as he walked to work on the morning of December 6.

Wyatt was accustomed to receiving work-related phone calls at all hours, but today there had been none to interrupt his breakfast or morning routine. Wyatt had no way of knowing that the phone calls, frantic and fearful, had started not long after he had left on his walk to work. As far as Wyatt knew, all was right with the world. However, as he neared the north gate of the Naval Dockyard, Wyatt could hear the distant clanging of fire alarm bells. He also saw the ominous cloud of black smoke that darkened the northern sky. He wondered what was burning. He would make inquiries when he got to his office.

Wyatt was crossing the railway tracks in front of the Naval Dockyard gates when one of his assistants came rushing out to meet him. Mate Roland Iceton was breathless. He had worked the overnight shift in the CXO's office, and an hour or so earlier he had stood on the deck of *Niobe* and watched the French munitions ship the SS *Mont-Blanc* as she steamed northward toward Bedford Basin. Back at his desk, Iceton dutifully recorded this information in preparation for the nine o'clock end of his shift. His plans changed abruptly the moment he learned the *Mont-Blanc* had been involved in a collision in the Narrows and was on fire and adrift in the harbour. Iceton knew, all too well, what the French ship was carrying. Panic was already welling up inside him when he rang Commander Wyatt's home.

"I'm sorry," the Wyatts' housekeeper had informed Iceton. "The commander has left for the office."

Iceton spent the next twenty minutes pacing and worrying. When he finally spotted Wyatt striding down Russell Street, he sprinted out to meet him. Iceton blurted out what he knew about the fire aboard the *Mont-Blanc.* As he listened, Wyatt's anxiety level grew. Like Iceton, the commander was well aware of the gravity of the situation. He also knew he had just one boat with firefighting equipment at his disposal. "My one thought was to get hold of the [*W.H.*] *Lee* to get down there," he said.

Hoping to find the naval motorboat there, the commander ran to the coaling wharf that was located just south of HMCS *Niobe.* Wyatt cussed when he saw that the boat was on the opposite side of the slip. However, seeing that the *Lee's* crew were already preparing to go battle the fire, the CXO called out to alert them that he wanted to go with them. He had no way of knowing it yet, but it was already too late to do anything to fight the fire.

AS COMMANADER WYATT WAITED for the *W.H. Lee* to head out, a half-mile to the north, Lieutenant James Murray aboard the tugboat *Hilford* had reached Pier 9. Kippers forgotten, Murray leapt the last few feet of water and hit the wharf running. He was desperate to reach the telephone in his office so he could sound the alarm. He knew that evacuating the entire area around Pier 6 as quickly as possible was the only way to avoid massive civilian casualties. The belief that he did not have a moment to spare would be the last thing James Murray would ever know.

LIKE SO MANY OTHER North End residents, Elizabeth Fraser was unaware of the emergency in the harbour. Not that she would have cared even if she had been told about it. She had other priorities. At age sixteen, Elizabeth was already working for a living, and she had a lot on her mind. There was nothing unusual about that, not for a young woman from a blue-collar family in 1917. Universities in Atlantic Canada were among the first in North America to admit co-eds, but most young women in Canada's Atlantic provinces left school after grade eight and married or went to work; only a minority attended high school. Even fewer young women went on to university; almost all of those who did were from well-to-do families.

In the decade between 1901 and 1911, the number of working women in Canada increased by fifty per cent. Women were paid just half of what males earned, prompting the National Council of Women of Canada in 1907 to adopt a resolution calling for "equal pay for equal work." That initiative still has a familiar ring to it.

"Owing to the prevailing ideology of separate spheres for men and women, of the male breadwinner and of woman's place in the home, it was mostly single women who held jobs in the prewar years; other women who took paid work were considered 'unfortunates'—widows, divorcées, deserted or separated women or wives of the unemployed."[6]

With the outbreak of war in 1914, many able-bodied men joined the military. To make up for the labour shortage, a growing number of women went out to work. "Most of the women who worked during the war were unmarried. . . . Despite the movement of women into a few new areas of the economy, domestic service remained the most common female occupation."[7]

That was true for Elizabeth Fraser, the second eldest of the seven children of Maude Fraser and her husband Arthur, an iron mold maker. With money being tight at home, she had left school in September 1914 at age thirteen to go to work in the Dominion Textile Factory. The money she earned helped support her family and allowed Elizabeth to feel she was doing her bit "for King and Country." After three years of making cloth for military uniforms, however, Elizabeth was ready for a change. So she took a job as a domestic helper, working for a young couple with four children, aged ten, eight, six, and three days old.

The morning of December 6 having dawned fair and mild, their mother had taken them out of the house for a few hours, and so Elizabeth planned to do some laundry. "But first the water had to be heated on the stove. This gave me time to start my dinner. Today, I was going to make a stew, and I was at the sink preparing the vegetables when *it* happened."[8]

THREE BLOCKS EAST of the Gottingen Street house where Elizabeth Fraser was busy with household chores, forty-five-year-old Vincent Coleman was at his desk in the rail yard of the Canadian Government Railways. Most Haligonians still referred to the utility as the Intercolonial Railway, as it had been known up until 1916, or colloquially as "the ICR."

Coleman was a familiar figure at the rail yard. A train dispatcher, he was also a devoted union man with an abiding sense of duty to his job and his workmates. Mustachioed, with a thick thatch of wavy hair, angular cheekbones, and a distinctive cleft chin, Coleman was still handsome at age forty-five for he was careful about his appearance.[9] He and his wife, Frances, were the parents of four children: the eldest was thirteen, the youngest one. All the children knew what their daddy did for a living; the Colemans lived at 31 Russell Street, a block west of the train tracks, five blocks south of the ICR rail yard, and a like distance from the North Street Station, the city's grand red-brick passenger terminal. The sounds of train whistles and shunting rail cars coupling and uncoupling were the soundtrack of everyday life in the Coleman household. Vincent Coleman set his watch by the arrival of the overnight express train No. 10 from Saint John, New Brunswick, which pulled into the North Street Station each morning at 8:55 a.m. Most days, Coleman was at work by then.

His office was a wooden shack located on the west side of the rail yard. If there were no trains parked on nearby sidings, Coleman had a clear view of Halifax harbour. Straight ahead, fifty yards distant, was a huge nautical freight complex made up of Piers 7, 8, and 9, while if Coleman looked to his right, he could see Pier 6, 100 yards to the south.

Vince Coleman used his telegraph key to coordinate the comings and goings of Halifax train traffic. Each day, those trains carried thousands of passengers to and from the North Street Station, delivered freight to Halifax's busy wharves, and carried troops embarking for the battlefields of Western Europe, as well as the thousands of men who came home wounded and broken. Vince Coleman's job was busy, and it was vital to the smooth and safe operation of the port.

TELEGRAPH OPERATOR VINCENT
COLEMAN. (NOVA SCOTIA ARCHIVES)

On the morning of December 6, Coleman was exchanging information with the night dispatcher when their conversation was interrupted by the sound of a muffled thud that seemed to come somewhere to the south. Both men wondered what had happened. Then, a minute or two later, came the screeching sound of metal grinding on metal. Whatever was going on, Vince Coleman knew it was nothing good. The huge billowing cloud of black smoke in the southeast sky soon affirmed that suspicion. Not long afterward, a co-worker poked his head in the door and advised Vince Coleman and the night dispatcher that two ships had collided in the Narrows, and one of them was now on fire. Coleman was still discussing this news a few minutes later with his boss, William Lovett, the Richmond rail yard's chief clerk, when a red-faced sailor in an RCN uniform appeared at the office door.

"Boys, you've got to get out of here. Run for it, right now!" the sailor shouted. "There's been a bad accident. A French munitions ship is on fire. The crew have abandoned her, an' she's adrift. She's up against Pier 6 and is going t' blow sky-high any second."

Coleman and Lovett stared at one another in disbelief. Then they quickly pulled on their coats. Lovett snatched up the telephone and called a terminal agent he dealt with to warn him of the danger. That done, both he and Coleman moved toward the door. But Coleman stopped and turned back to his desk. He had just remembered that passenger train No. 10, the overnighter from Saint John, chanced to be a few minutes late and would reach Halifax at any time. There might be as many as 300 people on board that train, and Coleman knew the track it would pass along was right next to Pier 6 and the French ship that was on fire there.

"For Chrissakes, Vince! What are you doin'?" Bill Lovett cried. "You heard the man. We've got t' get out of here right now, or we're as good as dead."

"You go, Bill. I'll be right behind you. I've got to send a quick message to Rockingham Station. The overnight train from Saint John is due here any minute. I've got to warn the crew, tell them to stay back."

Lovett gave no reply. He was gone in a wink, racing across the rail yard toward Campbell Road and whatever cover he could find there. Vince Coleman was too busy to watch him go. His heart was pounding as he sat down at his desk and began tapping away on his telegraph key. The dots and dashes of the Morse code message he sent to Rockingham Station, four miles to the north, read: "Hold up the train. Ammunition ship afire in harbour making for Pier 6 and will explode. Guess this will be my last message. Good-bye boys."[10]

CHAPTER 17

"A Sound for God to Make, Not Man"

Halifax Harbour, December 6, 1917, 9:04 a.m.

The hands of the Citadel Hill clock read 9:04 a.m. That was the exact moment of the great Halifax harbour explosion of 1917, which was destined to be the deadliest disaster in Canadian history. A primitive seismometer located in the basement of the old physics building at Dalhousie University recorded the event. However, the dispassionate scientific data—a few squiggly lines scratched on graph paper by a machine more than two miles from ground zero—told nothing of the human story of that fateful day: fear, horror, heartbreak, and drama.

The blast that obliterated the *Mont-Blanc*, claimed more than 2,000 lives, and devastated the city of Halifax was the most powerful "man-made" explosion in history, a distinction it held until the dropping of atomic bombs on Japan in 1945. Its reverberations shot through the soil, granite, and Precambrian slate bedrock beneath Halifax at a speed of more than four miles per second. That is twenty-three times the speed of sound.

The thunderclap that accompanied the explosion echoed up and down the length of the harbour channel. It boomed across the cities of Halifax and neighbouring Dartmouth, and it was audible much farther away.

The crew of the American cruiser the USS *Tacoma* heard the boom fifty miles out to sea. The warship's lookout had just sighted on the horizon the Devil's Island lighthouse, twelve miles southeast of the entrance to Halifax harbour. "At 9:05 heard heavy explosion in general direction of Halifax, observed great clouds of smoke high in air," the officer on watch recorded in the ship's logbook.[1]

The same rumble that drew the attention of the *Tacoma*'s crew was audible as far away as Cape Breton Island, 170 miles to the north. In Truro, 60 miles west of Halifax, the blast's concussive shock broke some windows and shook a clock off the wall in the railway dispatcher's office.[2] As one observer said, the rumble of the Halifax explosion was "a sound for God to make, not man."[3]

THE GREAT HALIFAX HARBOUR explosion of 1917 unleashed the energy equivalent of three kilotons of TNT. When detonated, a single kilogram of TNT releases a million calories of heat energy. *Kilo* being the Greek word for "a thousand," it follows that the calories of heat released in the explosion of one kiloton of TNT is a thousand times a million. A *billion* calories.

THE EXPLOSION CLOUD.

(COURTESY OF ANN FOREMAN)

The destructive power of a shock wave as intense as the one the Halifax harbour explosion generated is terrifying. On a bright, sunlit day, it is invisible, yet it can send human bodies and objects as big as a house flying like dry leaves in a gale. It can crush a person's internal organs, rupture eyeballs, and shatter eardrums. It can snap trees, lampposts, and telephone poles. It can level buildings that are close to ground zero, while those farther away that remain upright still see their doors blown off their hinges, roofs destroyed, and windows shattered; glass shards from broken windows fly like tiny arrows that maim, blind, and kill as they sever heads and limbs.

The pressure generated by the chemical reaction in the *Mont-Blanc*'s cargo hold amounted to thousands of "earth atmospheres"—the 14.70 pounds per square inch (psi) air pressure that is normal at sea level. (By comparison, the pressure at the wreck site of the *Titanic*, 2.5 miles deep, is about 6,500 psi.) At the same time, the air temperature flared to 9,000 degrees Fahrenheit (about 5,000 degrees Celsius), which is almost as hot as the surface of the sun, and was hot enough to vaporize the *Mont-Blanc*.

Just as a stone dropping into the still waters of a pond creates rings of disturbance, the destructive shock wave of the explosion surged outward for a mile in all directions and launched skyward molten remnants of the ship's hull and its cargo. Some bits of this shrapnel were as large as a refrigerator; others were the size of marbles. All were lethal, ripping into human flesh, slamming into wooden buildings, or perforating metal ships.

A piece of the *Mont-Blanc*'s 1,100-pound anchor soared through the air for two and a half miles before it crashed through a roof. The ship's 90-mm aft deck gun ended up near a small lake on the Dartmouth side of the harbour, three miles from ground zero. A large chunk of metal from one of the *Mont-Blanc*'s boilers smashed into the Royal Naval College of Canada, coming to rest in a lecture hall, where it flattened the master's dais and several student desks. Fortunately, the room was empty at the time.

THE HEAT OF THE EXPLOSION that obliterated the *Mont-Blanc* superheated the water around and under the ship, gasifying the sea to the harbour floor, twenty feet beneath. As water rushed in to fill the vacuum, it threw up a tsunami. The massive wall of water thirty feet high raced across the harbour to Dartmouth. It also roared up and down the harbour channel and far out into the Atlantic. In the confined space of the harbour, the impact was murderous. The tsunami battered ships, swamped boats, and tossed vessels of all sizes up onto the shore. It dragged people to their deaths when it washed over piers and sped waist-deep along streets on both sides of the harbour. "[The tsunami] boiled over the shore and climbed the [Fort Needham] hill as far as the third cross-street [Albert Street], carrying with it the wreckage of small boats, fragments of fish, and somewhere, lost in the thousands of tons of hissing brine, the bodies of men."[4]

Even then, the murderous wave was yet wreaking havoc. On its retreat, the water snatched up still more debris along with the bodies of explosion victims, some alive, others dead. And with them it carried off personal property, vegetation, animals, and the remains of crumpled homes and workplaces. There was still more misery to come.

In the wake of the tsunami's retreat, a towering cloud of noxious gases that billowed high into the sky drifted over Halifax. "For ten minutes after the explosion a 'black rain' was observed to fall from the sky. This was an oily soot, the unconsumed carbon of the explosives. It blackened clothing almost like liquid tar," recalled Archibald MacMechan, the Dalhousie English professor who would become the "official historian" of the explosion. "It blackened the faces and bodies of all it fell on. . . . It penetrated clothing to the skin and coated the ruins of the houses, until the snow and rain storms washed it away."[5]

AT GROUND ZERO in Halifax harbour, along with the *Mont-Blanc*, the explosion obliterated Pier 6 and Pier 8 and all the buildings on each of them. All disappeared. Aboard the SS *Picton*, which was moored at Pier 8, supervisor Francis Carew along with his two assistants and sixty-four dock workers and members of the ship's crew died instantly; fortunately, they had secured the ship's hatches before the blast and so the munitions in the cargo hold did not explode.

At Pier 6, nine of the ten Halifax firemen who had been battling the fire perished in that same instant. The crew of the *Patricia* were still positioning their fire hoses while driver Billy Wells was maneuvering the pumper truck to position it close to a fire hydrant when the *Mont-Blanc* blew up in a blinding flash. The searing fireball that blew outward from the blast's epicentre incinerated everything and everyone in its vicinity. With one exception.

THE EXPLOSION, WHICH CLAIMED THE LIVES OF CHIEF CONDON AND EIGHT OF HIS MEN, ALSO DESTROYED THE *PATRICIA* (LEFT) AND THE CHIEF'S 1911 MCLAUGHLIN ROADSTER (BELOW). (COURTESY OF TREVOR ADAMS/ *HALIFAX MAGAZINE*)

At the instant the explosion occurred, Billy Wells had been sitting in the driver's seat of the *Patricia*, his hands on the steering wheel. The next thing he knew, he was standing fifty yards from where Pier 6 had been, and he was naked. The blast had torn off his clothing, along with most of the flesh on his right arm. Although he felt no pain, the bones were exposed. In his left hand, Wells still clutched half of the *Patricia*'s steering wheel.

When he looked around for the fire truck and his mates, Billy saw nothing. They were all gone. But he had no time to make sense of any of this because in the next instant, the tsunami, a roiling wall of water thirty feet high, swept over him and carried him off.

It was a miracle that the wave did not claim Billy Wells' life. It was not his time to die. When he regained consciousness, he staggered westward, through the ruins of the rail yard and into what had been the Richmond neighbourhood. The damage and the carnage he saw all around him were nightmarish and horrifying. "[I] made my way to . . . Campbell Road. . . . The sight was awful . . . with people hanging out of windows dead. Some with their heads off and some [bodies] thrown over the overhead telegraph wires."[6]

THE SHOCK WAVE GENERATED by the explosion in Halifax harbour cut a 325-acre swatch across Halifax's North End. "People inside buildings during the blast endured one horror after another: shooting glass, tumbling ceilings and walls, [and] crashing furniture. With incredible speed, fire also added to the deadly work of the explosion."[7]

Its effects were most acute on the east-facing slope of Fort Needham hill, which overlooked ground zero. There the explosion levelled houses, shops, factories, and businesses.

All the workers who had climbed up to the roof of the Acadia Sugar Refinery for a bird's-eye view of the fire at Pier 6 perished when "the massive brick walls ... collapsed like a house of cards," as the *Halifax Herald* reported.[8] Twenty-seven children and the matron of the nearby Protestant Orphanage suffered a similar fate.

Meanwhile, 120 workers at the Naval Dockyard, as well as shopkeeper Constant Upham and the customers who had congregated outside his business, all died instantly.

A few blocks to the north, the blast cut down dozens of onlookers who were standing on a pedestrian bridge that spanned the Richmond rail yards at the foot of Duffus Street, 300 yards from Pier 6.

The Hillis and Sons Foundry, across the street from the Hinch family's home at 66 Veith Street, felt the full fury of the blast. The building crumpled, claiming forty-one victims; the foundry's manager, Frank Hillis Sr., and his son James, the assistant manager, were among them.

Sixty people perished at North Street Station, Halifax's main railway passenger terminal, when steel girders, concrete, and glass in the roof crashed down onto the platforms and tracks. "The station, a fine building with a glass dome, now stood open to the sky."[9]

THE RUINS OF THE HILLIS FOUNDRY, WHICH STOOD ACROSS THE STREET FROM THE HINCH FAMILY'S HOME ON ROOME STREET. (COURTESY OF ANN FOREMAN)

Damage at the nearby Richmond railway yard was also extensive. Train dispatcher Vince Coleman, who had remained at his post to send that one final telegram to warn off the No. 10 overnight passenger train from Saint John, died instantly. His boss, William Lovett, who had fled the rail yard moments before the explosion, was also among the more than fifty railway workers who perished.

THE RUINS OF NORTH STREET STATION, WHERE SIXTY PEOPLE PERISHED WHEN THE EXPLOSION COLLAPSED THE ROOF. (UNDERWOOD AND UNDERWOOD, NY)

All told, the great Halifax harbour explosion of 1917 destroyed more than 1,500 buildings and damaged 12,000 more. Six thousand Haligonians suddenly found themselves homeless, while more than 25,000 lacked adequate shelter. Almost 2,000 people in Halifax and surrounding areas would lose their lives, with hundreds of them perishing in less time than it takes for a single heartbeat.[10] The numbers are staggering. But numbers do not tell the full story of the agony, suffering, death, heroism, and incredible human courage of the people of Halifax and of those volunteers who came from far and wide to help with the emergency relief efforts and to help rebuild.

In the hours, days, and weeks after the disaster, many of those who had suffered grievous injuries in the blast died. Each of them left behind loved ones—family and friends—and unfulfilled hopes, dreams, and potential. There was also a tragic story behind every person who died so unexpectedly and so tragically.

Every survivor had a story of heartbreak, suffering, and loss to tell; all would recall the horrors they and their loved ones had endured. However, the story of the great Halifax harbour explosion of 1917 is, above all, a story of courage, perseverance, and the resilience of the human spirit. The people of Halifax endured unspeakable pain, yet they and their city emerged phoenix-like from the disaster to heal and rebuild their shattered lives and their city.

FEW OF THE PEOPLE who actually witnessed the great Halifax harbour explosion lived to tell the tale. Able Seaman Bert Griffith, aboard HMCS *Niobe*, was one of that select group.

Griffith and his mates were standing on the deck of the RCN's depot ship in the moments just before the blast. The thick pall of black smoke that hung over the water stung the eyes and made onlookers cough. It was akin to peering through a pane of smoked glass, but even though the fire was a half-mile to the north, the flames engulfing the *Mont-Blanc* were a sight to see. "All at once there was a most hideous noise [and] I saw the whole boat vanish, a moment after I saw something coming. [I] can't describe it," Griffith would recount in a letter home written a few days later.[11]

Charles Duggan Jr. was another eyewitness to the explosion. He made his living operating a nautical taxi service that catered to dockyard workers. Having dropped off his passengers and completed his early morning runs, the twenty-year-old had been back home having breakfast. Duggan, his eighteen-year-old wife, Rita, and their four-month-old son, Warren, lived with Charlie's parents and his siblings in a wood-frame house at

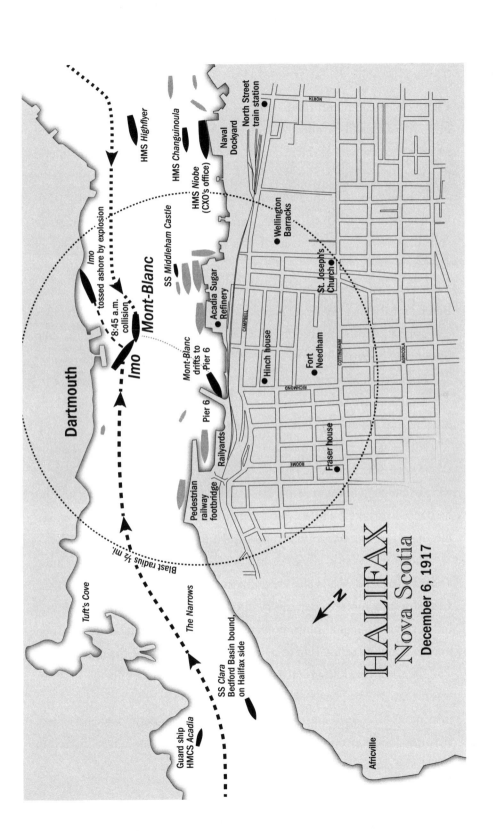

1329 Barrington Street. The Duggans were one of the many big, closely knit Irish Catholic families in Halifax's bustling North End. More than two dozen members of the extended Duggan family called the Richmond neighbourhood home.

The moment Charlie Duggan learned that two ships had collided in the harbour, he grabbed his hat and coat and ran out the door. After sprinting down Hanover Street, he crossed the railway tracks and reached the dock where he kept his thirty-six-foot trawler, the *Grace Darling*. With the boat's engine racing all out, Duggan sped toward the *Mont-Blanc* and the *Imo*. He was intent on helping in rescue efforts. "Before I had got halfway to the French boat, her deck had caught fire and the men of her crew were spilling over the side like rats," Duggan would recall.[12] The Frenchmen were madly rowing their two lifeboats toward Dartmouth, and Duggan instantly understood why; smoke from the fire clouded the air, stinging the eyes and searing the lungs when breathed in.

The heat from the fire and the booming explosions that periodically echoed across the harbour prompted Charlie Duggan to turn his boat and race for home. He was about to do so when curiosity got the better of him; he paused to take one final look at the burning ship. What he saw was mesmerizing. The flames were multi-hued and hissed as they burned.

Duggan was not alone in his fascination with the fire. The men aboard the *Stella Maris* and other boats that had been battling the blaze were similarly awestruck. Uncertain of what they were dealing with and increasingly wary of whatever dangers they were facing, the men had backed off while struggling to decide whether to resume the fight or flee.

The scene in Halifax harbour was surreal. The water in the harbour was placid. The sun continued to shine in a cloudless blue sky. That miasmic fog of oily, acrid smoke fouled the air. Yet an eerie calm prevailed. Was this the proverbial calm before the storm? That thought occurred to Charlie Duggan.

A bolt of fear, visceral and urgent, prickled the hair on the back of Duggan's neck and set his knees quivering. Call it premonition. Call it dread. But in that instant he sensed that he had to get as far away from that burning ship as possible, as quickly as he could. If he did not, he somehow knew he would die. "I bent over the engine trying to coax a little extra speed out of my boat and must have been half way across the harbour toward the Dartmouth side when the 'thing' occurred. I say 'thing' because I shall never find words to express what next happened.

"I was standing in the boat looking backward toward the *Mont-Blanc* when she appeared to settle in the water. A lurid yellowish-green spurt of flame rose toward the heavens and drove ahead of it a cloud of smoke, which must have risen 200 feet in the air. Then came the most appalling crash I have ever heard, and my boat went under my feet as if some supernatural power had stolen her from me while I myself was thrown into the harbour."[13]

CHAPTER 18

"MY, WHAT A RUSH OF WIND"

Halifax, Nova Scotia, December 6 1917, 9:04 a.m.

Confusion had reigned on the bridge of the *Imo* in the moments after the Norwegian ship's collision with the *Mont-Blanc*. Neither pilot William Hayes nor Captain Haakon From could quite believe his eyes.

Hayes had been a harbour pilot for more than twenty years. Until now, he had boasted of having an unblemished safety record. How could he ever explain what had happened this morning, even if he was blameless? Hayes knew the *Mont-Blanc* was hauling munitions, but miraculously the crash had not sparked an immediate explosion. For that, he thanked Heaven, but he also cursed his luck. He would face no end of trouble; the port's navy officials, the owners of the two ships involved in the collision, the shipping agents, the insurance companies, and their lawyers would see to that.

Haakon From was no less dismayed. He was also angry at the prospect of yet another delay in getting to New York. At this rate, he would never get home to Norway for Christmas, unless the damage the *Imo* had suffered was so minor that she could continue on her way. From dispatched Second Officer Peter B'Jönnas to check on the extent of the harm done while he and Hayes set about getting the *Imo* turned around for a return to Bedford Basin.

Down on the *Imo*'s deck, B'Jönnas found a half-dozen members of the ship's crew gathered near the bow of the ship. Like everyone else out on the water or gathered on the shore around the harbour that morning, the Norwegians focused their eyes on the *Mont-Blanc*. Shrouded in smoke, she was adrift some 300 yards off the *Imo*'s port bow. Through the haze, B'Jönnas could see the firefighters who were trying to battle the blaze. Their efforts seemed to be in vain; the puny stream of water they were directing toward the burning ship was having no discernable effect. How strange it all seemed to B'Jönnas and his mates. As yet, pilot Hayes was the only one aboard the *Imo* who knew the *Mont-Blanc* was laden with explosives. However, even he had no inkling of the destructive force about to be unleashed.

Slowly but surely, the bow of the *Imo* was turning as the ship swung starboard for her intended return to Bedford Basin. That never happened, for at that moment the *Mont-Blanc* blew apart with a roar that was so loud, so violent, so fiery that it seemed apocalyptic. Peter B'Jönnas did not see the actual blast. The only thing the *Imo*'s second officer would remember was the blinding flash and the boom that left his ears ringing for days. The concussive shock wave that came racing across the harbour a fraction of a second later sent B'Jönnas and his companions flying through the air. Two men—a boatswain and a carpenter—died instantly, as did two other crew members elsewhere on the ship. The shrieking barrage of white-hot metal bits that peppered the *Imo*'s hull perforated the *Imo*'s bridge and sheared off her funnel as the force of the blast was lifting the ship out of the water and hurling her toward the Dartmouth shore.

LIKE PETER B'JÖNNAS, *Imo* helmsman Johan Johansen had no idea the *Mont-Blanc* was about to explode. One moment, he was on the bridge, hands gripping the ship's wheel; the next, he felt himself flying through the air. "My, what a rush of wind when the explosion came. Blew me off just like a leaf. I didn't know what hit me . . . for a long time. Yes, the big wind blew off the other men, blew down the bridge, and most everything else aboard the *Imo*."[1]

Johansen suffered cuts and bruises to his legs, and he temporarily lost sight in his right eye. Despite being bloodied and dazed, he managed to free himself from the wreckage on the bridge when he came to. "[The] best I could do was to crawl along on my hands and knees and follow the ship rail. [It] seemed to me I crawled a mile, but when I had about decided my best stunt would be to drop into the bay, I heard voices."[2]

Johansen would have only the vaguest recollection of his shipmates helping him. The next thing he knew, it was several hours later and he was waking up in HMS *Highflyer's* sick bay.

Captain From, pilot William Hayes, and First Officer Ingvald Iverson were far less fortunate. The white-hot metal bits from the *Mont-Blanc* that tore through the *Imo's* bridge killed the three men instantly. The captain was decapitated, his corpse riddled with the jagged shrapnel. Hayes and Iverson suffered a similar fate.

Across the harbour from Halifax, the explosion shock wave delivered a devastating blow. Reverend C.W. Vernon, the minister at Emmanuel Anglican Church, would recall how in the wink of an eye "there were masses of ruins, houses converted into kindling wood, dead, dying, and wounded lying among the ruins, the injured flying in every direction, and fires at once beginning from blown down chimneys, overturned stoves, and live electrical wires."[3] The blast levelled Oland Brewery and various other Dartmouth businesses, partially collapsed the town's skating rink, and killed 100 people, including entire families, in the small Mi'kmaq

THE BRIDGE AREA OF THE *IMO* WAS DEVASTATED IN THE EXPLOSION.
(WRECK COMMISSION EXHIBIT)

village at Turtle Grove. The explosion virtually wiped out that community. It ceased to be. Only a few of the Mi'kmaq First Nation residents survived the disaster. Among them were young Aggie March and her baby, who had been on the front porch of her home when the crew of the *Mont-Blanc* came ashore seeking a place of refuge. The French sailor who had snatched Aggie's baby and ran toward the woods, with Aggie in hot pursuit, had probably saved the lives of both mother and child.

IN THE SPLIT SECOND before the *Mont-Blanc* blew apart, Francis Mackey had been marvelling at the intensity of the fire that was consuming the ship. Captain Le Médec was just about to tap him on the shoulder and remind him to take cover when the explosion happened. "Just as quick as that, we were knocked down," Mackey said. "I had a raincoat on . . . and it was taken off the same as if you had a rusty knife and cut it right around [my waist]. Trees fell over us, just like a miracle. The branches on it were bigger than my arm. . . . My cap was gone off of my head . . . and [Captain Le Médec's] coat was gone off."[4]

The force of the blast rendered Mackey unconscious. Luckily for him and for his companions, the tsunami thrown up by the explosion failed to reach the woods where the *Mont-Blanc* crew and those Dartmouth residents who had heeded the Frenchmen's warnings lay dazed and numb. Mackey was out for several minutes. When he finally came to, his face was bloody. The oily soot that rained down had streaked his body, and his clothes were in tatters. Yet miraculously, Mackey was otherwise unharmed. His thoughts immediately turned to his wife, Lillian, their five children, and the sixth who was on the way.

Mackey, still dazed and with his ears ringing, staggered to his feet as did Captain Le Médec. "*Mon Dieu!*" the captain muttered.

Le Médec and Mackey were struggling to decide their next move when Second Officer Joseph Leveque arrived with some bad news: a twenty-year-old sailor who was one of the *Mont-Blanc*'s gunners had suffered grave injuries. Yves Quequiner had a broken arm, and a chunk of flying metal had embedded itself deep into his back. He was bleeding heavily, and without urgent medical care, he would die.

Mackey, being the only one in the *Mont-Blanc*'s party who knew where to find a doctor in Dartmouth, acted as guide when Le Médec and some of his crewmen carried Quequiner into town. Unfortunately, he died on the way there and thus became the only member of the *Mont-Blanc*'s crew to perish as a result of the explosion.

By now, Mackey had decided he could do nothing more for Le Médec and his men, and so he bade the Frenchmen farewell. Mackey wanted only to get home as fast as possible, and although he was still woozy, he set off toward the Dartmouth ferry dock. Along the way, he encountered a man he knew, and he asked him, "Where can I buy a new cap? I've lost mine." Strange though this question was, the man explained that no shops in Dartmouth were open that morning; however, he removed his own cap and handed it to Mackey, who accepted with a hearty thank you.

Although he was bloodied, half-naked, and streaked from head to foot with oily soot, Francis Mackey sported new headwear. It topped his head as he crossed the harbour aboard the Halifax–Dartmouth ferry. Apart from some broken windows, the ferry continued to operate, its service uninterrupted. "The superintendent and other operators stayed at their posts, though they were anxious to find out what had happened to their homes."[5]

Mackey still had no real awareness of just how much death and destruction the *Mont-Blanc* explosion had caused. His first stop in Halifax was the pilotage office on Bedford Row. What he wanted to say, or even if anyone was in the office to receive his report, is unknown. Mackey would recall only that shards of broken window glass carpeted the street outside the pilotage office and other streets in the downtown, glittering like diamonds in the sunshine.

AFTER LEAVING THE PILOTAGE OFFICE, the route Francis Mackey followed on his twenty-minute walk home took him past the Halifax Common. Thousands of people had taken refuge there in the open air after a rumour made the rounds that there was going to be a second explosion. Mackey marvelled at the size of the crowd. He was staring with mouth agape when he heard someone call his name. Lizzie Brooks, his family's maid, waved and came running up to him. "[She] said, 'All down here, sir. All down here.' So she ran and got [Lillian and the children]."[6]

The Mackey family's reunion was joyous, but tearful. Francis Mackey explained his haggard appearance and did his best to reassure his wife and children that everything would be all right. To underscore that notion, he led the family on a return march to their Robie Street home, where they found soldiers patrolling the street outside their front door. The troops were there to maintain order and discourage looters. Mackey did a quick damage assessment and determined that apart from some minor damage and broken windows, the house was still habitable. Ignoring the orders of a soldier who insisted the Mackeys were not permitted to return to their home, they did so anyway.

Francis Mackey had piled the winter storm windows against the house a few days earlier. All nineteen of them were still intact. "So I got after them, got the fire [on], got some hot tea," he said. "From the time I started to put those windows on, I got them on at half past nine in the night—every one of them—and I was ready to lie down. I was bagged out."[7]

ACTING BOATSWAIN ALBERT MATTISON and a half-dozen of his shipmates who were riding in HMCS *Niobe*'s steam pinnace died instantly in the explosion. Searchers who went looking for them found no trace of their bodies or their boat.

Commander Tom Triggs from HMS *Highflyer* and the six Royal Navy sailors who were beside him in the Royal Navy warship's whaler also died. Incredibly, four of the men who were in the open boat somehow survived the blast; Able Seaman William Becker was one of them. When he resurfaced afterward, he found himself in the cloud of smoke and toxic vapour that hung over the harbour. Three of his comrades were treading water nearby, while bits of what little was left of the whaler floated around them. The stunned men swam to grab hold of wreckage. However, the near-freezing water was bone numbing. With each stroke Becker and his fellow survivors took, they could feel their strength ebbing; hypothermia was quickly setting in. Anyone unlucky enough to be immersed in such frigid water has fifteen minutes at most to live.

However, Becker was stunned, and so it was several agonizing, precious minutes before he regained his bearings. When he finally did so, he realized the sea had claimed two of his fellow survivors. Becker knew he would also die if he did not soon get out of the water. Summoning what little strength he had left, he began paddling toward Dartmouth. The shore, less than fifty yards away, was so close, yet so far. Becker's limbs were leaden. He had gone only a few yards when he came upon the only other man from the *Highflyer* whaler who was still afloat. Lieutenant James Ruffles was in a bad way and was fading fast. "Can you make it to the shore with me, sir?" Becker asked.

"No," came the weak reply. "I'm done for."

With that, the thirty-one-year old Englishman lost his grip on the chunk of wood he had been clinging to. When he slipped beneath the surface and disappeared, Becker was all alone in the icy water. Although he was only dimly aware of doing so, he continued to move his limbs. William Becker was determined not to die.

THE FORCE OF THE EXPLOSION in Halifax harbour hurled the salvage tug *Stella Maris* onto the shore near the spot where Pier 6 had stood. Captain Horatio H. Brannen and nineteen of his twenty-four-man crew perished. The captain's son Walter was among the five men who survived. Two of them were working belowdecks at the time of the explosion; two others were topside but chanced to be on the ship's leeward side. Ironically, the shock wave saved the younger Brannen's life, for it threw him down into the hold. "I was quite badly bruised [and] my eardrum was punctured," he would recall.[8] Physically, he was otherwise unharmed. Emotionally, his scars ran so deep they would never completely heal.

CAPTAIN FREDERICK PASCO had grown ever more frustrated in the minutes after the *Imo* and the *Mont-Blanc* collided in the harbour. He could only wonder about the whereabouts of superintendent Wyatt, the port of Halifax's CXO. Why had he not called to explain what was happening down in the harbour? Pasco, being the acting superintendent of the port, wanted answers, and he wanted them quickly. The captain was still pacing the floor of the home of the superintendent of the Naval Dockyard when the explosion happened a half-mile away. The shock wave that followed sent Pasco sprawling. Jagged glass from the window he had been peering out only moments before sprayed the room. Luckily for him, the captain suffered only a few "nicks around my eyes and . . . one or two on my hand. Superficial. [The blood] bunged up my eyes and [for] an hour or so afterward, I couldn't see."[9]

THE EXPLOSION SLAMMED HMCS *Niobe* hard, killing sixteen men. With ground zero barely half a mile to the north, the concussive shock wave struck the Canadian navy's depot ship with all its fury. The force sent Bert Griffith and his shipmates flying. "I got to my feet and ran with a whole lot of fellows," Griffith would recall. "My one fixed idea was to get below."[10] Many other men had the same idea. But there was just one ladder into the bowels of the warship, and so the sailors could only dive for cover as bits of white-hot metal from the *Mont-Blanc* rained down on them. They were still cowering moments later when the blast-generated tsunami slammed into *Niobe*. The explosion had snapped the ship's mooring cables, smashed her gangway, and damaged the adjacent wooden pier. Now the wall of water that swamped the ship swept men from the deck and threw them into the harbour. Many of them drowned.

Bert Griffith hung on in desperation. When the water receded, he scrambled ashore, soaking wet and still reeling from the shock. Military historian John Griffith Armstrong—Griffith's grandson—reports that at one point amid all the confusion "some officer heavy on tradition yelled thru a megaphone for all hands to stand fast, keep cool and everything will be all right, there's no immediate danger."[11] One of the anxious crewmen was unconvinced. He shouted back at the officer, "To Hell with you . . . we got wives and kids ashore!"[12] There followed a stampede of men intent on rushing home to check on the well-being of families and homes.

Bert Griffith was not among them, of course. Being from Red Deer, Alberta, he was a long way from home and had nowhere else to go. Griffith had come through this ordeal with no serious injuries, and so once he regained his senses, he began pitching in to help treat the wounded and to rescue sailors the tsunami had thrown into the harbour. He also helped to fight fires on shore. "By this time all the houses round the dockyard were on fire. I joined a party on the run to the ammunition magazines just on shore beside the jetty. . . . We worked like slaves, pulling out cases of cordite [and] shells of all kinds [and] dumped them in the water. It was a perfect miracle that they did not go off, as the [three] buildings where they were stored had been completely wrecked, but luckily had not caught fire."[13]

AT THE STERN of *Niobe*, the explosion had scattered the diving crew that had been working there. The shock wave upended Acting Gunner John Gammon, the group's leader. He was winded, but otherwise unhurt. His immediate concern was the fate of the two navy divers in the water. Their situation was instantly critical; Gammon knew they had only a minute or two at most before their oxygen would be gone and they would die.

Just one of the six men who had been working the air pump and ensuring the hoses did not tangle or kink remained on deck after the explosion. Able Seaman W.G. Critch, like Gammon, had escaped serious injury. Together, he and Gammon set about trying to rescue the two divers. The roof of the shed that housed the air pump had collapsed; however, Critch supported it with his left hand, his adrenaline surging, while he worked the pump with his right. Gammon helped the two divers return to the surface. The men were rattled but thankful—and fortunate to be alive.[14]

AS EFFORTS WERE UNDER WAY to prevent the store of ammunition located near *Niobe* from catching fire, a similar, even more menacing crisis was unfolding at the Wellington Barracks 300 yards west of the Naval Dockyard.

Located on a huge tract of land in Halifax's North End, the barracks included a parade square, an assortment of administrative buildings—one of which was Admiralty House (the erstwhile residence of the Royal Navy port commander, which in 1917 was serving as a military hospital)—residences for military personnel, and a wooden shed that housed the garrison's magazine.

At the very moment of the explosion, the garrison band and a contingent of army recruits were drilling and going through their paces in preparation for their deployment to France. The shock wave from the blast and the white-hot metal fragments that rained down across the north end of the city killed several soldiers and seriously wounded others. Among this latter group was twenty-seven-year-old orderly officer Lieutenant Harold Balcom, who was felled and would die from his injuries. Balcom's friend Lieutenant Charles A. McLennan of the Nova Scotia–based 76th Colchester and Hants Rifles militia regiment stepped forward to take charge.

When he did a quick tour of the grounds to check for casualties and damage to the facilities, McLennan was alarmed to discover that the explosion had severely damaged the hut that housed the magazine's furnace. "The door was blown in and smashed, the window frames were smashed on the floor, the roof were [sic] half off, the smoke pipe was blown from the heater," McLennan would report. "The hot-water heater itself had all its doors blown open and the coals scattered over the floor among the smashed woodwork. This was smouldering." [15] The hut's wooden floor was dangerously hot, as was the magazine itself. Lieutenant McLennan feared the building would catch fire. If it did, the flames could easily spread to the magazine.

Hoping to find a senior officer to assume command or provide him with orders, McLennan frantically sprinted across the parade square to the married officers' quarters. There he found a colonel who was caring for his wife, who had suffered serious cuts in the explosion. When McLennan explained the emergency at the magazine, the colonel reacted angrily. "To Hell with the military magazine!" he shouted. "My wife is bleeding to death. Get me a medical orderly."[16]

McLennan empathized with the colonel's concerns; however, he knew that if the barracks' magazine caught fire, the hundreds of kilograms of munitions stored there might explode, and many more people would die. Rushing back to the magazine, McLennan recruited a group of soldiers and sailors to clear away debris and empty the burning coals from the heater house's furnace. Meanwhile, he used a fire extinguisher to douse smouldering woodwork. This threw up a huge cloud of steam that escaped the building through holes in the damaged roof. The sight of the steam ignited a panic among the curious onlookers who had gathered outside the barracks fence; some of them mistook the steam for smoke. When someone shouted, "The magazine is on fire!" the stampede began. The rumour that the magazine was ablaze and about to explode spread quickly. Masses of people were soon on the move, rushing for Halifax Common and any other open space they could find. "The panic of both civilians and military personnel near Wellington Barracks was infectious," military historian John Griffith Armstrong would write. "The fleeing crowd expanded and spread. These circumstances underlie later intense controversy over the 'mysterious' origins of the widespread expectation of a second explosion and the spontaneous flight from shelter of thousands of Haligonians to open areas and Point Pleasant Park."[17] The situation in Halifax in the immediate aftermath of the explosion was beginning to spin out of control.

CHAPTER 19

Halifax, Nova Scotia, December 6, 1917, 9:04 a.m.

I s there such a thing as luck? If not, it must have been happenstance that
on this splendid, sun-drenched Thursday morning, Mary Jean Hinch
had managed to cheat death when all around her so many others were dying.

In a nanosecond, infinitely faster than the time it takes to blink, the
shock wave generated by the explosion in Halifax harbour "wrought
instant havoc everywhere. The force of it tore trees from the ground and
snapped telephone poles like toothpicks. [People] were thrown violently
into the air; houses collapsed on all sides."[1] Entire streets that had been
vital and alive one moment had all but ceased to be in the next. The force
of the explosion had flattened virtually all the buildings within 300 yards
of ground zero—what insurance adjusters in their cool, calculating
methodology would label as Zone One of the disaster.

In Zone Two—300 to 700 yards from ground zero—many buildings
suffered severe damage, or else they burned in the fires that were fed when
embers spilled out of shattered stoves and furnaces. Many unfortunate

souls who survived the explosion met a hideous end when they burned to death. "The dead lay thick among the ruins and in the streets, and for those trapped and buried under the wreckage [of buildings], the only sound was of the flames as they roared nearer and nearer."[2]

The dwelling occupied by Mary Jean Hinch's neighbours at 71 Veith Street—like the Hinches' home at 66 Veith Street—was one of the more than 12,000 houses the explosion destroyed. The force of the blast tore the Matthews family's two-storey wood-frame dwelling from its foundations and sent it hurtling across the street. All four members of the family who were home at the time died instantly. The bodies of thirty-four-year-old William Matthews, a machinist at the Naval Dockyard; his thirty-one-year-old wife, Clara, and their children, two-year-old Doris and nine-month-old Willie, would lie buried beneath the rubble of their home for several days before salvage workers recovered them.

The shock wave that claimed the Matthews family doubtless also would have killed Mary Jean Hinch had she not been in the lee of the Matthewses' house. However, as a large chunk of the west wall of her neighbours' house flew through the air, it struck Mary Jean with the fury of a giant's fist. The blow knocked her head-over-heels for ten yards. Her bloodied, unconscious body came to rest in a drainage ditch. There she would awake to find herself and the baby she carried buried under a mound of splintered lumber, downed plaster, smashed furniture, and broken glass. A heavy wooden beam pinned her legs, and she had a fractured hip and numerous cuts. Yet the same rubble that entombed Mary Jean Hinch also saved her life. It had shielded her from being swept away by the killer tsunami that washed up Fort Needham hill and over the ruins of Veith Street.

Mary Jean was aware of none of this, of course. She had no way of knowing that Veith Street had ceased to be or that the houses and all the people who lived in them were gone. The death rate on Veith Street was ninety-five per cent; of the 149 residents, all but seven perished in the explosion. Mary Jean's husband Joe and all her children, all ten of them, died when the explosion levelled their house. No family in all of Halifax suffered greater loss.

Those few residents of Veith Street who survived, like Mary Jean Hinch, were buried under piles of wreckage. No one knew this. No one knew these explosion survivors were trapped, in pain, and clinging to life by the slenderest of threads.

As Mary Jean drifted in and out of consciousness, in flickering moments of lucidity, she clutched the rosary she carried in her coat pocket. The prayer beads had been a gift from Father Walsh at St. Joseph's Church; he had given them to her on her wedding day back in 1893, when she had been a blushing sixteen-year-old bride. Mary Jean had carried the rosary beads with her and prayed every day since. Today was no different, except that today she prayed the beads would indeed protect her from Satan. She had reason to do so, for she could smell smoke and could hear the crackling of flames. The prospect of burning to death under a pile of blazing rubble was too terrifying to contemplate.

BAD LUCK SEEMED to follow Captain Henry Kendall. On the morning of December 6, 1917, the forty-three-year-old Englishman was the houseguest of some friends who lived about a mile from the harbour. Kendall had survived a shipwreck off the coast of Newfoundland in 1900, and in May 1914 he had been the master of the ill-fated RMS *Empress of Ireland* the night the huge passenger ship collided with a Norwegian collier and sank in the Gulf of the St. Lawrence, taking 1,012 people to the bottom with her.

The Halifax harbour explosion levelled the house in the North End where Kendall was staying. He escaped serious injury; however, when he crawled out from under the wreckage, the captain was staggered to see just a few yards from where he stood a sight that chilled him. There, embedded in the garden, was an unexploded artillery shell, most likely from the store of munitions that had been aboard the *Mont-Blanc*.[3] Talk about cheating death. Three months later, in March 1918, the captain survived yet another disaster—his third—when off the Ulster coast a German U-boat sank HMS *Calgarian*, the RN warship on which he was serving. Kendall was destined to die, not at sea or in battle, but rather in an English nursing home in 1965 at the ripe old age of ninety-one.

THIRTY-YEAR-OLD BERNIE ("KID") O'NEIL was a former boxer who had retired from the ring to take a clerk's job on the night shift at the Naval Dockyard. In December 1917, the Kid and his wife, Annie, were living with his wife's mother and her sister in an old wood-frame house on Campbell Road, not far from Pier 6. The sight of the *Mont-Blanc* ablaze and adrift had brought the Kid, his wife, and his in-laws to a fourth-storey window for it afforded a splendid view of the excitement that was taking place in the harbour. Few of them stood a chance when the ship exploded.

When Bernie O'Neil came to, he found himself lying in a pile of splintered lumber. The kitchen stove had landed atop his chest. He and Annie were the only two survivors in the house; sixteen other occupants had died instantly.

Annie O'Neil was horrified when she saw her husband's condition and his predicament, which was compounded and made urgent by the fact that the ruins of the building were ablaze. Annie staggered out into the street. There she hailed a passerby, a "big hulk of a man" who was in a bad way himself. When the zombie-like man ignored Annie's frantic pleas and staggered away, she resolved to do what she could to save her husband's life. "[Annie] comes back and battles and battles with that big stove," Bernie O'Neil would recall. "The fire is comin' near, an' my clothes begin to burn. My wife pulls an' drags at me until all the clothes is pulled off me; an' by God, I don't know how she does it, but that little woman has lifted the stove off'n me. And she weighs but 105 pounds."[4]

Ignoring her own injuries and the dangers of the situation, Annie O'Neil half-dragged, half-carried her husband out of the burning ruins of their home. She took him down to the water's edge, where she bathed him and cleaned his wounds in the icy salt water. Bernie was in dire condition. He had lost a huge chunk of muscle and much of the skin from his chest. Glass shards had peppered his body, and his legs were racked with pain. Yet he felt somewhat revived by the cold water. Supported by his wife, Bernie O'Neil found the strength to hobble along as the two of them went looking for help. He was naked but for a shoe and his wife's tattered skirt, which she had wrapped around him.

Fate smiled on the O'Neils. They encountered a policeman, who summoned some soldiers with a wagon. The men transported both of the O'Neils to a nearby hospital. Bernie O'Neil would later say of his wife, "She ought to have been a prize fighter herself."[5]

"A BLINDING LIGHT! Crash! Bang! Rumble! Rumble! Ohhhh! A thunderstorm? It's worse than that. That big cloud up there frothing at the edges must mean it's the end of the world," Jean Holder would recall. "Such were the thoughts of a six-year-old when the *Mont-Blanc* exploded."[6]

Although the Holders lived more than a mile from ground zero, Halifax's topography and urban landscape were such that the shock wave from the blast slammed the family's Robie Street dwelling hard. Jean and her sister Doris, who had just set foot outside the front door on their morning walk to school, were on the porch when they felt themselves flying through the air.

Frightened and bawling but otherwise unharmed, the girls picked themselves up and ran back inside. The damage there was extensive. The front door of their house had been blown off its hinges. All the windows were broken, and shards of flying glass had embedded themselves in the furnishings and interior walls. A built-in china cabinet in the sunroom was so badly rattled that all the dishes inside were smashed. The hot water heater, although still upright, sat tilted at a precarious angle. "It remained on its base, but the pipes broke so the kitchen started to flood."[7]

Fortunately, George Holder had military training, and he kept his cool. After determining that no one in the family was seriously injured, he told them to don their warmest winter clothing and be ready for whatever happened next. "When word came that there might be a second explosion [at Wellington Barracks] and people were advised to seek open spaces away from buildings, we were warmly dressed and ready to go," said Jean Holder. "[We took blankets with us] to the [Halifax] Commons so we didn't have to sit directly on the cold ground."[8]

THE MOMENT THAT NEWS of the explosion in Halifax reached Truro, Fred Rockwell knew what he had to do. Early next day, ignoring the advice of the local stationmaster, he bought a ticket for the morning train to Halifax; Rockwell was determined to learn the fate of a relative who lived in the stricken city.

There was no train service beyond the Rockingham Station, four miles from Halifax's devastated North Street Station. When Rockwell reached the end of the line, he had no choice but to walk the rest of the way into the city. While doing so, he wandered through streets knee-deep in snow, rubble, and despair. The magnitude of the destruction and the suffering was unlike anything he had ever seen. "A dozen people I passed . . . had no other marks on them except black eyes caused by the concussion [from the explosion], which in several cases I'm told popped their eyes right out," Rockwell reported in a December 12 letter he wrote to a family member.

"I heard of a chap going into a temporary dressing station in the North End with one of his eyes in his hand and inquiring whether they could do anything for him."[9]

IT WAS NOT AT ALL how Reverend Henry Cunningham of St. George's Anglican Church expected to start his day. On the morning of December 6, the minister was lingering over breakfast in the dining room of the church's Cornwallis Street rectory. The mantel clock across the hall in the study having just chimed nine times, the Reverend was musing about his schedule for the day. The lanky fifty-four-year-old Newfoundlander had a familiar routine.

Cunningham, quiet and studious, was well-suited to a clergyman's life. From the time he was a boy, he seemed predestined to follow in the footsteps of his cleric father; John Cunningham had been a missionary in the Anglican Church's Society for the Propagation of the Gospel. The elder Cunningham was stationed in the isolated fishing village of Burgeo (population 650), on Newfoundland's south coast, when his son was born in August 1862. At the time, Newfoundland was a British colony. So young Henry went away to England for his early education, and there he won first-class honours in clerical examinations that were set by Oxford and Cambridge universities. Following his 1883 ordination, Cunningham returned to Newfoundland to begin his clerical career. But then in 1892, he moved to Illinois, where he ministered with the Episcopal Church and served as the chaplain of former governor Richard Oglesby, who had been a close friend of Abraham Lincoln.

Cunningham returned to Canada and the Anglican fold in 1900 when he became the minister of the historic "old round church of St. George's," one of Halifax's oldest parishes. A few years later, when the church offered him a bishopric, he declined. "It's a wise man who knows his own limitations," Cunningham explained.[10]

The Reverend, his St. John's–born wife, Augusta, and their four children felt very much at home in Halifax. By all accounts, the parishioners of St. George's liked Reverend Cunningham as much as he enjoyed ministering to them. Cunningham would spend thirty-seven years at St. George's and would experience many memorable times there. In April 1912, he was deeply involved in efforts to arrange funerals for the more than 120 victims of the *Titanic* disaster who were buried in Halifax cemeteries. Afterward, in a gesture of appreciation, searchers who had retrieved the bodies presented the Reverend with the only deck chair to be salvaged from the sunken ship's debris field.[11]

As extraordinary as Cunningham's experiences in April and May of 1912 were, they would be supplanted in his personal memories by the disaster that devastated Halifax on December 6, 1917. Life for him, his family, and the parishioners of St. George's would be forever changed.

"My wife had just handed me a cup of coffee when we heard a deep boom," Cunningham would recall. "It sounded far away, in the distance. Three seconds later, there came a loud crash and a mighty rush of air that shattered the windows in the rectory and blew in the curtains. The force of it sent me to the floor, and I felt shards of glass cutting my neck."[12]

For a few moments, Cunningham lay sprawled on the carpet under the table. As the fog cleared from his brain, he realized there had been an explosion. The dining room was a mess. Chunks of broken window glass littered the room. Books had tumbled from the shelves on the wall, and chunks of plaster had fallen from the ceiling and walls. From outside came the sounds of children shrieking. The blast had also wreaked havoc across the street at Alexandra School.

Cunningham was unhurt, save for a few minor cuts. Clambering to his feet, he adjusted his wire-frame glasses and collar, and wiped the blood from his face and balding head. Where were his wife and the family's female lodger? Both had been in the dining room when the crash came.

The force of the blast had thrown both women into the adjacent kitchen. Fearful that there were more explosions to come, the women had scrambled down the basement stairs in search of a refuge. Reverend Cunningham found the tearful women huddling near the coal bin. They were rattled but otherwise unharmed.

Like his wife, Cunningham assumed Halifax had come under bombardment from German warships or one of the Zeppelin airships he had been reading about in the newspaper; the flying machines had recently started appearing in the skies over London. "I thought to myself, 'What's the use of keeping the city dark [at night]?'"[13] The war, which until now had seemed far away from Halifax, suddenly had become close and all too real.

Upstairs in the rectory, Cunningham discovered that the blast had sent furniture flying and dislodged huge patches of plaster from the walls and ceilings. Shards of window glass were embedded in the walls and furnishings. "What sort of people would wreck my house like that?" Reverend Cunningham wondered.[14]

Although St. George's was on the periphery of the Richmond neighbourhood, the Reverend worried that the explosion had damaged the church. One look at the building was all he needed to confirm that fear. The church hall had suffered extensive structural damage, and every window in the church itself was broken. The front doors were askew; the chimney had collapsed, and the pipe organ was beyond repair. However, Cunningham thanked the Lord that the church was salvageable. Ironically, St. George's Anglican Church had escaped worse damage only because nearby St. Patrick's Roman Catholic Church had shielded it from the blast's worst effects. St. Patrick's was a pile of rubble.

Cunningham, with the help of some parish volunteers, provided suddenly homeless fellow parishioners and others from the neighbourhood with emergency shelter in the church and in the rectory; sadly, twenty-five members of St. George's congregation—seven of them children—had lost their lives in the explosion.

THE FORCE OF THE EXPLOSION in Halifax harbour destroyed the stained glass windows in churches and other houses of worship throughout the city; those in the Richmond neighbourhood of North Halifax fared worst of all. All four churches there suffered extensive damage. St. Mark's Anglican, Kaye Street Methodist, Grove Street Presbyterian (whose congregation had only the night before celebrated paying off the last of the church's debts), and even St. Joseph's, which was of sturdy stone construction, lay in ruins. The North End churches lost many parishioners: St. Joseph's, 404; St. Mark's, 200; Grove Street Presbyterian, 148; and Kaye Street Methodist, 91. Outside the explosion's one-mile blast radius, Starr Street synagogue also suffered severe damages, although its all-important ark, which held the Torah scrolls, survived.

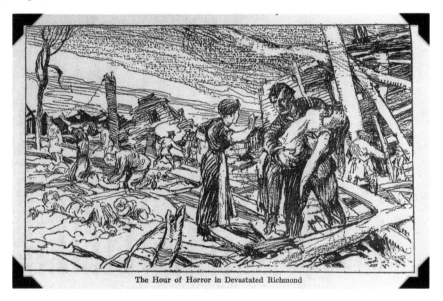

The Hour of Horror in Devastated Richmond

"THE HOUR OF HORROR IN DEVASTATED RICHMOND" IS ONE OF ARTHUR LISMER'S SKETCHES OF THE DISASTER. (COLLECTION OF ALAN RUFFMAN)

Thirty-two-year-old Arthur Lismer, a future founding member of the legendary Group of Seven, was in Halifax working as principal of the Victoria School of Art and Design. In the aftermath of the disaster, Lismer created a series of sketches for *The Canadian Courier* magazine that convey a sense of the pathos and the horror of the scenes he witnessed.

ONE MOMENT, ELIZABETH FRASER was in the kitchen of the house where she worked as a domestic. The next thing she knew, she was waking up "outside in the yard, unharmed as far as I could tell."[15] However, there was chaos all around her. It was nightmarish. On all sides, buildings were

THE RUINS OF ST. JOSEPH'S ROMAN CATHOLIC CHURCH.
(UNDERWOOD AND UNDERWOOD, NY)

in ruins. Some were ablaze. The force of the blast had ripped trees and telephone poles out of the ground. Dazed and bloodied people wandered aimlessly through the rubble-strewn streets—men, women, and children, young and old. Many of them were in various states of exposure, the force of the explosion having shredded or peeled away their garments.

Elizabeth had no idea what had just happened, only that it was something bad. Very bad. Her thoughts immediately turned to her family. She wanted to get home as quickly as possible to find out if they were safe. Along Gottingen Street she ran, tears streaming down her face. "I saw my poor father on all fours crawling like an animal, moaning and crying, but I didn't stop. I had to get home even though I expected to find them all dead. My path was strewn with debris of all sort, fallen wires and trees, and even dead bodies."[16]

It was a scene of heartbreaking sorrow that greeted Elizabeth when she reached 105 Roome Street. Minutes earlier, the wood-frame house she had called home had stood just three blocks from the harbour. Now it was a pile of smoking rubble. The killer tsunami that had washed up Fort Needham hill in the explosion's wake had not come this far.

Elizabeth's mother, her seven sisters, and her aunt Sophie had all survived, but they were in shock. Sophie was bleeding from her eyes and

clutching one of her children. The women wailed as they lay on the cold
ground in the dooryard, next to the ruins of the house. Elizabeth, the only
family member who was uninjured and still able to function, felt her desperation growing. She realized that her brother was missing; eleven-year-
old Arthur was her favourite sibling.

When Elizabeth asked how her brother was, her mother gestured toward
the ruins of the family's home. She said nothing; she did not need to. The
emptiness in her eyes spoke for her. Arthur Fraser lay beneath a mound
of smouldering lumber, downed plaster, and broken glass. Elizabeth
Fraser had no way of knowing if her brother was alive or dead, but she
wept for him. She cried, too, for her aunt Sophie, who was in a bad way.

Elizabeth's uncle James was serving overseas in the Canadian military, and so his pregnant wife was caring for their three children on her
own. The explosion at Pier 6 had levelled the family's Campbell Road
home. Elizabeth's aunt Sophie had survived the explosion, but she was
horribly injured and blinded. Somehow, she had managed to claw her way
out of the rubble and stagger to the Frasers' house on Roome Street. She
did so "dragging her little six-year-old boy [Colin] by the hand," said
Elizabeth Fraser. "[Sophie's] eyes were both blown out of her head, and she
was telling [Colin] to hurry; he was dead, but she didn't know."[17]

It was a gut-wrenching scene. The Frasers were huddled together "like
lost sheep, bewildered and not knowing what might happen next."[18] The air
was thick with smoke. Arthur Fraser, although unable to walk, had crawled
all the way home. Exhausted, he now lay on the ground. He had no strength
to help Elizabeth offer comfort to family members, let alone to relieve their
suffering. Numbed and bloodied, their hands, clothing, and faces blackened
with oily soot, the Frasers waited. For what, they had no idea.

Every few minutes, a dazed, bloody figure in tattered clothing came
staggering along what earlier that morning had been Roome Street. In the
distance, Elizabeth Fraser could hear voices calling in vain for help. When
finally some soldiers on horseback appeared, it was only to advise the

family to head for open ground; there might be another explosion coming. The Frasers were too exhausted, too confused, too frightened to care.

There was no second explosion, but it was several more hours before help arrived. Other soldiers, these ones with a horse-drawn wagon, transported the Frasers and as many of their injured neighbours as could be carried to the Rockhead Hospital. Located at the extreme north end of the city,

THE EXPLOSION LEVELLED THE PUBLIC SCHOOL ON ROOME STREET.
(NOVA SCOTIA ARCHIVES)

the building was on a bluff overlooking the black community of Africville and the Bedford Basin. Originally built to serve the "poorest of the poor" and run ancillary to Rockhead Prison, in December 1917 the facility was being used as a convalescent home for war veterans. The reinforced concrete building had withstood the explosion and remained serviceable; however, most of the windows were broken, the heat and electricity were off, and there were gaping holes in the roof. Compounding the crisis, with telephone lines down, "Rockhead Hospital was entirely cut off from communication with the city by the burning district. The nurses had all been hurt, the medical supplies blown up."[19]

Like every other medical-care facility in the city, Rockhead was overflowing with the injured and the dying. The situation there could only get worse. And it did.

CHAPTER 20

Courage in the Face of Death

Halifax, December 6, 1917, 11:30 a.m.

Henry Stubbs Colwell, the fifty-four-year-old proprietor of Colwell Brothers ("The English Shop for Men"), Halifax's finest and oldest men's clothier, was a soft-spoken man. However, H.S.—as his family, friends, and business associates called him—was a go-getter. Slightly built, with delicate features and fair hair, his most distinguishing aspect was a toothbrush moustache, which gave him an air of gravitas. The Saint John, New Brunswick, native was a veteran of the Canadian army, having served during the Northwest Rebellion of 1885. After returning to the east coast, he had settled in Halifax and joined with his brother to start a men's clothing shop. In 1915, Colwell got involved in municipal politics and quickly emerged as a rising star at City Hall, and when Mayor Peter Martin was away, Colwell stood in as deputy mayor. It was a role he took seriously and relished.

The Colwell home was on South Park Street, a few blocks from Halifax Public Gardens. Most days, H.S. made the twenty-minute commute on

H.S. COLWELL.
(COURTESY OF JOHN COLWELL)

foot to and from his Barrington Street clothing shop. The cane he carried on his perambulations was more for genteel effect than out of physical necessity; like many residents of Halifax's upper-crust South End, Colwell was unabashedly pro-British and subscribed to British customs.

As he walked to work on the morning of December 6, Colwell's thoughts were preoccupied by that great cloud of black smoke that was filling the northern sky. It was an ominous, brooding presence on such a splendid morning. Colwell wondered where the fire was. With Mayor Martin away and H.S. filling in as deputy mayor, he felt it was his job to make some phone calls to learn what was happening. A few blocks from his shop, H.S. paused to look skyward and then glanced quickly at his pocket watch: it read 9:04 a.m. He was still fumbling with the fob so as to slip the watch back into his waistcoat when it happened.

Colwell felt the earth rumble beneath his feet. A split second later, the concussive shock wave that radiated outward from Pier 6 in Halifax harbour surged along Barrington Street. Like a scythe, "the Thing"—as some people would call it—mowed down pedestrians, shattered windows, overturned delivery wagons, and hurled leaves and bits of debris high into the air. Colwell felt as if an invisible hand had punched him in the stomach; he went down hard. He was fortunate, however. His heavy tweed overcoat absorbed some of the blow and cushioned his fall. After staggering to his feet and retrieving his fedora and cane, he took a moment to steady himself. Colwell's first coherent thoughts in the wake of the explosion—like those of so many other Haligonians—were of family. He set off running for home.

IN 1917, RELATIVELY FEW HOMES in Halifax, or elsewhere in Canada, had a telephone; there was just one for every 15.5 Canadians.[1] And, of course, there were no radio or television broadcasts to keep people informed. It would be another two years before Canada's first radio station—an experimental set-up owned by the Marconi Company—began broadcasting in Montreal. It would be thirty-three years after that—in 1952—until the country's first television stations went on the air in Toronto and Montreal.

In the second decade of the twentieth century, print publications were "the media" in Halifax and elsewhere. Halifax had five daily newspapers: the *Morning Chronicle* and the afternoon *Daily Echo*, both of which were owned by Halifax lawyer G. Fred Pearson; the rival morning *Halifax Herald* and the *Evening Mail*, owned by Senator William Dennis; and the evening *Acadian Recorder*. In addition, there was a weekly newspaper called the *Patriot*. All the city's newspapers experienced production delays owing to the damage wrought by the great explosion on the morning of December 6. The windows of newsrooms and business offices were shattered, and the buildings that housed the printing presses were in a shambles. It was only with dogged determination that the staffs of all five dailies managed to put out hand-printed one-page editions on December 7, the day after the disaster. Most of the news that day consisted of preliminary lists of the names of the dead and requests for information about the whereabouts and well-being of those who were missing.

STAFF MANAGED TO PUT OUT A ONE-PAGE EDITION OF THE *HERALD* ON DECEMBER 7, 1917. (*HALIFAX HERALD*)

Try though they did, Halifax newspapers could not hope to keep up with the pace of fast-changing events; word of mouth became most people's primary "social medium." Not surprisingly, with perspectives being limited, rumours ran rampant.

The tram service that most city residents used to get around was suspended, and it was all but impossible for motor vehicles and horse-drawn wagons to navigate the streets. That was especially so in the Richmond neighbourhood, where collapsed buildings, downed electrical and telephone wires, fires burning out of control, and the bodies of people and animals blocked the way. With so many familiar landmark buildings flattened, it was difficult for anyone—would-be rescuers or disaster survivors—to get their bearings or to have any sense of the full scope of the damage. This was something Reverend Henry Cunningham of St. George's Anglican Church discovered when he ventured onto North End streets in the hours after the explosion. "I had the impression that I was in a strange country where I'd never been before. It was all terribly unfamiliar. You saw nothing to remind you that you were in Richmond."[2]

HALIFAX'S HARBOUR SITS IN A HOLLOW, and so the explosion's shock wave roared up and down the channel. To the north, the concussive impact died in the openness of Bedford Basin. To the south, the hillside and the thick stone walls of the Halifax Citadel atop it deflected the blast's full impact. However, in the streets to the east of the Citadel "not a single building escaped, all [lost] their windows," the *Herald* would report, "and telephones were instantly and inevitably out of commission so that it was impossible to ascertain quickly whence came the death-dealing blow."[3]

The explosion's impact was relatively light in two areas of Halifax. One was the city's relatively affluent South End; the other, ironically, was the impoverished black neighbourhood of Africville at the far end of north Halifax. Because the community was on the northern slope of the drumlin that is Fort Needham hill, it escaped the worst effects of the blast. Many of the flimsy buildings in Africville received structural damage, but only a few residents died.

In Halifax's residential South End, the shock wave from the explosion felled some telephone poles, snapped limbs off trees, shattered windows, and rattled doors in the homes of residents such as Deputy Mayor Henry Colwell, port of Halifax CXO Commander Frederick Wyatt, harbour pilot Francis Mackey, and Rear Admiral Bertram Chambers, the senior RN officer in Halifax.

Chambers had just finished breakfast when the explosion happened. His first thought was that the soldiers at the fortifications atop nearby Citadel Hill had fired their guns; there was nothing to worry about, he assured his wife. "Before I had finished speaking—an interval of possibly ten seconds—there came a second crash," Chambers would recall. "This time the floor seemed to rise up and the room filled with dust and soot, though luckily, the windows which were double and facing away from the explosion stood."[4]

Mrs. Chambers cried out. She feared a bomb had exploded in the garden. Her husband suspected it might have been a gas-line explosion. "On reaching the hall I saw that the big double front doors had been burst wide open. I ran toward them, and there, right in front of the house... was rising into the air a most wonderful cauliflower-like plume of white smoke, twisting and twirling and changing colour in the brilliant sunshine of a perfect Canadian early winter morning."[5]

Overall, the damage to the Chamberses' home and to others in Halifax's South End was light. In fact, most residents of the fashionable thoroughfares in the area of Point Pleasant Park initially had no idea what had happened down in the harbour, much less the extent of the mayhem and carnage there.

THE FIRST DISASTER RELIEF EFFORTS in Halifax's North End and across the harbour in Dartmouth were neighbourhood focused; people helped each other. Those public buildings that were still serviceable opened their doors and became emergency care shelters. "Immediate rescue efforts were largely uncoordinated, though policemen, firemen, and soldiers were on hand surprisingly soon after the blast. Vehicles of all kinds—horse-drawn drays, cars, army trucks—transported victims to the nearest hospitals, where the living rubbed shoulders with the dead."[6]

Makeshift medical clinics began popping up all over the city, often in the offices or homes of doctors or nurses. So many medical people got involved in these impromptu initiatives that Halifax hospitals—four public, four military, and seven private facilities, which provided from a handful of beds to as many as 300—faced a staff shortage. One doctor who worked at Camp Hill Hospital lamented, "The local doctors just weren't there. Why? . . . They were so busy with their own patients at homes and offices, they couldn't get away."[7]

Typical was Dr. Lewis Thomas, who lived just south of the Halifax Citadel. So overwhelmed was Thomas by the number of injured people who turned up at his door that he told some of them to hobble off down the street to the home of his colleague and friend Dr. Murdock Chisholm. Thomas was stunned when one of the walking wounded informed him that the sixty-eight-year-old Chisholm, who was one of Halifax's most prominent and beloved physicians, was dead; his name was among the list of casualties that had appeared in that morning's edition of the *Chronicle*.

Thomas could not believe the news, *refused* to believe it. Taking a break from his labours, he rushed over to Murdock Chisholm's house. There he found his old friend unconscious in a pool of blood on his office floor. A shard of window glass had sliced one of Chisholm's arteries. Thomas cleaned and stitched the wound, revived his friend, and got him to hospital. Chisholm's medical colleagues gave him a blood transfusion and special care. Within a few days, Dr. Chisholm had recovered enough that he was able to sit up and read his own obituary, which had appeared in one of the city's newspapers.[8]

IT WAS LESS THAN THIRTY MINUTES after the *Mont-Blanc* exploded when Rear Admiral Bertram Chambers set out aboard the tugboat *Maggie* on an emergency tour of the harbour. An oily black soot was still raining down on Halifax. As the port convoy officer and senior Royal Navy man in Halifax, Chambers had two immediate priorities. One was assessing the damage the explosion had caused; the other was ensuring that the port remained operational and convoys continued to leave for Europe. Halifax was vital to the Allied war effort. The arrival in port the previous night of a hospital ship carrying 200 wounded soldiers from France was a stark reminder of that reality.[9]

Chambers' first stops were the Royal Navy cruiser HMS *Highflyer* and the armed merchant cruiser HMS *Changuinola*, both of which had sustained explosion damage. Next, the rear admiral visited Bedford Basin, where he saw there were thirty-one ships at anchor.[10] Chambers wanted to check on the condition of the ships slated to be included in a convoy that would sail for Europe next morning; this was the same convoy Captain Le Médec of the ill-fated *Mont-Blanc* had hoped to join. Chambers found that the merchant vessels in the Bedford Basin marshalling area had escaped damage in the morning's explosion; however, he concluded that with HMS *Highflyer* being unseaworthy—let alone combat-ready—he would have to delay the departure of the Friday convoy until repairs on the warship were made.

With the port's telephone and telegraph lines down and the navy's radio transmission capabilities seriously limited, Chambers had difficulty alerting the Admiralty in London to the situation in Halifax. *Highflyer*'s radio room was in a shambles; Chambers prayed that the equipment aboard the depot ship HMCS *Niobe* was still working. On the way there to find out, he spotted a sailor frantically waving from the shore. It turned out the man was a member of the crew of the *Hilford*, one of the RCN's locally chartered tugboats. The explosion had destroyed the vessel, hurling its wreckage onto Pier 9 on the Halifax side of the harbour. When Chambers went ashore to investigate, what he found left him feeling horrified. "Amidst the ruins wandered a few dazed creatures, blood-stained and in rags. They were the remains of the military guard stationed on the pier. Many of [them] were in dying condition; others had been pinned to the ground by flying masses of timber. Beneath one of the largest piles I could distinguish the body of my very capable second assistant, Lieutenant-Commander T.A. Murray . . . who had been making a telephonic report to the convoy office at the time the explosion took place."[11]

Only after the *Maggie* had transported the most seriously injured men from Pier 9 to *Highflyer* and Chambers had alerted Captain Herbert N.

Garnett, the ship's master, to the emergency conditions at Pier 9 did the rear admiral resume his journey to *Niobe*. It was about noon when he finally arrived aboard the depot ship, where he hoped to send a wireless message to London. Captain George Eldridge, the depot ship's naval intelligence officer, assured him that he would transmit the dispatch as quickly as possible. Eldridge was true to his word, but only because a motorcycle courier raced twelve miles south to the Marconi facility at Camperdown, near the mouth of Halifax harbour. From here, a message transmission was sent to Sydney, and from there it was relayed on to Ottawa.

AT 9:04 A.M. JEAN ROSS, a fourth-year student at Dalhousie, was working on an academic assignment when the explosion rattled the library in which she was sitting. Afterward, even as all the dramatic events were taking place down in the harbour, she carried on with her normal routine. It was only later in the day, after teatime, that she became aware of the seriousness of the situation unfolding elsewhere in the city. "Some girl came for volunteers for Camp Hill Hospital," [12] Ross would recall. At first, she declined to get involved, even though she had received first-aid training. "I thought it was ridiculous sentiment and nothing more, and what could girls do there, still more, I who hate all sickness. Besides, I was so tired, I could barely stand." [13]

Scores of other Dalhousie students, male and female, who had also trained with the Voluntary Aid Detachment of the St. John's Ambulance Brigade, stepped forward to serve in the hospitals and the impromptu emergency medical clinics that were springing up all across Halifax. It was only the next day, Friday morning, when a friend told Jean Ross about her experiences caring for injured people that Ross relented. She and another Dalhousie co-ed then volunteered and made their way over to Camp Hill Hospital. That facility, "a low, two-storey affair of light construction," [14] had been open for only two weeks and was supposed to serve as a convalescent home for war veterans. Prior to the disaster, patients occupied just seventy of the 300 beds. By noon on December 6, more than 1,600 civilians had gone there seeking emergency medical care. Many of the veterans who were mobile gave up their beds and went to work as nurses, orderlies, and porters. "The injured were being laid down anywhere space could be found—on the few beds, on the floors of the corridors, on the long kitchen tables, bundled in gray army blankets And every sort of wrap rags," said one young female first-aid worker. "And from bundle to bundle the frantic people went, looking into the ashen faces of the injured and the dying, seeking their own."[15]

For the first two days after the explosion, there was only minimal organization of medical relief efforts at Camp Hill. Chaos reigned, and conditions were appalling. The hospital became "almost a synonym for horror."[16] Many of the injured who arrived there, on foot or by ambulance, had suffered grievous injuries—broken bones, burns, horrendous cuts, and eye injuries. Most of the wounded were bloody, and many bore the residue of the oily black soot that had rained down on areas of the city after the explosion. Providing even the most basic care for the needy was difficult. Camp Hill was not equipped for surgeries, and vital medical supplies such as antiseptic, morphine, and bandages were scarce. Making matters worse, there was no X-ray machine on site. In fact, there were only three units in Halifax in 1917. Regardless, the injured kept on coming to Camp Hill Hospital.

Among those who arrived was Billy Wells, the sole survivor from the firefighting crew that had been on Pier 6 when the explosion happened. Wells was in dire condition, clinging to life. The sheer force of the blast had stripped most of the flesh from his right arm, exposing the bones. In addition, he had suffered lacerations and bruises too numerous to count, and he was coated with the black sooty residue that had fallen from the sky. It was a miracle Wells survived the explosion, let alone made it to hospital. Given the limited medical care available, it was an even greater miracle that he survived at all. "[Wells'] life was probably saved by the use of a then-new development, Dakin's Solution, which had been perfected for burns and gangrene overseas."[17] His care providers doused his wounds with the antiseptic, which cleansed them and hastened the separation of dead from living tissue.

CONDITIONS AT CAMP HILL HOSPITAL were grim, yet when Jean Ross and her girlfriend arrived there on Friday morning, an elderly female patient advised the young women, "We don't need you here. We have our arms and legs. Go North!"

Jean, her friend, and two other co-ed volunteers heeded that advice. They hiked north along Robie Street, two and a half miles to Rockhead Hospital. Here the two doctors who were attempting to cope with the emergency on their own warmly welcomed the four young women. As "wounded refugees began to pour in from the surrounding district"[18] in the hours after the explosion, the situation had quickly become desperate. The Dalhousie co-eds set to work cleaning wounds, caring for the scores of injured, feeding patients, and helping the doctors as best they could.

Many Haligonians—young and old, rich and poor, male and female— volunteered their time and energies to the cause. They persevered despite the physical discomforts they endured and the emotional trauma of being knee-deep in blood, suffering, and death. "It is impossible to relate in detail what happened in all the hospitals," official explosion historian Archibald MacMechan would write. "It was the same story everywhere of the injured swamping the accommodation and being tended by heroic doctors, nurses, and voluntary helpers who labored day and night in their unceasing ministry of mercy."[19]

WHEN DR. FRED TOOKE, a prominent Montreal ophthalmologist, arrived at Camp Hill Hospital on Friday morning, he set to work treating the scores of people who had suffered eye injuries. With no operating room available to him, Tooke did the best he could while working behind a makeshift screen at one end of a ward. Here, "eyes were being removed, without anesthetic."[20]

Trauma counselling was unheard of in 1917, and so it is no small wonder that many of those who provided medical aid to victims of the Halifax explosion—trained medical workers as well as community volunteers—incurred emotional distress. In some cases, the pain of seeing such sights as buckets of enucleated eyeballs was profound and enduring.[21] So haunted by his experiences at Camp Hill was one young doctor that later he reportedly committed suicide, hanging himself in his surgery.

CHAPTER 21

"HALIFAX HAS HAD ITS FIRST TASTE OF WAR . . ."

Halifax, December 6, 1917, Noon

"What we see depends mainly on what we look for," or so the saying goes. Thus, on the morning of December 6, many Haligonians—especially those whose homes were relatively intact and who had not lost family members—felt that whatever misfortune had befallen their city could not be very serious. "People who could not see the harbour assumed that wherever they were was the center of the disaster."[1]

At Morris Street School in downtown Halifax, morning classes had just started when fifteen-year-old Robert L. ("Ginger") Fraser felt the building shake, and then the windows of the second-floor classroom shattered, fortunately without causing any serious injuries to anyone. The teacher in charge, a young man whom the students jeeringly referred to as "Slacker" because he was not in uniform, led the young people to safety. A few minutes later, when the principal dismissed them, he told them to go home immediately. Ginger and his pal Everett Covey heard that advice, but they ignored it.

"Above the North End, a fantastic cloud was rising and swelling. A grey mushroom on a thick pallid stalk, silver-edged, black and purple lined, splendid but malignant, writhing evilly as it climbed and spread."[2] Such a sight was too much for teenage boys to resist, especially when they were volunteer members of the military cadet corps; Ginger Fraser and his pal figured the city must be under German attack.

Both Fraser and Covey were full of the bravado of testosterone-fuelled would-be warriors. Intent on adventure, they made a beeline for Citadel Hill, where they hoped for a prime view of whatever battle was under way. However, as the pair neared City Hall, trucks and wagons loaded with heaps of bloodied corpses came racing toward them. A driver told the lads, "A ship blew up in the harbour, and the North End has been levelled. Everyone there is dead!"

Ginger and Everett refused to believe it. How could *everyone* in Richmond be dead? The boys carried on past the Citadel, walking toward Wellington Barracks. It was only when they reached the North Street Station that the enormity of the disaster that had hit Halifax became clear and undeniable. The station, an imposing two-and-a-half-storey red-brick structure with a mansard roof, Romanesque windows, and an expansive glass roof above the passenger platforms, was now a smoking pile of bricks and rubble. The collapse had killed railway workers and train passengers. Sixty bodies lay beneath the rubble. The boys felt shaken, but they were still undeterred. Ignoring the bloodied and frightened people they saw rushing in the opposite direction, Ginger Fraser and Everett Covey pressed on; neither one wanted to be the one to give in to their fears. Their bravado disappeared only when a soldier stopped them and asked where they were going. "The magazine at Wellington Barracks is on fire, an' she's going t' explode at any minute. Unless you want t' die you two lads had better get down t' Point Pleasant Park or some other open space where you'll be safe." Ginger Fraser and Everett Covey heeded the soldier's warning.

"We didn't have to be told twice, and [so we] watched our chance to jump on one of the flat wagons going [south on] Barrington Street," Fraser would recall. "There were quite a number of people on it, some moaning and most of them bleeding quite badly."[3]

"ALTHOUGH A NEWSPAPERMAN's imagination is usually lively, nothing approximating the magnitude of the horror that faced us in the Richmond district had been pictured in our minds," a visiting journalist reported. "For nearly two square miles there was an incredible mass of debris, houses flattened and crumbled like matchwood in some giant hand: beds, stoves, kettles, pots, pans, and furniture smashed and twisted, giving the impression of a huge junking yard. Stout telegraph poles were levelled to the ground like stalks of wheat in a rainstorm, the wires trailing on the ground to mark the direction of what had once been a street."[4]

THE HALIFAX WATERFRONT IN THE AREA OF GROUND ZERO WAS A
WASTELAND FOLLOWING THE EXPLOSION. (NAVAL HISTORY AND
HERITAGE COMMAND CENTRE)

North End residents looked instinctively to one another for help. In the South End, where it took a while for the true extent of the emergency to become apparent, people's response to the situation was markedly different. The knee-jerk reaction of many well-to-do Haligonians and middle-class residents was to look to the municipal and provincial governments and the military for direction and leadership.

The war years in Canada, 1914–1918, saw the rapid growth of big government and state-sanctioned intrusions into people's everyday lives. It was during the four years of conflict that the federal government introduced a series of bold new initiatives, among them: income and corporate taxes, conscription, prohibition, daylight savings time, and a 1918 "anti-loafing act" that made it a legal requirement for all able-bodied adult men to be gainfully employed.[5]

Most Canadians accepted such dictates as a necessary evil, viewing them as being part and parcel of the Allied war effort. Similarly, at least some Halifax residents regarded the explosion as a predictable consequence of events in Europe, collateral damage. "Halifax has had its first taste of war," an editorial in the *Herald* opined. "Though it does not compare to what the people of Belgium and France suffered the past three years, it will nonetheless give our people a slight idea of what war really means and what we may expect in Canada if the huns [sic] reach our shores."[6]

That grim message resonated with upper- and middle-class burghers in Halifax. In the wake of the events of the morning of December 6, "the city appeared chaotic and dangerous [to them], and they valiantly wielded telephones, typewriters, and pencils in an exhausting battle against disorder and confusion. The chaos they envisioned was a product of their centralized knowledge being insufficient to the task. To these managers, order was by definition created by central committees and the logic of central commands. To some extent, this was a result of a municipal political culture that revolved around the military and its centralized power structure."[7]

Deputy Mayor Colwell almost certainly subscribed to that notion. H.S.'s first concern was the safety of his family. It was only after assuring himself that his wife, Bessie, and the couple's three teenage children were safe—their eldest child, twenty-one-year-old son Garnet, was a lieutenant in the 66th Halifax Regiment, based at Wellington Barracks[8]—that Colwell struck out for City Hall. He still was not exactly sure of the nature of the disaster, but he knew that as deputy mayor he should be downtown. "I realized I held the most important [municipal] position in Halifax."[9]

City Hall, located at the north end of the historic Grand Parade square—Canada's oldest public square—is an imposing three-storey edifice of red brick and granite. "Completed [between 1887 and 1890] in an eclectic late-Victorian version of the Second Empire style,"[10] the building is one of Nova Scotia's largest public buildings. It is also one of the most visually intriguing, being a smorgasbord of nineteenth-century architectural embellishments topped off with a seven-storey clock tower.

It was about 9:45 a.m., a little more than forty minutes after the explosion, when Henry Colwell reached City Hall. He found the building all but deserted. Although the sun was shining brightly, City Hall was ice cold inside; the explosion had smashed all the windows. Colwell could see his breath as he moved around. Loose papers were scattered everywhere on the floors, and Colwell's footsteps echoed in the empty hallways. The scene had an eerie post-apocalyptic aura to it. Colwell found just two officials at their desks: City Clerk Fred Monaghan and Police Chief Frank Hanrahan; the latter would play a key role in Colwell's efforts to get a handle on the situation and to organize the city's disaster relief efforts.

Hanrahan, a forty-seven-year-old native of the nearby fishing port of Ferguson's Cove, had joined the Halifax police force in 1892 as a rookie patrol officer. A big, barrel-chested man with a thick, full handlebar moustache, he was the quintessential Irish cop. He was plain-talking, tough, and principled, "a strict disciplinarian, but fair."[11] Hanrahan could boast of having won a well-deserved international reputation as a brilliant detective. He was proficient at and delighted in running down lawbreakers and maintaining "the King's peace." Hanrahan's rise through the ranks of the Halifax police department had been steady, and he was a popular choice to become chief. People trusted Frank Hanrahan and looked to him for advice and leadership. Deputy Mayor Henry Colwell certainly did.

Hanrahan briefed Henry Colwell on what he knew about the morning's events. After receiving the grim report, Colwell began to understand the scale of the emergency Halifax now faced; it was unprecedented and far bigger than anything the city could hope to handle on its own. "The machinery for reserving order and protection against fire had broken down; and there was no ready-made machinery to bring about large measure of relief . . . [so] the Deputy Mayor turned at once to the organization that had plenty of men and full control of them—the Military." [12]

Colwell, Hanrahan, and Monaghan hiked over to military headquarters, which was on Spring Garden Road. There they conferred with Colonel W.E. ("Ernie") Thompson, the assistant adjutant-general of the Halifax Citadel. Thompson, a lawyer in civilian life, was a burly man who brought to soldiering the same gung-ho approach he had carried into play as a university football player. As Halifax explosion historian Archibald MacMechan noted, "He is the kind of man who gets things done." [13]

To the surprise of his City Hall visitors, Thompson seemed almost gleeful at the prospect of marshalling the militia troops under his command to meet the emergency. Thompson obviously was a reader of the *Herald*'s editorial page. "At last the war has come to us. I'm glad!" he exclaimed. "People will know we're in it." [14]

The colonel readily agreed to the request that the city's militia units set up and equip tents on the Halifax Common to serve as emergency shelter for the homeless. "Colonel Thompson responded at once, and in the most forceful way, issuing orders and dispatching mounted men in all directions"[15] to do what they could to help keep the peace, rescue victims of the explosion, and begin the grim task of recovering bodies.

COLWELL AND HIS COMPANIONS were about to return to City Hall from military headquarters when W.A. Duff, the assistant chief engineer of the Canadian Government Railways, approached them. Duff announced he was ready to help the city in any way he could. He was, he explained, in town on business that Thursday morning, and after the explosion, he had borrowed a motor car in hopes of touring the Richmond neighbourhood to assess the situation at the rail yards there. Stunned by the extent of the devastation, Duff had dashed off a telegram to Moncton asking for emergency medical assistance for Halifax.

At the time he did this, Duff was unaware that another railway executive, George Graham, the general manager of Dominion Atlantic Railway (DAR), had also sounded the alarm. Graham and his daughter had been having breakfast in his private railcar, on a siding near the Halifax rail yard, when the explosion occurred. Like Duff, Graham recognized the scale of the disaster and the urgency of the need for emergency aid; all told, more than 120 railway workers had lost their lives. The blast had wrecked scores of locomotives and railcars, rendered the tracks impassable, and downed telegraph and telephone lines. Graham hiked to the train station in the hamlet of Rockingham, on the western shore of Bedford Basin. There he had sent a telegram to DAR headquarters in Kentville. "Organize a relief train and send word to Wolfville and Windsor to round up all doctors, nurses, and Red Cross supplies possible to obtain," Graham said. "No time to explain details but list of casualties is enormous."[16]

Graham's cryptic message may have set DAR staff wondering what had happened in Halifax, but they dutifully obeyed his request that they relay the appeal for help to the towns of Wolfville and Windsor. For good measure, the DAR staff also included Truro and New Glasgow in the alert. The appeal for emergency assistance would eventually spread far and wide, finding its way to scores of other cities and towns throughout Atlantic Canada and the northeastern United States.

Henry Colwell, who knew nothing of any of this, grew increasingly concerned as he listened to W.A. Duff's eyewitness account of the situation in the North End. "For God's sake, send out more messages," he implored Duff. "Send them to every town in Nova Scotia and New Brunswick. Ask for help, and sign it 'Mayor of Halifax.'"[17]

That decision was prudent, and it proved to be pivotal. The railway men's telegrams elicited swift responses. Their pleas "put in motion the most powerful machinery for the aid of Halifax at the earliest moment, nothing short of the whole activity of the Canadian Government Railway system."[18] Within hours, firefighters and emergency relief trains loaded with doctors, nurses, and medical supplies were rushing toward Halifax. However, there were problems. Much of the equipment firefighters brought with them to Halifax was useless; many of the hoses were the wrong size to be connected to the city's fire hydrants. At the same time, "Since all the IRC [Intercolonial Railway] facilities in Halifax were located in the part of the city devastated by the explosion, the railway was temporarily paralyzed."[19]

The same was true for the port of Halifax. Rear Admiral Chambers had toured the harbour less than an hour after the explosion. While passing through the narrows, he noted how "it was necessary to exercise caution on account of the floating wreckage that almost blocked the way."[20] There were chunks of lumber, stray barrels, the wreckage of small boats, all type and manner of trash, items of people's personal property, dead animals, and the corpses of the victims of the explosion and the tsunami. The devastation was overwhelming.

JOHN REID, THE FEDERAL MINISTER of Railways and Canals, had made it known that getting the railways and the port up and running again as quickly as possible was a national priority. To that end, railway officials who were in Halifax set about moving ahead with opening a new set of tracks into the city. Construction crews had spent several years working on the "South Cut," a rail line intended to serve an ocean terminal complex that was being built in Halifax's South End. The six miles of new tracks ran down the west side of the Halifax Peninsula, on the shore of the Northwest Arm. The South Cut was not due to open until the spring of 1918, and there was no station or other facilities; however, the project was fast-tracked, literally and figuratively. Until repairs to the main network of tracks and the Richmond rail yard were completed and both were back in service, the new tracks filled a vital need in emergency relief efforts.

RUINS OF THE HALIFAX RAIL YARD. (NOVA SCOTIA ARCHIVES)

DEPUTY MAYOR COLWELL, Police Chief Hanrahan, and City Clerk Monaghan were still discussing next steps in their disaster relief strategy when a new crisis came to light. "The magazine at the Wellington Barracks is going to explode at any minute," a soldier messenger advised them.

The already nightmarish situation in Halifax only seemed to be getting worse. Colwell, Hanrahan, Monaghan, and Duff scattered. Colwell and the police chief joined the throng of people who were rushing toward Point Pleasant Park in the city's South End, hoping to get there before the next big explosion. Colwell and Hanrahan stared in astonishment at the wave of humanity they saw surging southward. Many of these terrified people were in dire need of medical care. Colwell was more than a little out of his comfort zone, but he knew what he had to do: ignoring the risk, he and Hanrahan decided they must return to City Hall to organize an emergency care plan for Halifax hospitals. If a second explosion occurred, the deputy mayor and police chief would have to take their chances on surviving it.

They had not gone far when Colwell heard a familiar voice calling out to him. Robert MacIlreith, who was a former mayor (1905–1908), and another man were waving from across the street. The silver-haired man at MacIlreith's side was MacCallum Grant, Nova Scotia's seventy-two-year-old Lieutenant Governor.

After explaining that he and Chief Hanrahan were returning to City Hall to organize a plan for emergency medical care, Colwell asked Grant and MacIlreith, a lawyer by profession, to join them. When the two men agreed to do so, Grant also accepted Colwell's invitation to chair an impromptu organizational meeting of a disaster relief committee.

Those rumours of a second explosion would prove to be false, and at 11:30 a.m. Colwell, Grant, MacIlreith, and Hanrahan met with three members of city council and two controllers who had arrived at City Hall. The men gathered in the second-floor office of the city's tax collector, "it being the only room in the building not so badly wrecked by the Explosion as to be unfit for the purpose."[21] Grant chaired the meeting, while Colwell served as secretary. It is a measure of Colwell's uncertainties and his respect for process that he kept detailed minutes of this "joint meeting of the Members of City Council present and citizens in attendance."[22] The eight men discussed what emergency measures were necessary, and they made several key decisions. One was to strike committees to oversee five specific aspects of disaster relief: transportation, finance, housing, food, and the mortuary. They also decided to call an emergency session of city council for that afternoon at three o'clock.

In attendance then were the councillors, a dozen citizens, and two military men—Major-General Thomas Benson, the senior army officer in the city, and Rear Admiral Bertram Chambers, the port of Halifax's convoy officer and its top Royal Navy officer. The group quickly vetted the proposed membership of the various volunteer committees and approved the general direction of the initial relief efforts. Afterward, the five subcommittees of the larger body that was now being referred to as the Halifax Relief Committee set to work, as did Deputy Mayor Colwell, who "moved into the City Auditor's room, where he was 'nailed down to a table.' For four days and four nights he did not leave the building."[23]

In a report to his Admiralty Office superiors in London that he wrote later that same day, Chambers described that City Hall meeting as "a remarkable experience—held in the shattered town hall amidst splintered woodwork and floors covered with broken glass."[24]

Despite the destruction, death, and chaos that were everywhere, Chambers noted that he had "left the building with the impression that order was already beginning to arise out of the chaos, and that what could be done would be done."[25]

The rear admiral was correct. City Hall became the focal point of relief efforts in those crucial first few days after the disaster. City staff and community volunteers distributed food, clothing, and other emergency supplies to needy citizens.

At the same time, by the evening—less than twelve hours after the explosion—city staff had devised an ad hoc transportation system. Necessity being the mother of invention, Lieutenant Governor MacCallum Grant issued an Order-in-Council commandeering all private cars and other vehicles, putting them at the service of the emergency relief committee. "Its legality might not have stood much testing, but it was sufficient at a time when red tape was dispensed with."[26]

It is worth noting that female volunteers shouldered much of the burden for the relief work that originated out of City Hall. "In all the activities [there], women had a large and important part," Archibald MacMechan noted. "They showed initiative, organization and endurance."[27]

SEARCHERS COULD NOT COME soon enough for those explosion survivors who found themselves trapped under the wreckage of collapsed buildings in the city's North End. Time was of the essence for most of them; that was definitely so for Mary Jean Hinch.

She figured she had been lying for several hours in that Veith Street draining ditch, just a few doors from home. She had no way of knowing that 66 Veith Street was now a smoking pile of rubble or that her husband, Joe, and her ten children were all dead. The only thing Mary Jean Hinch knew for sure was that each time she tried to move, the pain of her broken hip was so intense that she passed out. Without the miracle she was desperately praying for, this was where she and the baby she carried would die. It was not fair. She was not even sure how she had gotten where she was, under the smoking rubble of a collapsed building. Had the Germans bombarded Halifax? Yes, that must have been what happened, she decided. Her husband, Joe, had often warned her about the possibility of a German

WOMEN SEARCHING THE RUINS OF NORTH END HOUSES DESTROYED BY THE EXPLOSION. (WILLIAM JAMES FAMILY FONDS, CITY OF TORONTO ARCHIVES)

attack. "If the Huns start shelling the city, take the children down into the basement," he had advised. Mary Jean wished she had stayed home instead of going out to see the fire in the harbour. As she drifted in and out of consciousness, Mary Jean thought she could hear trickling water and muffled voices. She figured there must be people nearby, or perhaps someone was digging through the rubble above her. Could it be her husband? she wondered. Mary Jean wanted to call out, but she could not. So weak was she that it took every ounce of her remaining strength to make any sound at all emerge from her lips. Her pain was excruciating and ever-present.

When Mary Jean was next aware, it was the cries of a child wailing that had summoned her back to the world of the living. She listened intently for several minutes, until the crying rose to a fever pitch of terror. Then it stopped, having given way to a curious crackling sound. It sounded like wood burning. Mary Jean did not dare to think about it. So she clutched her rosary and prayed. "When you pray, you're never alone," Father Walsh always said. She found comfort in that thought.

FOLLOWING THE EMERGENCY city council meeting held at City Hall on the afternoon of December 6, acting on the request of Deputy Mayor Henry Colwell, Robert MacIlreith and his long-time friend, Colonel Paul Weatherbe of the militia, an engineer by profession, divided the city into medical-care districts. They assigned doctors, nurses, and other health care professionals who had volunteered their services to work in the various facilities. MacIlreith and City Engineer Henry Johnson also ventured out on a quick trip up to the North End. Their mission: find a public building that was suitable for use as a temporary morgue. MacIlreith knew what to look for; he had experience in dealing with mass casualties, having been involved with organizing the city's role in identifying and processing the bodies of more than 200 victims of the April 1912 *Titanic* disaster.

MacIlreith and Johnson visited three schools. It took them only a half-hour to settle on a suitable venue for use as a temporary morgue. Chebucto School was ideal. Located on Chebucto Road, in a fast-growing residential neighbourhood just to the west of devastated Richmond, the school, a sturdy five-year-old building atop Fort Needham hill, had survived the blast with only minor structural damage. The explosion had shattered windows and caused some pipes to burst, but the building itself remained serviceable. The classrooms offered ample office space, and the commodious basement featured two sets of double doors, each with an outside ramp that would make it easy to move bodies, coffins, and equipment into or out of the building.

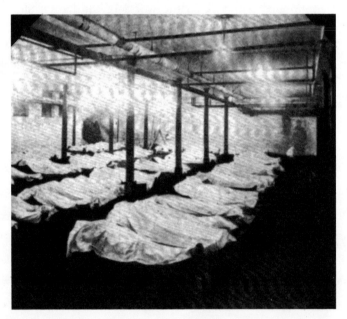

THE BASEMENT OF THE CHEBUCTO SCHOOL BECAME AN ERSATZ MORGUE. (*THE BOOK OF VIEWS*, SOUVENIR POSTCARD BOOK, 1918)

Thus, the morgue at Chebucto School "became the stage for many scenes of distress as the vain search for the missing ended among the long rows of sheeted dead."[28] It would take until next day for a crew of forty men working all out to ready the building to serve as a morgue—the largest one ever in Canada. The nightmarish task of collecting and identifying the victims of the Halifax harbour explosion had begun and was now proceeding in earnest. City Hall had sent out a request to all Halifax funeral homes: deliver any unidentified bodies to the new morgue. The goal was to make it as easy as possible for the relatives and friends of missing persons to find and identify their loved ones. The bodies of explosion victims, parts of bodies, and the charred, unidentifiable remains of those who just a few hours earlier had been living, loving, and loved began to arrive at Chebucto School even before repairs to the building were completed. As one of the sisters of St. Jospeh's School and Convent mused in verse, "But the twinkle of an eye / But the draught of a breath / From the blossom of life / to the paleness of death."[29]

ARTHUR R. BARNSTEAD, the registrar of deaths for Halifax, was initially in charge of operations at the Chebucto School morgue. You could say that death was the Barnstead family's business. Arthur Barnstead's father, Dr. John Henry Barnstead, was a prominent Halifax physician who had supervised identification of the bodies of the *Titanic* disaster victims that recovery workers had brought to Halifax in April 1912. Faced with identifying so many nameless victims, John Barnstead had developed the first methodology for identifying the dead in any mass-casualty situation. He devised a numbering system and made use of mortuary bags to hold a deceased's clothing and personal effects. Now, five years later, Arthur Barnstead adopted his father's methodology to help identify and keep track of the dead from the Halifax harbour explosion.

Morgue operations would be refined still further a few days later when a forensics specialist arrived from Toronto to take over as director. Working with a team of doctors and soldiers, Professor R.N. Stone organized the processing of corpses, the completion of death certificates whenever possible, and the embalming and release of bodies for burial.

When explosion historian Archibald MacMechan, who was a member of the medical relief committee, visited the morgue, he noted that paperwork was being done in the upstairs offices. Clothing and personal effects recovered from bodies were piled on children's school desks to await labelling and cataloguing. A huge wall chart indicated the location of each body that was downstairs in the morgue area. Soldiers and cadet volunteers—schoolboy Ginger Fraser among them—drew the task of escorting people who came there searching for the bodies of loved ones. The soldiers lifted a cotton sheet to reveal each corpse. It was grim, sobering work, but as MacMechan noted, the staff became inured to the horrors of it. "The attendants are very pale and tired, with low-pitched voices, as if always ready to answer the same hopeless question," MacMechan wrote. "Yet [upstairs in the offices] some of the stenographers are giggling, and a box of chocolates is being passed around."

The professor also toured the embalming room. He found the experience chilling. "It is a mysterious, awful place. Thick steam clouds limit the vision to a few inches. Through the mist loom the indistinct contours of nude corpses above which ghoul-like figures bend with eerie implements and vessels."[30]

The work of processing, identifying, and embalming the bodies of the dead would continue for three long, difficult weeks. Of the almost 1,200 corpses that arrived at the Chebucto School morgue, fifteen per cent had carried identification, and the staff worked diligently to identify about sixty per cent of the remaining bodies. The final twenty-five per cent—almost 300 people—were in such poor condition when recovered that they went unidentified. City workers would bury them in a common grave.

No traces were ever found of another 400 people who were unaccounted for. Some of them lived alone; others were transient workers who may or may not have been in town when the disaster occurred. As a result, the exact death toll of the great Halifax harbour explosion of 1917 will never be known.

CHAPTER 22

THE MILITARY TO THE RESCUE

Halifax, December 6, 1917, 2:00 p.m.

Captain Frederick Pasco was in a bad way. The force of the explosion had pitched him across the room at the dockyard superintendent's house. The dwelling was still unfamiliar to him, for he had been staying there only a few days. Now dazed and bloodied, his uniform in disarray, he felt his way downstairs. There he encountered Captain Martin's housekeeper, who led him outside via the back door; debris had blocked the house's main entrance. "I went out . . . to see what was going on and where the explosion was," said Pasco. "The impression in my mind was . . . [that] the cruiser *Highflyer* had gone up."[1]

Compounding Pasco's confusion was the fact he had been in Halifax less than a week and was still getting his bearings when the disaster occurred. He knew only that his first priorities as acting dockyard superintendent were to secure the facilities under his command and to initiate the search for survivors and victims of the explosion. The captain was "a nasty sight" as he made his way down to the water's edge. "I could see on the ground, but not horizontally," he would recall.[2]

At Pier 3, Pasco came upon a milling crowd of sailors and civilian dockyard workers. Many of the men were injured; all felt shaken and disoriented. Those navy boats that were still afloat served as emergency first-aid posts or nautical ambulances; efforts were under way to triage the wounded. "They tried to pull me on board one of those trawlers for first aid, and I told them there was nothing the matter," said Pasco.[3]

Over his protests, a couple of sailors cleaned and bandaged the captain's wounds. Afterward, he issued a few preliminary orders and then stumbled back to the Naval Dockyard commander's house. He reasoned that anyone who was looking for him would show up there. Sure enough, Pasco soon encountered Captain Walter Hose, his second-in-command. "[Hose and I] together took up a stand in front of the Captain's house and [in] sort of a central position, where people could report."[4]

Despite his relative youth, the forty-two-year-old Hose was an experienced, well-respected naval officer. Like Pasco and Evan Wyatt, he was a senior Royal Navy officer who had transferred into the fledgling RCN when war began. Having recently married, like Wyatt, Hose welcomed the pay boost that came with his transfer to the RCN.

Although he was not a big man, the captain's chiselled, hawk-like facial features and his penetrating gaze served advance notice that he was not someone to trifle with. Hose had arrived in Halifax from Sydney a few months earlier, when the RN had adopted the convoy system as a means of protecting Allied shipping against attacks by German U-boats. Halifax had become the winter marshalling point for convoys, and Hose was in charge of the port's anti-submarine patrols.

Frederick Pasco knew and trusted Walter Hose. So when Pasco realized that, owing to his injuries and his unfamiliarity with naval operations in Halifax, he was not up to the challenges of fulfilling his duties as superintendent of the Naval Dockyard in this time of emergency, he advised

Captain Hose, "I don't think it's any use my pretending to be in charge any longer. You'd better take charge."[5] Hose did so, albeit reluctantly.

EARLY IN THE AFTERNOON of December 6, the two highest-ranking military commanders in Halifax met to exchange information and discuss how best to coordinate their relief efforts. Major-General Thomas Benson was the commander of the Canadian army in Halifax. Rear Admiral Bertram Chambers was the port of Halifax's convoy officer and its senior RN man. He was also acting as superintendent of the Naval Dockyard; just hours after agreeing to take on the job, Captain Walter Hose had asked Chambers to relieve him. As a result, Chambers was sitting down with Major-General Benson at military headquarters to plan and coordinate the military response to the disaster.

Some 3,300 Halifax-based soldiers, most of them older, married, and less fit for service than front-line troops, were responsible for defending the port. When Canadian recruits and other troops who were awaiting transport to Europe and 600 army medical-aid personnel—doctors, nurses, and orderlies—were included, Benson commanded about 5,000 soldiers. In those first chaotic hours after the explosion, these troops really were the only group in position to mount organized rescue operations, serve as stretcher-bearers, recover the bodies of the dead, and help fight the fires that were raging in the North End. Within days, the army would set up a network of thirteen field hospitals, while teenage army cadets served as couriers, carrying messages and delivering food baskets to the hungry.

One detail of troops from the 63rd Regiment, the Halifax Rifles, worked for seventy-two hours straight. "The [army] units in Halifax, comprised for the most part of militia battalions that had been called out for active service in 1914 in defence of the port, were to really prove themselves in the days following the explosion."[6]

Another way they did so was by maintaining law and order in Halifax. As is so often the case in the wake of any disaster, the best and the worst of human nature were on display. The vast majority of city residents came together to help each other and work for the common good. To that end, people selflessly volunteered their time, energies, and resources to the relief effort. However, there also were those who sought to take advantage of the situation, preying upon explosion victims alive and dead.

"Few folk thought that Halifax harboured any would-be ghouls or vultures. The disaster showed how many," one explosion survivor recalled. "Men clambered over the bodies of the dead to get beer in the shattered breweries. Men taking advantage of the flight from the city because of the possibility of another explosion went into houses and shops, and [they] took whatever their thieving fingers could lay hold of. Then there were the nightly prowlers among the ruins who rifled the pockets of the dead and dying, and snatched rings from icy fingers."[7]

An American newspaper published an interview with one J.A. Meisner, a former Halifax resident who was visiting friends there on December 6. Meisner's account of events in the stricken city had a chilling ring to it. "There has been looting, and it has gone hard with those caught at it," said Meisner. "The papers [in Halifax] do not say much about this, but a soldier told me that he found a negro with four fingers in one of his pockets, which he had cut off for the rings. He was cutting a fifth finger from a woman when seen by a soldier who raised his gun and fired. The four fingers were then taken from the dead man's pocket."[8]

Looting was not the only crime that police, soldiers, and residents reportedly had to deal with. Stories made the rounds about "white slavers" who were supposedly prowling the streets, taking advantage of the chaos to snatch young women; if this ever happened there was no proof if it—it may have been the 1917 equivalent of scary clowns.

CONFUSION AND FEAR gripped Halifax in the days following the disaster. Understandably so. With so many telegraph and telephone lines down, communications were disrupted. The world first learned of the explosion via sketchy, inaccurate reports that began "rippling across Canada and the United States,"[9] as one historian would put it. For example, the *Washington Times* reported that a Royal Navy cruiser had collided with an American munitions ship in Halifax harbour. In Hawaii, half a world away from Nova Scotia, an article in the *Honolulu Star-Bulletin* claimed that the Halifax death toll was "300 or 350."[10]

In Ottawa, Canada's chief press censor (CPC) began hearing about such reports, and he grew concerned; news of the disaster was spreading quickly. Within two hours of the explosion, Lieutenant-Colonel Ernest Chambers' office received a telegram from the editor of the newspaper in Sydney asking for permission to report on the events in Halifax. The CPC wasted no time in replying. "No objection publication of all facts you can get regarding Halifax explosion. Thanks for query," he wrote.[11] Chambers had wisely concluded that it was best to let the basic facts come out rather than to let rumours take root; suspicion that the explosion had been the result of German sabotage was already widespread and growing.

Chambers promptly contacted Canada's two telegraph companies— the Great North Western Telegraph Company and Canadian Pacific Railway Telegraph Company—to request that they give priority to the transmission of press reports written by the Halifax bureau chief of the Canadian Press (CP) news service. Chambers knew the CP had a reciprocal agreement with Associated Press, its American counterpart. As a result, some CP articles that appeared in newspapers across Canada were shared with AP in New York. Those that were of wide general interest— such as news of the catastrophic explosion at Halifax—would be distributed to newspapers across the United States.

With this in mind, Chambers instructed Colonel A.E. Curren, Halifax's military censor, to allow the Canadian and American journalists who were rushing to the stricken city to write and cable their reports with a minimum of official interference. However, local censorship rules remained in effect, as did prohibitions on photos of the port and it facilities.

NOT SURPRISINGLY, REPORTERS for Halifax's five daily newspapers were quick to report on all aspects of the great Halifax harbour explosion. Too quick, in at least one case. When John ("Jack") Ronayne, the *Daily Echo*'s twenty-three-year-old marine reporter, saw the smoke that was billowing from the fire aboard the *Mont-Blanc*, he rushed down to Pier 6. The story of the incredible scene he saw was one Ronayne was destined never to write. The journalist was among the dozens of ill-fated onlookers who were watching the fire from the pedestrian footbridge that spanned the train tracks at the foot of Duffus Street. All died instantly in the blast.

For Ronayne's colleagues and peers, the story of the historic disaster would be the biggest, most memorable of their careers. That was so for Peter Lawson, the Bermuda-born editor of the *Herald*.

Lawson, who worked nights, was sleeping at 9:04 a.m. when the blast occurred. The shock wave shattered the windows of his boarding house, blew in the doors, and roused Lawson from his slumber. His first thought was that Halifax had come under bombardment from a German U-boat. Lawson was still musing about that when a messenger arrived with a note from Senator William Dennis, the *Herald*'s publisher. Dennis, staunchly pro-British, pro-war, and a crony of Prime Minister Robert Borden, was a "key figure in the system of local patronage. That made him no friend of federal or provincial officials such as Admiral Kingsmill [the head of the RCN], who endeavoured to eschew political considerations in making appointments and spending tax dollars."[12] Dennis told Lawson to "get on" the explosion story as soon as possible. The senator hoped that whatever had happened would embarrass Kingsmill.

Lawson did as ordered. Leaving his Buckingham Street boarding house, he endured the oily rain that was falling as he gathered a few of the basic facts before hiking four miles through the smoking ruins of the North End to reach the Rockingham train station. There, he was able to send to Truro a cable that was one of the first news reports of the explosion.

AT LEAST IN THE FIRST FEW DAYS after the Halifax disaster, the articles that appeared in Canadian newspapers tended to be more accurate than those in foreign newspapers. But not always. For example, a CP article written by a journalist in Halifax that supposedly appeared in a Toronto newspaper stated that "One looter was shot, his body strapped to a post over which was affixed a flaming legend which stated, 'This was a looter.'"[13] If this incident ever happened, there is no firm evidence of it. Regardless, similar articles appeared in Toronto newspapers. The *Globe*— which, in 1917, like the *Herald*, was not known for the subtlety of its news coverage or editorials—reported that looters in Halifax were busy breaking into railway boxcars to steal cases of booze.[14] Similarly, the *Toronto Star* published a news story reporting that Halifax police were on the "look out for a man who speaks with a German accent, who has been suspected of looting."[15] This was not the first time—nor would it be the last—that the media stirred up paranoia about the perfidy of the city's German-Canadian population. One widely circulated rumour "was that the pilot of the Belgian relief ship, a man [who] had taken in and out of the Straits thousands of ships without an accident, had been found murdered and the collision was foul play."[16]

There was no end of such rumours or of incendiary news reports, both of which fanned the flames of suspicion and anger. Halifax newspapers—the *Herald*, in particular—were among the worst offenders in this regard. As military historian John Griffith Armstrong would point out, they had "a penchant for scare paragraphs."[17] When CPC Ernest Chambers visited Halifax on December 14, he held a closed-door meeting with representatives from the city's daily newspapers and the local CP bureau chief to remind the journalists of their rights and their responsibilities. There was, after all, still a war going on.

THOSE URGENT TELEGRAMS sent on the morning of December 6 by railway executives W.A. Duff and George Graham requesting that emergency aid be sent to Halifax had the desired effect. Within hours of the explosion, trains loaded with doctors, nurses, and medical supplies were racing toward Halifax from New Glasgow, Wolfville, Truro, and other towns across Nova Scotia, neighbouring New Brunswick, and the New England states.

The closest undamaged station to the Richmond rail yards and the devastated North Street Station was the one at Rockingham, on the main line leading north out of Halifax. The first regularly scheduled train to arrive there post-disaster came from Wolfville, fifty-five miles to the northwest. When it pulled into the station, George Graham was waiting on the platform. "Are there any doctors or nurses aboard this train?" he called out.

Graham was in luck; there was. Major Avery DeWitt stepped forward and introduced himself. DeWitt, a thirty-six-year-old member of the Canadian Army Medical Corps, was the scion of a prominent Wolfville family. His father, Dr. George DeWitt, was a graduate of Harvard medical school, while his sister Nellie was a trained nurse. In 1917, Avery DeWitt was working as the doctor at Camp Aldershot in the Annapolis Valley. On the morning of December 6, he chanced to be travelling to Halifax on business.

George Graham hastily arranged for a locomotive to carry DeWitt as close as possible to what was left of the Richmond rail yard. When he got there, DeWitt found parked on a siding the No. 10 overnight passenger train from Saint John, New Brunswick—the train that dispatcher Vince Coleman had lost his life trying to warn off. As it happened, the No. 10 had already passed Rockingham Station on the morning of December 6 when the shock wave from the explosion hit it. The blast had smashed the windows of the passenger cars, and the entire train had rocked precariously before settling back on the rails, damaged but still operational. The only person on board to suffer injury was the engineer. Although badly shaken, he insisted on remaining on the job. It was fortunate he did so, for his decision saved lives.

No sooner had the train come to a halt after the explosion than scores of injured people descended upon it. Many of them were bleeding; some had suffered eye injuries; others had broken limbs and were barely able to walk. By the time Avery DeWitt arrived on the scene, even more injured people had appeared at the rail yard. "Men, women, and children were lying round on the ground on boards, broken beds, doors, or anything they could get and suffering untold agonies."[18]

J.C. Gillespie, the conductor of the No. 10 train, had taken charge of the situation, doing the best he could. With help from some railway workers, a few soldiers who happened along, and several of the able-bodied train passengers, he had loaded the train with 112 of the most seriously injured people. The question he then faced was what to do next. Gillespie had been struggling to find an answer when Dr. DeWitt arrived, like a godsend. After discussing the situation with DeWitt, the conductor concluded their only viable option was to move the train to Truro. There was no hospital there, but the town had a population of about 6,000 and Gillespie figured there would be somewhere to unload and treat the wounded. He knew that if they remained on the train, many of them would die.

Avery DeWitt stayed on board for the two-hour journey to Truro and did his best to treat and comfort the injured. Using forceps and a pair of scissors—the only tools he had at hand—the doctor also performed emergency surgeries, including the removal of several patients' badly damaged eyeballs. Despite DeWitt's best efforts, three children succumbed to their injuries while in transit. The death toll might have been even higher if it had not been for the efforts of a second doctor and a nurse who boarded the train at Windsor Junction. Because they got on at the end opposite to the passenger car in which DeWitt was working, he had no idea of their identities.

It was only when the train reached Truro that DeWitt discovered that his own father and sister were the mystery medical pair. Now, in Truro, the three DeWitts were the only medical personnel in the town; all the local physicians had rushed off to Halifax to help with emergency relief efforts. The DeWitts continued to work alongside local volunteers night and day for five days. "The great exploit of Truro was the astonishingly rapid transformation of three of its public buildings [the courthouse, a school, and the fire hall] into hospitals on the very day of the disaster, and having them ready for the patients when No. 10 train arrived." [19]

CHAPTER 23

THE BLAME GAME BEGINS

Halifax, December 6, 1917, 3:00 p.m.

In addition to the *Mont-Blanc* and the *Imo*, twenty-six of the ships and boats in Halifax harbour on the morning of December 6 suffered damages, while the explosion sank three others.[1] Both HMCS *Niobe* and HMS *Highflyer*, two of the largest and most visible warships in the harbour, were among the vessels damaged.

Wreckage littered *Niobe*'s deck. Two of the ship's four funnels were down, and there were gaping holes in her superstructure and stanchions. Some of the nineteen men felled by the blast were still alive, but others had died instantly. Their crewmates who had escaped serious injury quickly set about cleaning up the damage, tending to the wounded, and recovering the bodies of the dead. Other men helped deal with emergencies in the Naval Dockyard and surrounding area. Teams of sailors working under the direction of Captain Walter Hose, CXO Evan Wyatt, and other RCN officers battled fires, rescued blast survivors, and recovered bodies. A contingent of sailors—Able Seaman Bert Griffith among them—volunteered to help remove explosives from the Wellington Barracks magazine, which was ablaze.

Although *Highflyer* was a front-line fighting ship with armour plating six inches thick in places, she suffered damage to her superstructure. The explosion tore a hole on the ship's starboard side and wrecked the captain's upper deck cabin and the chart house. Fifty sailors had suffered injuries, while three men died. In addition, Commander Tom Triggs and those half-dozen sailors who had ventured out in *Highflyer*'s whaler to help fight the fire aboard the *Mont-Blanc* were missing and presumed dead. Their mates, who searched for them later, found "no trace of [most of] . . . the whaler's crew."[2] Searchers did find Able Seaman William Becker, who was more dead than alive after washing up on the Dartmouth shore. Unconscious and in shock, he suffered from hypothermia. His rescuers carried him to some nearby railway tracks where they saved his life by warming his body with heat from a locomotive's firebox.

It was also in Dartmouth that the British naval search party encountered the crew of the *Mont-Blanc*. The British sailors escorted the Frenchmen to *Highflyer*, where they joined the crew of the *Imo* in protective custody. Later that afternoon, Le Médec and his men would take refuge in the home of the French consul while they waited to learn what would happen next. In far-off Ottawa, that decision had already been made.

WITHIN HOURS OF the news of the explosion in Halifax, federal government bureaucrats were scrambling to formulate plans for a public inquiry. Crew members from both the *Imo* and the *Mont-Blanc* would be called on to testify before they would be allowed to go home.

Alexander Johnston, a deputy minister in the Ministry of Marine and Fisheries, was quick to set the wheels in motion to launch such a review of the events of December 6. Johnston, a fifty-year-old Cape Breton native, had served as the local member in both the Nova Scotia House of

Assembly and the federal Parliament. He also owned the daily newspaper in Sydney. As such, he was well aware of the political situation in his home province; with a bitter election campaign under way, Prime Minister Robert Borden was in a delicate position. Halifax was Borden's home, and it was his former riding. "Arguably [he had] failed to protect his people from terrible harm. Should blame be laid at federal feet, there would be huge financial and political consequences."[3]

Johnston called Captain Louis Auguste Demers, "the redoubtable and much feared" Dominion Wreck Commissioner.[4] His job was to investigate shipping accidents that happened in Canadian waters, and he did so with the zeal of an inquisitor rooting out heresy. When an incident was minor, Demers held a hearing over which he or a delegate would preside. If there was considerable damage and loss of life, or if the accident was high profile—the 1914 sinking in the St. Lawrence River of the passenger liner *Empress of Ireland* being a prime example—the process was more complicated.

The Canada Shipping Act gave the minister of Marine and Fisheries discretionary authority to launch a formal inquiry.[5] When that happened, Demers helped the deputy minister organize proceedings, and if needed, he acted as a nautical advisor to the presiding judge.

In the wake of the disaster in Halifax, Johnston and Demers immediately began making plans for an inquiry. Johnston had been a deputy minister for seven years and knew that his boss, Minister of Marine and Fisheries Charles C. Ballantyne, was a political novice. When Borden appointed him to cabinet in October 1917, the Montreal businessman was still trying to win a seat in Parliament; he would be one of the handful of Unionist MPs from Quebec who won their seats in the election on December 17. Given his inexperience, Ballantyne had no choice but to depend on his deputy ministers for guidance; George Desbarats was in charge of Naval Services; Alexander Johnston oversaw Marine and Fisheries.

Time was of the essence for Ballantyne and the Borden government in terms of coming to grips with the disaster in Halifax. In addition to the domestic political concerns, Halifax was Canada's most important port in the Allied war effort. Thus, "pressure came directly from the top, with instructions from Prime Minister Borden to Minister of Marine [Charles] Ballantyne that the investigation be instituted without delay."[6] Left unsaid, but understood by everyone involved, was the implicit message that the "blame game" had begun in earnest.

SENIOR BRITISH AND CANADIAN naval officials, politicians, Halifax newspapers, and the city residents were all demanding an explanation of how things could ever have gone so horribly wrong in Halifax harbour. Rumours ran rampant.

With German U-boat activity in the North Atlantic spiking, many people suspected the explosion was the work of saboteurs. To unsophisticated ears in Halifax, the accents of the *Imo*'s Norwegian crewmen sounded German. That notion added fuel to suspicions that a German agent had murdered pilot William Hayes and that the killer had been in control of the Norwegian ship as it entered the Narrows. Others in Halifax believed—or wanted to believe—that the *Mont-Blanc*'s captain and crew were responsible for the collision. "Only four months earlier, Canada had passed a Conscription Act despite strong opposition from the province of Quebec. It was easy for the local populace to focus its anti-French sentiments on the *Mont-Blanc*."[7] Captain Le Médec and his crew, well aware of the hostility, kept a low profile and welcomed police protection. On the afternoon of December 6, having made his way to the home of Emile Gaboury, the French consul in Halifax, Le Médec set about organizing his defence to the questions he would inevitably be obliged to answer. Le Médec had initially declined to speak with journalists; however, on December 10 he issued a three-page written statement in hopes of countering some of the malicious rumours about the role he and pilot Mackey had played in the events of December 6. The captain's statement—which he would repeat almost verbatim when he was called to the witness stand at the public inquiry into the disaster—was published in the *Boston Herald-Journal* on December 11 and reprinted in newspapers across the United States and Canada.[8]

NO LESS DISMAYING than concerns about *how* the disaster in Halifax had happened were a couple of vexing questions. For one, why had the French ship, a rusting tramp steamer laden with a devil's cargo of munitions, ever been allowed to enter Halifax harbour? For another—and this question cut to the core of the matter: *who* was at fault for the collision? Apart from the political imperatives that were in play, the answer to that latter question was vital for both moral and legal reasons. Knowing who had been responsible would channel people's anger and would dictate who would ultimately pay when it came time to assess liability.

Wreck Commission inquiries did not normally make findings of negligence. "Marine inquiries were entrenched within the judicial system and often [were] the prelude to corrective action, resolution of insurance claims, and subsequent litigation."[9] However, the legal distinction between an inquiry and a trial to determine "who done it" was lost on most people. In the disaster's aftermath, officials in Ottawa knew that a public inquiry would divert attention and shift blame away from the federal government and senior naval commanders in Halifax. Both wore a measure of blame for the disaster. They had been lax in enforcing safety regulations that would have prevented a munitions ship such as the *Mont-Blanc* from ever entering the harbour; they had failed to clarify—let alone define—the chain of naval command in Halifax or the relationship between senior naval officers and the civilian harbour commission and pilots. Given the federal government's priorities and political motivations, it was inevitable that there would be an inquiry sooner rather than later, and also that there would be enormous pressure on the presiding judge to have an expanded mandate.

THE LOGISTICAL DETAILS to be sorted out before a Wreck Commission inquiry could begin were myriad. Time was of the essence, and so the day after the disaster, Deputy Minister Johnston retained Halifax lawyer William A. Henry to act as Crown counsel at the inquiry. Johnston wanted the proceedings to begin just six days hence, on December 13. It was a tall order, but Henry was up to the challenge.

The fifty-four-year-old Antigonish native was one of Halifax's most prominent and skilled lawyers. The son of a Father of Confederation who had also served as one of the inaugural judges of the Supreme Court of Canada, William Henry had received his early education in France and Scotland before studying law at Harvard, Cambridge, and Dalhousie. By 1917, he had been a lawyer for thirty-seven years. His role in organizing the Wreck Commission inquiry would be one of the biggest challenges of his career.

Provincial and municipal politicians, the public, and the media, in particular the ever-strident *Herald* newspaper, were demanding that the proceeding focus on the question of guilt—who had been responsible for the disaster?—and why the *Mont-Blanc* and her deadly cargo had been allowed into Halifax harbour. Part and parcel with both concerns, there were loud calls for sweeping reform of the port's pilotage system.

Henry wrote to Deputy Minister Johnston to caution him how "improper" it would be for the Wreck Commission—or any Canadian government inquiry—to delve into issues relating to the details of how Allied ships were transporting munitions to Europe in wartime. Halifax was a Canadian port, but Rear Admiral Chambers and his RN officers directed all convoy operations originating there. As for the *Mont-Blanc*,

Henry reminded Johnston that the French ship had been carrying American-made munitions, which had been loaded in New York. Further complicating matters, the *Mont-Blanc* had sailed under British Admiralty orders. "The war interests . . . of our greatest allies are involved, which would make, I think, the holding of . . . an investigation a very delicate matter," Henry advised.[10]

He went on to advise the deputy minister that any reorganization of the Halifax harbour pilotage—sorely needed though it might be—was a matter beyond the Wreck Commission's jurisdiction. If Ottawa was intent on broaching such a thorny issue, Henry recommended that it do so in a separate proceeding. As for the suggestion that the planned inquiry should affix blame for the Halifax harbour explosion, Henry was more sanguine. There was nothing, he opined, to stand in the way of the Wreck Commission rendering a verdict. That view was shared by Judge Arthur Drysdale, the jurist who would preside over the inquiry. Drysdale already had some very definite ideas on what matters the Wreck Commission inquiry could and should deal with. Like most Haligonians, he demanded to know who had been responsible for the events of December 6.

CHAPTER 24

THE YANKS ARE COMING

Halifax Harbour, December 6, 1917, 3:15 p.m.

The unexpected but timely arrival in Halifax harbour of two American warships provided a welcome boost to initial disaster relief efforts. The cruiser USS *Tacoma* and the armed troop carrier USS *Von Steuben*, a former German raider ship that had been seized by the American government in 1917, chanced to be passing Halifax the morning the explosion happened. The lookouts on both vessels heard the thunderous boom and sighted the towering black mushroom cloud that hovered over Halifax. The ships had been travelling independently, but both abruptly changed course and raced to Halifax.

By late afternoon, the *Tacoma* and the *Von Steuben* were anchored in Halifax harbour. Captain Powers ("Pete") Symington of the *Tacoma*, the senior American naval commander on hand, immediately tendered the services of the crews of both American ships to do whatever they could to help in rescue and relief efforts that were getting under way. "Sent a party of seventy-seven men and five officers ashore for patrol duty," the officer responsible wrote in the ship's logbook that evening.[1]

For the next three days, hundreds of sailors—"bluejackets"—from the *Tacoma* and the *Von Steuben* rescued survivors and recovered bodies from the still-smouldering ruins of North End buildings, helped maintain security, and assisted in building emergency homeless shelters.

Equally important were the contributions of the crew of the USS *Old Colony.* The ship, a refurbished coastal passenger vessel, had been England-bound when she had stopped in Halifax a few days earlier for engine repairs. In the wake of the explosion, R.M. Hayes, the ship's medical officer, oversaw the transformation of the *Old Colony* into a makeshift floating hospital. Several parties of the ship's crew went ashore, and within two hours, they had brought fifty-four explosion survivors to the ship for medical care.[2]

THE USS *OLD COLONY*, IN PORT FOR REPAIRS AT THE TIME OF THE EXPLOSION, QUICKLY BECAME A HOSPITAL SHIP. (U.S. NAVAL HISTORICAL CENTER)

Surgeons from the *Tacoma*, the *Von Steuben*, the U.S. Coast Guard cutter *Morrill*, and the armed merchant cruiser HMS *Changuinola*, assisted by nurses and female volunteers from Halifax, performed emergency surgeries and dressed wounds. Meanwhile, down in the ship's galley, the staff served up hot meals to one and all, 24/7.

NEWS OF THE EXPLOSION in Halifax reached Boston within two hours of the disaster. Fragmentary though the initial reports were, they set alarm bells ringing at Massachusetts State House. The ties that bind Canada's Atlantic provinces—and the city of Halifax, in particular—to New England were deep and pervasive. In the days of sailing ships, the Nova Scotia port had looked south, not west to central Canada, for much of its trade and economic activity. That habit continued in the post-Confederation era. Despite the political divide that sometimes separated Canada from the United States, the trade, migration, and family ties between Nova Scotia and New England long had fostered a profound sense of community on both sides of the border. Samuel McCall, Massachusetts' Republican governor, was Pennsylvania born and had been in office for only about a year, but he understood the uniqueness of this cross-border relationship.

McCall dashed off a telegram to the mayor of Halifax offering whatever help the stricken city needed. He also mobilized the Massachusetts Committee on Public Safety (MCPS); state government officials and concerned citizens had organized that wartime emergency response team in February 1917. When McCall contacted Henry B. Endicott, the wealthy Bostonian who chaired the MCPS's executive committee, Endicott agreed that the state should send emergency aid to Halifax. "And I know just the man for the job. Let's ask Cap Ratshesky if he's willing to take this on." McCall seconded the idea, enthusiastically.

Abraham Captain Ratshesky—"Cap" to family and friends—was someone both McCall and Endicott knew well. The fifty-three-year-old businessman and philanthropist was a human dynamo with a reputation for fair-mindedness, integrity, and an unwavering commitment to good causes. McCall and Endicott were confident Ratshesky could quickly organize and then supervise an MCPS emergency relief team for Halifax.

Dark-haired, bespectacled Ratshesky was a son of Jewish immigrants. He had served three years as a Republican member of the

Massachusetts Senate (1892–1895) but had opted not to seek re-election after he got married in 1894; his wife, Edith, was not much for politics. Turning his talents instead to business, Cap Ratshesky and his brother founded a trust company with an innovative business plan: they would provide loans, mortgages, and other financial services to the wave of immigrants who were flooding into the cities of the northeastern United States at the time. In particular, the Ratshesky brothers catered to Jewish people who could find no other bank willing to handle their money. The U.S. Trust and Loan Company proved to be an inspired initiative that made Ratshesky and his brother rich. Through it all, Cap maintained his commitments to philanthropy and public service. He helped organize emergency relief for the victims of massive fires that razed the Massachusetts towns of Chelsea (1908) and Salem (1914). He also started his own hospital in Boston and celebrated his fiftieth birthday by endowing his own charitable foundation.[3]

Those who knew Ratshesky were not surprised that he agreed to drop everything and accept the role of commissioner in charge of the MCPS Halifax disaster-relief team. The only question he asked was "When do you want me to leave?" As it would happen, the answer was "As soon as possible."

Governor McCall had received no reply to two telegrams he had sent to the mayor of Halifax. This led him to conclude that the rumours were true: Halifax had been hard hit, and many people there were dead. The governor and MCPS chair Endicott agreed that the state's relief team should leave for Halifax immediately. And so it did. The special five-car "Train of Mercy," as the Boston Post dubbed it,[4] left the city's North Union Station a few minutes after ten o'clock on Thursday night. This was just fourteen hours after the explosion in Halifax.

The weather in Boston was damp and seasonally cool at the time, and there was heavy snow in the forecast for the next day. The outlook for New Brunswick and Nova Scotia was even more ominous. Cap Ratshesky understood that he and his team would be travelling into a storm, possibly even a full-scale blizzard. But they were undeterred.

Joining Ratshesky aboard the Train of Mercy were thirty other volunteer members of the official party—eleven doctors, ten nurses, and members of the Massachusetts State Guard's medical unit. Also travelling with the relief expedition were six representatives of the American Red Cross, four railway officials, and reporters from Boston's five daily newspapers.

The overnight train ride from Boston to Halifax normally took twenty-seven hours. However, time being of the essence, on this occasion the engineer of the MCPS relief train carried a blanket permission from American and Canadian railway officials that gave him the right-of-way over all other rail traffic. The hope was that the relief train could reach its destination in just twenty-two hours. That, however, would prove to be impossible.

AS THE MCPS RELIEF TRAIN was chugging northward, in Halifax, the daytime temperature, which had hovered a few degrees above freezing, was dropping by the hour. A winter wind blowing in from the North Atlantic brought with it snow-laden pewter skies. A raging blizzard, the first of the winter and one of the worst to hit Halifax in years, was on the way. It could not have done so at a worse time.

The electricity was off all across Halifax. In the cold and gathering darkness, residents worked by the light of lanterns and candles to seal broken windows and doors in those buildings that were still habitable. People nailed up anything they could find—blankets, scraps of wood, tarpaper, and cardboard—to keep out the snow and wind. "Halifax had become in a trice a city of dead bodies, ruined homes, and blasted hopes."[5]

IT WAS DARK BY THE TIME George Smith set out on an emergency tour of Halifax harbour. The local representative of the Pickford & Black shipping agency had a job to do. It was one he dreaded but could not avoid. Smith was obliged to send damage reports to clients of the shipping agency whose ships had been in port when the explosion occurred. Thus, Smith's job was to discover which ships were still afloat and assess damages.

The situation in the harbour had remained chaotic for much of the day. That is why it was six o'clock when the *Booton*, a chartered tugboat Smith used to travel around the harbour, finally arrived at the Pickford & Black wharf. There waiting with Smith and several of his men were Hervey Jones, the twenty-five-year-old editor of the *Echo* newspaper, and a trio of veteran harbour pilots. LaMont Power, Charles Martin, and Henry Latter were all intent on accompanying Smith when he boarded the wreck of the *Imo*. The pilots hoped to recover the body of their friend and colleague William Hayes.[6]

It was slow going out on the water at night. The only light visible for miles around came from the flickering fires that still burned among the piles of rubble on Fort Needham hillside. Captain David Rudderham at the helm of the *Booton* proceeded slowly, picking his way through debris and the wreckage of sunken ships and boats.

First stop was British cargo carrier the SS *Middleham Castle*, which had incurred heavy damage. Jones waited on board the *Booton* while George Smith and his men searched the abandoned ship. When they reappeared, Jones was eager to hear what Smith had found. "The damage is pretty bad," said Smith. "We found a dead man who's quite a sight. I'd advise you not to look when we bring the body on board."

THE MERCHANT SHIP SS *MIDDLEHAM CASTLE* SUFFERED HEAVY DAMAGE IN THE HALIFAX EXPLOSION. (COURTESY OF ANN FOREMAN)

Although he knew he should heed Smith's advice, Jones snuck a peek. He immediately regretted doing so. "As the corpse was slowly lowered over the side of the *Middleham Castle*, it was tied to a board. One end was tilted downward, and some of the dead man's brains fell onto the deck of the *Booton*, narrowly missing one of the men standing near me."[7]

The situation was no less macabre when Smith and his party crossed the harbour to Dartmouth to explore the wreckage of the *Imo*. The relief ship was a forlorn sight. Her four masts had withstood the explosion, but much of the superstructure was smashed flat, and the ship's funnel was missing. The crumpled hull, which had come to rest in the shallows, listed twenty-five degrees to starboard, with her stern low in the water.

THE WRECKAGE OF THE *IMO* ENDED UP BEACHED ON THE DARTMOUTH SHORE, WHERE IT LAY UNTIL SALVAGERS REFLOATED THE SHIP IN APRIL 1918. (NOVA SCOTIA ARCHIVES)

The surviving members of the *Imo*'s crew had departed hastily, having accompanied a rescue crew from HMS *Highflyer* back to the British warship. The *Imo*, broken and forlorn, was now a ghost ship. Smith, his

Pickford & Black helpers, and Captain Rudderham from the *Booton* boarded her to assess the damage. Meanwhile, the three harbour pilots went off to search for the body of William Hayes. Despite the gruesome scene he had witnessed aboard the *Middleham Castle*, Hervey Jones smelled a good story, and so he tagged along with Smith and his men. However, Jones was quickly unnerved again, for in the darkness he almost tripped over two corpses that were lying on the deck of the forecastle. Neither body was that of William Hayes.

Jones received another fright when the searchers heard a baleful moan. Thinking they'd found a survivor, one of the Pickford & Black men opened the door to the captain's cabin. As he did so, out of the darkness an animal let out a menacing, guttural snarl. The hair on Hervey Jones' neck bristled. Terrified, he jumped back. One of the other searchers bolted and ran back to the tug as fast as his legs would carry him.

When repeated efforts to calm Captain From's terrified dog and dislodge it from its hiding place proved fruitless, one of the searchers quickly ended the impasse with a single rifle shot. A subsequent search of the captain's wrecked cabin turned up no sign of Haakon From or of pilot Hayes. "We found Hayes' body near what was left of the bridge," Jones would recall. "He appeared to have been crouching under a lifeboat, as if he had been trying to find shelter from the effects of the explosion."[8]

It was also on the *Imo*'s bridge that the searchers discovered Captain From's body. The lethal spray of white-hot metal bits loosed by the explosion had cut down the captain, William Hayes, and First Officer Ingvald Iverson. The three men had died instantly.

Captain From's remains were shipped home to Norway. A huge crowd of family, friends, and colleagues—"more than the chapel could hold"— would attend a February 2, 1918, funeral service in Sandefjord.[9]

William Hayes' body was returned from Halifax to nearby Herring Cove, where it was buried in St. Paul's New Cemetery.

Remarkably, in the spring of 1918, salvagers would succeed in refloating the *Imo*. After being refurbished and rechristened in 1920 as the *Guvernøren* (*Governor*), she would serve as a whale oil tanker. On November 30, 1921, while en route to the Antarctic, the ship went onto the rocks off the Falkland Islands. The captain and crew safely abandoned ship; however, the vessel herself would be lost to the sea.

AT THE SAME TIME the search party was recovering the bodies of Haakon From, William Hayes, Ingvald Iverson, and other men from the wreckage of the *Imo*, an eerie calm prevailed in the North End of Halifax. The military had thrown up a cordon around the devastated neighbourhood. Apart from the fires that continued to burn among the ruins of what looked like a Western Front battlefield, the only visible light came from bobbing lanterns—beacons of hope amid the gloom—carried by those rescue workers who persisted in their labours. "As the evening wore on there were still moans and cries from shattered homes, but there were little means of reaching the victims lying within."[10]

For Mary Jean Hinch and other wounded explosion survivors who found themselves trapped under the rubble and clinging to life by the flimsiest of threads, time was running out. Very quickly.

CHAPTER 25

THE STORM

Halifax, Nova Scotia, December 7, 8:00 a.m.

As Friday morning dawned, the winter storm closing in on Halifax was growing in intensity. As the first flakes of snow began to fall, the temperature dropped. Soon it would be a frigid seventeen degrees Fahrenheit (minus eight Celsius), and the gale-force wind that blew in off the ocean cut exposed skin like an icy knife.

Sixteen inches of snow would fall on this day. By nightfall, the waist-high drifts smothered the last of the fires that had been burning in the city. The charred landscape in the North End now took on the monochromatic beauty of a winter wonderland. A few days earlier, such a scene would have evoked thoughts of a Currier and Ives print. Not today. The driving snow made almost impossible the already perilous job of the rescue workers who continued to search for survivors and the bodies of the dead in the ruins of collapsed buildings. "The narrow tracks cleared through the rubble of the devastated area were quickly blocked. Troops now had the added task of shovelling to try to keep a passageway open and of digging through the deep drifts covering the ruins to find out what lay underneath."[1]

Nineteen-year-old Hugh Mills had been over in Dartmouth when the explosion occurred on Thursday morning. After responding to the call for volunteers, he had spent the afternoon in Richmond as a member of one of the search-and-rescue crews poking through the wreckage of buildings on Barrington Street in Halifax. The unpleasantness of the work—grim and dangerous to begin with—was compounded by the weather and by a shortage of tools; searchers had only their hands to work with.

THE SEARCH FOR VICTIMS AND SURVIVORS IN THE DEVASTATED RICHMOND NEIGHBOURHOOD WAS DIFFICULT, COLD, AND DANGEROUS WORK. (WILLIAM JAMES FAMILY FONDS, CITY OF TORONTO ARCHIVES)

Hugh Mills had toiled until after dark on the evening of December 6. Lean as a beanpole and slight of build, he felt exhausted. After spending a long, miserable night in the ruins of an abandoned house, he emerged at daybreak. Spotting a bonfire in the distance, he made his way over to it. The men whom Hugh found huddled around the fire welcomed him with a mug of hot tea. The liquid left Hugh feeling only slightly revived; he was still tired, cold, and feeling increasingly downcast. So far he had found no one alive in the rubble.

The men invited Hugh to join them in their search for survivors, but he declined. He wanted to go to Veith Street. "I know some people who live . . . or *lived* there," he explained

Veith Street was in ruins, and a pall-like silence prevailed. The explosion down at Pier 6, barely 200 yards away, had flattened every building. Here and there, a listing telephone pole or the skeletal remnants of a tree remained upright, like hands of the dead reaching skyward from their graves. The only identifiable landmark still standing along the street's two-block length was one wall of the Hillis foundry. Scores of people had worked in the building, but there were no signs of life now.

With the wind picking up and the snow falling ever harder, Hugh Mills' spirits were sinking fast. Inside his tattered mittens, his hands were numb. That was a blessing of a sort, for it dulled the ache caused by wood splinters and cuts he endured while picking through the rubble.

Hugh was ready to go home. However, as he was clambering over yet another pile of splintered, broken lumber, he heard a strange noise. At first, he thought it might be a squeaky board, or maybe the wind was playing tricks. "Hello," he called. "Is there someone there?"

The sound came again; this time Hugh realized it was beneath his feet. Dropping down on all fours, his adrenaline level rising, Hugh frantically began sweeping aside the snow and tearing at the lumber below with his bare hands. As he did so, he immediately knew there was more wood than he could ever move by himself. His pulse racing, his heart pounding, he stood tall and shouted for help. His cries drew a couple of American sailors, who came wading through the knee-deep snow to reach him. The men, burly bluejackets from the crew of the hospital ship the USS *Old Colony*, were much stronger and fresher than Hugh was.

Together, the men cleared away the snow and debris. Hugh Mills was the first to spot the body that lay trapped beneath the pile. "It's a woman!" he cried. "Oh, my God! It's Mrs. Hinch. She lives here on Veith Street."

When her rescuers pulled a bloodied and bruised Mary Jean Hinch from the wreckage, she was semi-conscious and barely alive. The bluejackets loaded her onto a makeshift stretcher and transported her to the emergency medical clinic aboard the USS *Old Colony*.

EVEN AS THE BLIZZARD RAGED over Halifax, a massive relief effort was starting to take shape and build momentum. Trains carrying doctors, nurses, Red Cross workers, firefighters, tradespeople, and hundreds of volunteers ready to do whatever it took to help with rescue operations arrived daily. The explosion in Halifax harbour had made the headlines far and wide. In addition to the relief trains from Boston, others from Rhode Island; Bangor, Maine; and New York City were speeding toward Halifax.

Governments were the first to answer the city's urgent pleas for dollars to fund relief efforts, and they would emerge as the biggest donors to the cause. Canada's federal government provided more than $18 million in emergency relief money; in today's currency, that would be about $350 million. In 1917, when a loaf of bread cost six cents, and twenty-five dollars was a solid weekly wage for a blue-collar worker, a dollar went much farther than it does today.

The American and British governments also stepped up, each providing gifts of $5 million to the relief fund. Smaller donations flowed in from far and wide. Among them were $250,000 from Australia, $50,000 from New Zealand, and a like amount from St. John's, Newfoundland, which at the time was still a British colony.[2]

In Montreal, the first season of the newly formed National Hockey League (NHL) was about to get under way, and the Montreal Wanderers and Montreal Canadiens played an exhibition game, with proceeds going to the Halifax relief fund. Some hockey historians claim this was the first game played in NHL history—"or at least, the first game contested by players belonging to NHL teams."[3] Although there is no record of how much money the game raised, the gesture itself is noteworthy.

The Massachusetts–Halifax Relief Committee had much loftier fundraising ambitions than did the hockey players. The Massachusetts agency launched a campaign to raise a million dollars. Community relief drives collected pennies from schoolchildren and dollars from their parents. A thousand Boston women took to the streets for "Halifax Tag Day," which raised $10,000 for the Halifax relief fund.[4] Legendary Scottish music hall performer Sir Harry Lauder was among the celebrity donors at a luncheon that raised more than $2,000. Opera fans contributed to the cause by attending a benefit concert "given for the Relief of Sufferers from the Recent Disaster in Nova Scotia." The performance featured members of the Boston Symphony Orchestra, celebrated Australian soprano Dame Nellie Melba, and Austrian violinist Fritz Kreisler. Boston's largesse did not stop there.

Cap Ratshesky had sent a telegram home asking for window glass and glaziers to install it. The glaziers, accompanied by twenty-five doctors and sixty-five nurses, would reach Halifax aboard another relief train on the afternoon of Sunday, December 9. That same day, the first of two Halifax-bound ships carrying more window glass, glaziers, emergency food supplies, blankets, and winter clothing would sail from Boston. When the American Red Cross issued an appeal for donations, the public response was so enthusiastic that officials had to halt the collection; the hall where people were dropping off donations overflowed with piles, bundles, and boxes of incoming goods.

In Chicago, a citizens' committee chaired by former Halifax resident James B. Forgan, an aide to the Chicago mayor, held a public meeting where attendees donated $43,000 to the cause.[5]

Heeding the adage that charity begins at home, towns, villages, churches, and chapters of the Red Cross from across Nova Scotia, the neighbouring provinces of New Brunswick and Prince Edward Island, and the New England states donated to the Halifax relief fund. Trains carrying doctors, nurses, firefighters, and rescue workers sped to Halifax from communities all over Nova Scotia—among others, Wolfville, Truro, Amherst, Sydney, and New Glasgow—and from Moncton, St. John, and Campbellton in neighbouring New Brunswick. Individuals across Atlantic Canada donated money, articles of winter clothing, and anything else they could spare. "The country folk sent in gifts of butter, cream, eggs, and poultry," Archibald MacMechan reported.[6]

AMONG THE MOST VULNERABLE victims of the explosion on December 6 were children, thousands of whom suffered serious injuries, while hundreds were orphaned. Establishing the identities of babies and toddlers proved to be an especially difficult task.

In 1917, with so many men—the breadwinners for their families—fighting overseas, the wives of men in uniform often struggled to make ends meet. When the women were unable to do so, their children sometimes ended up in an orphanage. There were six in Halifax. Four were Roman Catholic, two were Protestant. All received funding from private donations and local churches.

In the wake of the explosion, "upwards of 500 families, including more than 1,500 children"[7] were in need of emergency relief. In response, the Liberal provincial government of Premier George Murray organized an emergency relief committee headed by Ernest H. Blois, the provincial Superintendent of Neglected and Delinquent Children. Blois, a forty-nine-year-old former teacher, was a staunch advocate of government involvement in child welfare matters. A big man with imposing physical presence and a personality to match, Blois had very definite ideas about how to do his job.[8] For that reason, he refused to allow American Red Cross officials to be members of the committee he headed, despite their expertise in disaster relief and child welfare. The Americans complained that Blois was "inflexible and went so far as to call him jealous of the rehabilitation workers."[9] Their comments were like water off a duck's back to Blois, who forged ahead with his own agenda.

The Blois committee provided Halifax newspapers with lists of the names of "unclaimed" children. "Out of 617 Robie Street, a little boy with light hair and dark brown eyes, aged about 2½ years," a typical announcement read. "He can give no account of himself or his people other than that 'Daddy is at war.'"[10]

In some cases, one or both parents of needy children were dead or had suffered serious explosion-related injuries. No less tragic were those situations in which youngsters and parents found themselves separated. This was the case with scores of injured children who convalesced in smaller cities and towns in Nova Scotia and neighbouring New Brunswick. With the blessing of provincial child welfare officials, families who helped care for the children eventually adopted some of them. This sometimes proved problematic. That was so in the case of thirteen-year-old Fred Kidd.

The grade seven student at Bloomfield School in Halifax suffered a head injury in the explosion. After Fred had spent four days in an emergency first-aid clinic, an administrator asked the lad and some of the other children if they would like "to go for a little trip."[11] When they agreed, they soon found themselves on a train bound for Campbellton, New Brunswick, 340 miles to the northwest. The children celebrated Christmas there, and afterward they learned they would be "placed" with local farm families. By this time, Fred Kidd's mind had cleared, and he rejected this plan. He raised such a fuss that the provincial child welfare officials put Fred and all the children who had come to Campbellton with him on a train back to Halifax. When they arrived, Fred was reunited with his family, who had been searching for him.

All turned out well for Fred Kidd, but many other Halifax youngsters were less fortunate. Some children, mostly toddlers and babies, simply disappeared in the post-disaster whirl of confusion, and their parents never saw them again. That was the fate of the three children of Lottie and William Moore.

The explosion on December 6 destroyed the Barrington Street home in which Lottie and William and their three children lived. When soldiers dug twenty-six-year-old Lottie out from under the rubble, she learned that her two daughters, nine-year-old Hazel Moore and six-month-old Hilda, and her five-year-old son Gerald had disappeared. The Moores spent years hunting for the children; however, their efforts were in vain. The names of the two older children—or those of others with the same names—appeared on the ledger of a ship that served as a temporary shelter for explosion survivors, but there the trail went cold. Were the Moore children alive or dead? No one could say for certain, and so their names were ultimately included in the Halifax Explosion Book of Remembrance. [12]

Lottie Moore could never bring herself to accept that Hazel, Gerald, and Hilda were dead. For her and for her husband, there was and could be no closure. The couple never gave up hope of finding their precious children. "Had I known they were dead, I could have put it to rest in my mind," she would often say. [13]

DESPITE THE PALL THAT LINGERED OVER HALIFAX IN THE WAKE OF THE DISASTER, SMALL CHRISTMAS PARTIES WERE HELD FOR AT LEAST SOME OF HALIFAX'S ORPHANED CHILDREN. (WILLIAM JAMES FAMILY FONDS, CITY OF TORONTO ARCHIVES)

CHAPTER 26

Bringing Order to Chaos

Halifax, Nova Scotia, December 8, 1917

By noon on Friday, December 7, the Train of Mercy from Boston had travelled more than 400 miles, arriving in Saint John, New Brunswick, in the midst of a blinding snowstorm. "For hours today [we] ran through country a foot deep in snow that whirled over the field in a cutting north wind," the *Boston Evening Transcript*'s correspondent reported.[1]

At stations all along the route northward, crowds greeted the MCPS train. Cap Ratshesky found himself besieged with requests from people who were eager to come on board for the ride to Halifax. He did his best to accommodate them. "I instructed those in charge of the train to fill every available space, giving doctors and nurses the preference."[2]

The scale and severity of the disaster in Halifax began to come into sharper focus at the Saint John train station. There the Massachusetts relief team encountered an ambulance train that had just arrived from Halifax. Aboard were fifty injured children with "their heads bandaged and their little arms in slings."[3] The spectacle was so sobering that Ratshesky ordered that additional stores of drugs and medical supplies be taken on board before the MCPS train left Saint John. And after hearing that the explosion had broken almost every window in Halifax, he wired Boston to ask that large quantities of glass and putty be shipped north as soon as possible. Ratshesky knew how essential windows were in the Nova Scotian winter.

As the Train of Mercy continued its rush northward, it was delayed for several hours near Truro, Nova Scotia, when the locomotive broke down. Then shortly after the train got going again, seventy-five miles north of Halifax, a massive snowdrift that towered higher than the doors of the baggage car blocked the tracks. Canadian railway officials announced that the Americans would have to wait for the storm to die down and workers to clear the tracks. However, patience was not one of Cap Ratshesky's virtues; he "pleaded with them to do everything in their power known to railway men to clear the track."[4] They did so, and Ratshesky was pleased that "within an hour by hard shovelling, the use of steam and ramming, and amid great cheers from all on board we went through the drift."[5]

The MCPS train rolled into Rockingham Station, the last stop before Halifax, at 3:00 a.m. on Saturday, December 8—thirty hours after departing Boston. The snow had finally stopped, the wind had died, and the sky was clear and starry. Ratshesky, who had been up all night making plans for his arrival in Halifax, was dismayed to discover that no local officials were there to meet the American relief team. What's more, the tracks were impassable because of the deep snow. A Canadian railway official who had boarded the MCPS train for the final leg of its journey into Halifax sent for a snow plow to clear a path to the end of the line, six miles distant. As he waited, Ratshesky could only bide his time. Never being one to sit idle, he "roused all who had retired and ordered an early breakfast."[6]

It was 7:00 a.m. when the Train of Mercy finally reached Halifax—or as close to the city as it was possible for any train to get for now. There to greet the Americans when their train came to a stop was C.A. Hayes, general manager of the Canadian Government Railways. Hayes afforded Ratshesky a hero's welcome and arranged for him to meet the Canadian "premier," as the media referred to the prime minister at that time. Sir Robert Borden had arrived in Halifax during the night, and his private railway car now sat on a siding near the one where the MCPS relief train had parked.

Borden, sixty-three years old, silver-haired, and mustachioed, was the leader of Canada's Conservative Party. A native of Nova Scotia's Annapolis Valley and a "self-made man," he had been a teacher before studying law and answering the call to the provincial bar in 1878. Borden was, by all accounts, a brilliant lawyer and an astute politician. He won election to Parliament in 1896, and again in 1901, when the Conservative caucus chose him to head the party. He became prime minister in 1911 and was destined in 1917 to lead the Conservatives and their "Unionist" allies to a resounding victory in the December 17 general election, one of the most hard-fought and bitter in Canadian history. Borden won re-election in the Kings electoral district.

Borden had been campaigning on Prince Edward Island on December 6. Upon hearing of the explosion in Halifax, he immediately dropped what he was doing and set off for the city. "I arrived [late Friday night] in the midst of one of the most terrible blizzards I ever experienced," he would recall in his memoirs.[7]

Next morning, December 8, Borden was up and dressed and ready for a nine o'clock meeting at City Hall with the members of the Halifax Relief Committee. Informed that a trainload of doctors, nurses, and Red Cross workers from Boston had arrived during the night, he waded through the snow to the MCPS train and came on board to introduce himself to the Americans. In more settled times or with advance notice, this would have been a "photo op" for a prime minister. However, on this day and on this occasion, there were no cameras there to record the moment. Borden shook the Americans' hands and thanked them for coming to Halifax's aid so quickly. Their relief train, he told them, was the first to arrive in the city. That was not true. Ever the deft politician, Borden failed to add the qualifying words "from the United States." Trains from across Nova Scotia and New Brunswick had already arrived.

When Ratshesky, who by now was more anxious than ever to get to work, asked Borden what he and his relief team could do first, the prime minister shrugged. "I don't know," he replied. "It's all confusion."[8] Borden invited Ratshesky and senior members of his team to accompany him to City Hall for a meeting with local organizers of the relief efforts. The deputy mayor of Halifax, the city's police chief, Nova Scotia's Lieutenant Governor, and Liberal premier George H. Murray would all be there to provide briefings on the status of the relief efforts already under way. Borden planned to use the occasion to announce the federal government's intention to provide Halifax with $500,000 in emergency funding, with more money to follow as needed.

Borden, Ratshesky, and senior members of the MCPS relief team piled into a sleigh that disaster relief workers had been using to transport the wounded to hospital and the dead to the morgue. Muddy slush and dried blood had soiled the seats on which Borden and his guests sat in their fine greatcoats. The young man who drove the sleigh advised his passengers that he had been on the job for twenty-four hours straight and was dog-tired. However, he wanted to stay busy; his wife and four children had all died in the explosion, and he did not want to stop for fear he would surrender to his grief. It was, as Cap Ratshesky put it, "a gruesome start" to his stay in Halifax.[9]

The sun was shining, the wind was light, and the temperature was a crisp fourteen degrees Fahrenheit (minus ten Celsius), yet the mile-and-a-half ride downtown took more than an hour. The snowdrifts were waist-high, and in places along Barrington Street, it was necessary to set aside explosion debris before traffic could pass.

When finally the prime minister and his party reached City Hall, "an awful sight presented itself," Ratshesky would recall. "Buildings shattered on all sides; chaos apparent; no order existed."[10] That assessment was unduly harsh; appearances were somewhat deceiving. Deputy Mayor Henry Colwell, the members of the Halifax Relief Committee, and other city officials had made some progress toward stabilizing the situation. They had done their best in difficult circumstances; however, to a person they were exhausted. Colwell himself had slept for just two hours in the previous three days; many of his colleagues were in the same situation.

The hub of the City Hall relief efforts was a couple of rooms where staff had boarded up the broken windows. The workspace was now jammed with the city staff and volunteers who were doing their best to bring order to the chaos, but their efforts were producing mixed results at best. Most of the rooms in City Hall were ice cold. "Women and children filed through the building's wretched and snow-covered offices and corridors all day long with blankets under their arms."[11] When Cap Ratshesky saw this, he felt stunned. "Everything was in turmoil, and apparently the first necessity was organization," he concluded.[12]

When he broached the subject with Deputy Mayor Henry Colwell and other local officials, Ratshesky did so "very carefully, as the situation was delicate and we did not wish to appear as intruders."[13]

Fortunately, John Moors, an American Red Cross official who was a member of the Massachusetts relief team, had experience in disaster relief work—having helped restore order after the great San Francisco earthquake of 1906. At Ratshesky's urging, Moors tactfully suggested that "the good men and women of Halifax" who had gotten the emergency operations started deserved a rest. Moors floated the idea that perhaps it was time to move the city's relief headquarters to a quieter, more suitable venue. When heads around the meeting table nodded in agreement, someone suggested that the City Club, a fine building a block to the south, might be suitable. The members of the Halifax Relief Committee along with Ratshesky and his team went to investigate.

There were two private "gentlemen's clubs" in Halifax in 1917: the City Club and the Halifax Club. The former, a block from City Hall along Barrington Street, was the choice of Halifax's managerial class. The latter, on nearby Hollis Street, had been established in 1862 by a group of fifteen of the city's leading business leaders. In socially stratified Halifax, the upscale, exclusive Halifax Club was the preferred choice of the city's elite—among them were Prime Minister Robert Borden and the men who owned businesses that members of the City Club managed on their behalf.

Interestingly, Cap Ratshesky, the doctors in his team, the Red Cross officials, and the newspaper reporters from Boston settled in at the Halifax Club for the duration of what would be a five-day stay. Robert Borden made all the arrangements. "The club ordinarily had no sleeping facilities, and I am told that it is the first time in its history that beds have been set up," Ratshesky noted in a report he wrote for Governor McCall of Massachusetts. [14]

Whether or not he knew it is unclear, but the Halifax Club—like most such establishments for gentlemen in other cities across North America in 1917—did not accept Jews as members. However, these were extraordinary times in Halifax, after all.

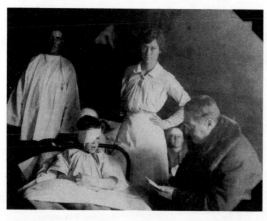

CAP RATSHESKY (RIGHT), THE SPECIAL REPRESENTATIVE OF MASSACHUSETTS GOVERNOR SAMUEL MCCALL, WAS A PIVOTAL FIGURE IN ESTABLISHING EMERGENCY MEDICAL CARE IN HALIFAX IN THE DAYS AFTER THE DISASTER. (JEWISH HERITAGE CENTER AT THE NEW ENGLAND HISTORIC GENEALOGICAL SOCIETY)

THE TEMPORARY MORGUE at Chebucto School was a grim place; morgues tend to be that way. Haligonians who visited in the days following the explosion came reluctantly and with fear in their hearts. They came seeking something they desperately wanted, yet dreaded finding: the sense of closure that came with recovering the remains of missing loved ones. It was with that in mind that Ada Moore paid a visit.

She was a member of the Jackson clan, one of the eight children of Elizabeth and James Jackson. At age thirty-nine, she was a younger sister of Mary Jean Hinch. In some regards, the women were alike; in others, they could not have been more different.

Both were married. Both were the mothers of large broods—Mary Jean had given birth to ten children, Ada to nine. Both were strong-willed and determined. However, while Mary Jean was a devout Roman Catholic who revelled in her role as mother, wife, and homemaker, her sister Ada had rejected her religious faith. She questioned the patriarchal nature of the Church and no longer attended church or bothered with confession. Her intellectual rebellion did not end there. She was a feminist long before the word came into vogue.

Ada Moore made no secret of her resentment of the notion that society expected, demanded even, that women were tied to home, hearth, and children, while men were free to come and go as they pleased and had the vote.

Despite her feisty demeanour and her skepticism about religion, Ada still cared deeply for her sister and for her family. "Quick and clever, she also had a passion for organization, and most of the Jacksons were content to sit back and let Ada take charge of the constant stream of family weddings, births, birthdays, and anniversaries."[15] In the years after the great Halifax harbour explosion, there would be a lot fewer such events in that area of the Richmond neighbourhood—from Veith Street over to Duffus Street—that Ada, only somewhat in jest, referred to as "Jacksonville."[16]

The explosion had decimated this entire area, and Ada had suffered crushing, almost unbelievable loss. Of the eight siblings, four brothers and at least two sisters had perished; Ada remained unsure about the fate of her remaining sister, Mary Jean. The death toll among family members in Ada's own household had been no less horrific. The explosion had levelled her family home at 1496 Barrington Street, killing her husband Charlie and five of Ada's nine children; the other four had suffered serious injuries. Ada was one of the few members of the extended Jackson family who had come through the disaster without serious injury. In total, forty-six of her kinfolk were gone. The majority of those who survived had sustained serious injuries. Ada knew the explosion had destroyed the Hinch house on Veith Street, and so she assumed her sister Mary Jean and her entire family all were dead.[17]

Ada had cried until she could cry no more. She had then steeled herself and set to work comforting family members and searching for the bodies of those who had died. She wanted to make sure all of them received proper funerals. Ada was viewing bodies in the basement of the Chebucto School morgue when she felt a tap on her shoulder. To her surprise, her greeter was Hugh Mills. Ada had seen him around on Veith Street; he was nineteen, the same age as her sister Mary Jean's eldest daughter.

Hugh Mills explained that he was a volunteer worker at the morgue. Today he was helping to unload newly recovered bodies from the trucks. The work was difficult and emotionally draining, but he wanted to do what he could to help.

"Mrs. Moore, I don't know whether you know it or not, but your sister, Mrs. Hinch, is alive," said Hugh.[18]

Ada gasped. She could scarcely believe her ears as Hugh Mills recounted how he and the two American sailors had rescued Mary Jean from under a pile of rubble on Veith Street. She was in bad shape, Hugh said, but medical staff aboard the American hospital ship the *Old Colony* were caring for her, and she seemed to be on the road to recovery. Ada was overjoyed that her sister was alive. She immediately rushed over to Pier 4 at the Naval Dockyard, where the *Old Colony* sat moored. There she met with an American navy doctor who explained that debris thrown up by the explosion shock wave had struck Mary Jean. The haematoma she had suffered on the right side of her body was, the doctor said, the worst such injury he had ever seen. The force of the trauma had also fractured Mary Jean's hip, but amazingly neither that injury nor any of the myriad cuts and bruises she had suffered were life threatening. Mary Jean faced a long, painful, and difficult recuperation, but she would recover from her injuries. That she did. Four months after the disaster,

DESPITE HER TERRIBLE
INJURIES, MARY JEAN HINCH
SURVIVED HER EXPLOSION
ORDEAL AND LIVED TO THE
AGE OF EIGHTY-ONE, DYING
OF CANCER IN 1958.
(COURTESY OF DIANE WALKER/
ROWENA MAHAR)

she would give birth to the baby boy she had been carrying on December 6.

Ada Moore's reunion with her sister was tearful but joyous. Both women were saddened beyond measure by the losses they had endured. Ada drew upon her inner strength for solace, whereas Mary Jean found comfort in her religious faith. She mentioned to sister Ada that Hugh Mills and the two American sailors who had rescued her had visited several times and brought "little treats." A Catholic priest had also come by her bed to offer communion and hear her confession.

"Ada's first reaction was one of frustration. Confession? How in hell could Dude commit any sins lying in bed unable to even stand up?"[19] It was not easy for her to do so, but Ada Moore bit her tongue and made no comment. She was delighted that her sister was alive, and really, that was the only thing that mattered.

THE HOLDER FAMILY, like so many other Halifax families, was home-less after the explosion. The two Holder girls who were of school age, eight-year-old Doris and six-year-old Jean, were almost as distraught that Chebucto School was closed for the foreseeable future as they were that their family home at 488 Robie Street had suffered heavy damage. The base-ment of the girls' school was now a temporary morgue. Jean Holder knew this because when she and her mother walked by the school one day, they saw a "low sleigh piled high with the load covered with [a] tarpaulin . . . [that] didn't hide the fact that the load was bodies. I thought that all the legs and arms were covered with black stockings. It was years later that I realized there were no black stockings—that was burned or frozen human flesh."[20] Small wonder that when classes eventually resumed, Jean Holder was reluctant to return to her school. "I'd go . . . but once I was there I wouldn't enter the school." When the morning bell rang and the other children went to their classroom, Jean Holder ran home. This behaviour lasted for several months, until she missed her friends so much that she returned to school. However, when she did so, she refused to ever go into the basement.

SEARCHERS USED SLEDS TO TRANSPORT TO THE MORGUE BODIES OF THE DEAD THAT WERE COLLECTED ON THE SNOWY STREETS OF HALIFAX. (BAIN COLLECTION, U.S. LIBRARY OF CONGRESS)

THE CITY CLUB proved to be the ideal location for the administrative headqua rters of Halifax emergency relief operations. Once the group of officials who had trekked over from City Hall made the decision to set up shop here, they quickly went to work. Their first order of business was a pep talk from Cap Ratshesky, who was nothing if not energetic and bubbling with all the certainty and "can-do" spirit that characterized Americans of the day. Next, John Moors of the American Red Cross stressed that he and his colleagues were there to help and offer advice, not to run the relief operation or serve on committees. Moors was sensitive to the need for him to stay in the background and not be pushy or arrogant, but he did offer several suggestions that proved invaluable. He urged the members of the executive of the Halifax Relief Committee to maintain tight control over subcommittees, and he stressed the need for centralized control of admin-istra tive functions—in particular, finances and the distribution and approval processes for official records.

Cap Ratshesky seconded Moors' message about the need for organiza-tion and "process." However, being a man of action, he had a far more immediate and pressing concern: he wanted to find a building the Americans could use as their base of operations and as a temporary hospital. Ratshesky found what he was seeking in Bellevue Mansion, a tumbledown Regency-era townhouse in the city's downtown. Located on the northeast corner of Queen Street and Spring Garden Road, the century-old building had recently served as a club for army officers from the local garrison. Bellevue had s uffered some explosion damage, but the structure itself remained sound and serviceable. When Ratshesky asked to use it, Major-General Benson, the senior militiaman in Halifax, made it happen.

"Under Ratshesky's direction, Canadian officials—as well as Major Harold Giddings of the Massachusetts State Guard, Lieutenant-Colonel Frede rick McKelvey Bell, assistant director of medical services for the Canadian armed forces, and fifty of the crew of the *Old Colony* managed to turn old Bellevue Mansion into Bellevue Hospital."[21] After clearing out the furniture, the sailors set about fixing broken windows and doors. They scrubbed floors and walls and moved in hospital beds, tables, desks, and medical supplies.

Word quickly got around that the American medical team were planning to open their hospital, and by nightfall on Sunday, December 9, patients already occupied sixty-five of the facility's 100 beds. When Prime Minister Borden dropped by for a quick visit, he grew tearful. "[He] went from cot to cot, speaking to the wounded men, women, and children, many of whom he knew personally." [22]

Above the front door of Bellevue Hospital, a Stars and Stripes flag fluttered in the breeze. Passersby who saw it nodded their understanding, for that flag brought to mind a popular patriotic song of the day. The refr ain by American tunesmith George M. Cohan proclaimed, "The Yanks are coming." Now in Halifax, as in Europe, the Yanks had arrived. And they were making a difference—a huge one. [23]

THE MASSACHUSETTS STATE GUARD MEDICAL UNIT POSED FOR A PHOTO IN FRONT OF THE TEMPORARY AMERICAN HOSPITAL ON SPRING GARDEN ROAD. (NOVA SCOTIA ARCHIVES)

CHAPTER 27

The people of Nova Scotia—like all residents of Canada's Atlantic provinces—are nothing if not resilient. Yet, life in Halifax would, indeed could, never be the same after the tragic events of December 6.

No city in 1917 was ready to deal with a crisis as extraordinary, devastating, or nightmarish as the one Halifax faced. Halifax simply did not have the resources to cope with a disaster that was—and thankfully remains—unprecedented in Canadian history in terms of the number of lives lost, the staggering injury toll, and the amount of property damage incurred.

The military assumed the lion's share of the responsibility for restoring order, fighting fires, rescuing the injured, and recovering the bodies of the dead. "The [Halifax] garrison had an organizational structure and trained manpower on the spot, including medical services, engineers, transport, logistics, administration, security, and other services," historian John Griffith Armstrong would observe. "While the point is hardly profound, neither is it necessarily obvious: soldiers train for war; war is a disaster. The Halifax explosion was a disaster, and in the short term the militia organizational structure provided a template for effective reaction to the crisis."[1]

By Saturday, December 8, just two days after the explosion, Rear Admiral Chambers advised his superiors in London that "despite the deep wounds, Halifax is operational as a naval base and as a port."[2] With repair work at the Naval Dockyard under way in earnest, "convoy work can be carried out immediately."[3]

Some aspects of everyday life in Halifax were back up and running as soon as the military were able to stabilize conditions in the city and reopen the port. Despite the stormy weather, rail service between Halifax and Montreal was back on track the day after the disaster. By Sunday, work crews had cleared and repaired the train tracks leading to the ruins of the North Street Station.

Although the post office in the Richmond neighbourhood suffered extensive damage and the postmaster and one of his carriers were dead, postal service in Halifax resumed on Monday, December 10. Some banks opened for business that same day, as did those stores that had escaped major damage from the explosion, the ensuing fires, or looters. One shop-keeper, the proprietor of "a small shop of the corner variety" on Veith Street, lost her business, but because it was not open when the explosion levelled the building, she escaped injury. The woman accepted her loss and invited customers to take whatever stock they could recover from the ruins of her shop. "I can go to service again," she said.[4]

For the first ten days after the disaster, food was in short supply in Halifax and rationing was in effect. Military-run food depots distributed more than 16,000 meals daily. It was not until December 17 that disaster relief officials announced that those who had registered for food rations could begin to shop in the stores again. Other aspects of everyday life took longer to return.

Government officials postponed voting in the December 17 federal election until January 28.[5] And to the delight of many children—at least initially—school board officials announced that Halifax schools would remain closed until March 1918. Sunday church services went ahead only in those neighbourhoods where property damage was relatively light. Churches in the city's North End that were in ruins and those houses of worship that were still standing in other areas of the city remained closed until repairs were completed; in many cases this would take months to happen. Even on Christmas Day, one of the most joyful celebrations on the Christian calendar, churches held few services. Yuletide festivities were restrained; few people felt much like celebrating.

Halifax's tram system provided limited service for several weeks after the explosion. Work crews had partially repaired the electrical grid within days of the disaster, but it took longer for workers to clear the debris from the tracks. Likewise, the availability of telephone and telegraph service remained limited, although workers did manage to restore one emergency line within an hour of the disaster.

Despite the snow and cold of one of the most severe Halifax winters in recent memory at that time, the search for victims in the surreal landscape of the Richmond neighbourhood ruins continued throughout the holiday season and into the new year. A week after the explosion, hundreds of corpses remained unclaimed at the Chebucto School morgue. City officials pegged December 16 as the last day residents could stop by to search for and claim the bodies of their loved ones. All of Halifax's daily newspapers had resumed publishing by the weekend of December 8–9, with lists of the names of the dead and missing filling many pages. This made for sobering reading, especially the detailed accounts of the remains of the unidentified. "No. 471. Female. Age about four years," read a typical listing. "Face completely disfigured. Light brown hair, blue sweater, black-and-white striped underwear, black-and-brown striped dress. Envelope found on body addressed Mrs. Julia Carroll, 1419 Barrington Street. Inside envelope receipt from Singer Sewing Machine Company, Halifax, issued 27 August 1917."[6]

That description of someone's child, cold impersonal words on a page, offered only hints as to the identity of such a young victim and a tantalizing glimpse into lives that the explosion had cut short so suddenly, so needlessly, and so tragically. More than 250 youngsters under the age of five died in the Halifax explosion. Scores more were gravely injured. Among them was thirty-month-old Eric Davidson, who was the youngest person to lose his sight in the disaster. Hundreds of other Haligonians suffered serious eye injuries. Fortunately, Halifax had a school for the blind, and director Sir Frederick Fraser hired extra staff to help treat the wounded. Fraser also launched a fundraising campaign that eventually raised about $72,000 for care and programming. Meanwhile, the American Red Cross provided funding for a husband-and-wife team from New York City, experts in caring for the blind, to visit Halifax for a few weeks. They accorded special attention to the thirty-seven Haligonians who were blinded as a result of explosion-related injuries; twenty of them were women between the ages of twenty-one and forty.

AMERICAN RED CROSS CANTEEN WORKERS WERE AMONG THE MEDICAL AID WORKERS WHO RUSHED TO HALIFAX IN THE WAKE OF THE EXPLOSION. (U.S. LIBRARY OF CONGRESS)

A dozen "oculists"—as ophthalmologists were known at the time—had provided emergency medical care to 592 patients in Halifax. Those same doctors performed 249 enucleations, removing eyeballs too badly damaged to be saved. Sixteen people had both eyes removed.[7]

THE EFFORTS OF the medical relief team from Massachusetts continued all out as Halifax's recovery began building momentum. A second group of doctors and nurses had arrived from Boston on December 9, and the next day a train carrying a 105-member Red Cross unit from Rhode Island and a Christian Science medical team from Boston reached Halifax. However, it was the Massachusetts–Halifax expedition team that continued to garner much of the media attention. In good measure that was because of Cap Ratshesky. He was here, there, and everywhere in Halifax. In doing so, he won the respect and trust of the locals he worked with and praise from the media. Halifax newspapers applauded Ratshesky and "lauded the [Massachusetts relief team] . . . as a shining example of 'American efficiency,'"[8] while in the words of the *Boston Post*'s correspondent, Ratshesky was "practically [a] dictator in the relief work in this city."[9]

Lieutenant-Colonel Frederick McKelvey Bell, the chair of the Halifax medical relief committee and head of the military hospitals in Halifax, echoed that praise; however, "hidden beneath Bell's words . . . was a certain resentment towards the Americans."[10] The men and women of the Canadian Army Medical Corps were providing much of the emergency medical care to the people of Halifax, yet the American visitors were basking in a disproportionate share of media attention.

The relationship between the Canadian military—the RCN, in particular—and Halifax was as complex as it was curious. There was much skepticism in Halifax about the value and integrity of the RCN; "the aversion of Admiral Kingsmill [the head of the RCN] for traditional political patronage in purchasing and in granting Canadian contracts did little to improve local opinion [of him]."[11]

It is a measure of the degree of Kingsmill's unpopularity in Halifax—with the mayor and the local media, the *Herald* newspaper in particular—that when the admiral visited the city on December 10–11, he slipped in and out of town with no fanfare. Kingsmill came to assess the situation at the Naval Dockyard and to check on the condition of his son, who was in the military and had sustained injuries in the explosion. Kingsmill took the young man with him when he returned to Ottawa.

IN ADDITION TO emergency medical care for the injured, food and shelter were the most urgent needs of the people of Halifax in the wake of the disaster. The military were quick to feed the hungry at hastily erected emergency field kitchens, and within a few days of the disaster, needy families were receiving food hampers provided by the city and private donors. Although City Hall was no longer the headquarters of the Halifax Relief Committee, the building continued to be both a depot for food collection and distribution and an organizational hub for emergency medical care. It also was the venue for intrigue. When in the hours after the explosion bottles of confiscated alcohol disappeared from the office of Edwin Tracey, the province's Temperance Act inspector, he suspected the heist was "an inside job." A special City Hall committee was formed to investigate. Halifax newspapers reported the heist, and police questioned city officials and councillors. However, in the end, the thirsty thieves were never caught, and the matter was soon forgotten.[12] There were far more pressing matters to deal with. As the days passed, the nature of the care being provided began to change. Not all injuries Haligonians had suffered were physical.

The disaster had left thousands of people homeless and in mental distress. Dr. William McDonald, a neurologist visiting from Boston, spent his time in Halifax treating patients who were suffering from what today would be diagnosed as post-traumatic stress disorder (PTSD). And before McDonald returned home after several weeks in Halifax, he handed off his patient caseload to local doctors. A clinic at the city's YMCA was caring for more than 1,200 patients. The stress that many people were feeling would become chronic. The problems this created were myriad and significant.

Initially, the homeless found refuge in "the less damaged public buildings, such as the theatres. . . . In addition, countless private citizens offered to house the shelterless in their own homes, specifying the number of families or of individuals they could take in."[13] A longer-term solution to the housing shortage began taking shape on December 8, when members of the Halifax Relief Committee created a sub-committee to oversee housing reconstruction efforts. Chaired by lawyer G.F. Pearson and managed by army colonel Robert S. Low, who had experience designing army camps, this group set to work compiling ledgers in which canvassers recorded information on the properties that the explosion had damaged or destroyed. Low also involved himself when soldiers began erecting tent housing for 1,000 homeless people on Halifax Common. Monthly rents here began at five dollars for a basic two-room unit.

That initiative signalled the start of a flurry of activity that led to the construction of three temporary tenement-style housing projects on public lands. The architects of these developments designed them to have a five-year lifespan and to be demolished quickly. The reconstruction committee, which was a subcommittee of the Halifax Relief Committee, hired workers and tradespeople to erect these buildings and to repair damaged homes. Before long, "construction was taking place at such speed that the reconstruction department reckoned that one apartment was being built every hour."[14]

The most ambitious of the new housing projects rose on the Halifax Exhibition Grounds in the city's North End. At the time, it was reputed to be the world's largest apartment complex. Paid for and largely furnished with money provided by the Massachusetts–Halifax Relief Fund, the sprawling Governor McCall apartment "settlement" consisted of thirty-five individual buildings. Workers took just thirteen days to build each of these jury-rigged, two-storey frame structures. Although they were not much to look at—a letter writer to the *Herald* newspaper described them as "temporary shacks"[15]—they were functional. Monthly rents in the twelve-unit buildings, which housed 2,200 people, was twelve dollars for a four-room flat.

Many of the tenants in the McCall apartments and the other emergency accommodations were so delighted to have a place to call home again that they wrote thank-you letters to the Massachusetts–Halifax Relief Committee. "I might say, dear sir, that the one bright spot in this awful year of trouble has been what those generous people of Massachusetts have done for us," said one letter-writer.[16] "I now write these few lines to try and thank-you for your great kindness in helping us to furnish a little home after losing all we had," said another.[17]

THE THIRTY-FIVE BUILDINGS IN THE SPRAWLING GOVERNOR MCCALL APARTMENT COMPLEX, ERECTED DURING THE WINTER OF 1917–1918, PROVIDED TEMPORARY HOUSING FOR 2,200 PEOPLE. (WILLIAM JAMES FAMILY FONDS, CITY OF TORONTO ARCHIVES)

Despite such expressions of gratitude, tenants had many problems and complaints. The threat of infectious diseases—tuberculosis and influenza in particular—was a constant concern in such crowded living conditions, and recreational facilities were in short supply. Even more problematic was the resentment and anger that festered when rumours began making the rounds that some people were receiving preferential treatment that gave them first pick of the emergency housing and generous cash allowances to cover losses they claimed to have suffered. Such concerns took on new life after the Borden government in Ottawa, acting on requests from the city of Halifax and the province of Nova Scotia, issued an Order-in-Council under the War Measures Act to establish the Halifax Relief Commission.[18]

This new agency, which replaced the volunteer committee that had formed impulsively on December 6, assumed long-term responsibility for four vital aspects of disaster relief efforts: medical aid, rehabilitation, reconstruction, and finance. The HRC, under the leadership of lawyer T. Sherman Rogers, also took control of the purse strings of $21 million in relief money the various governments, corporations, and individuals had donated. This development took on added significance when the Nova Scotia legislature began considering a bill to broaden the commission's powers, authorizing the agency to "repair, rebuild or restore any building or property damaged, destroyed or lost in or by reason of the said disaster, or compensate the owner thereof, or any person having an interest therein."[19]

Both the federal and provincial governments supported the HRC; however, many Halifax residents and some city council members—the people with the most at stake—had reservations. A large and raucous crowd turned out when a committee of the provincial House of Assembly held a town hall–type meeting to "state their opinions on Bill No. 82, An Act to Incorporate the Halifax Relief Commission."[20] A majority of the attendees were unhappy North End residents. "If there was a man or

MASSACHUSETTS GOVERNOR SAMUEL MCCALL (CENTRE, WEARING DERBY HAT) VISITED HALIFAX IN
NOVEMBER 1918 TO TOUR THE TEMPORARY HOUSING COMPLEX THAT BORE HIS NAME AND TO ACCEPT
AN HONORARY DEGREE FROM DALHOUSIE UNIVERSITY. (NOVA SCOTIA ARCHIVES)

woman who had a favourable opinion regarding the proposed legislation, that opinion remained unexpressed, while applause of various degrees of intensity greeted every adverse criticism of the bill,"[21] the *Herald* reported.

In particular, many of the meeting attendees attacked the HRC because of a widespread and growing public perception that commission officials were drawing fat salaries and living "high on the hog" in hotels while many of those who had lost everything in the disaster remained homeless. That latter notion arose because HRC staff were working out of rented space in Halifax hotels while a new headquarters for the commission was under construction.

Another sore point with some people was the HRC's plan to expropriate a huge parcel of land in the North End to make way for the redevelopment of a "planned community." The original owners of affected properties were to receive compensation, but they feared it would not be for fair-market value. Others were concerned that they had no opportunity to offer input on what the HRC had in mind for the neighbourhood. Among the protesters was Dr. Arthur Hawkins, a prominent North End physician who was a candidate in the upcoming mayoralty election. When Hawkins stood up at an April meeting, he argued that it was "unjust that this government should attempt to take money which has been contributed to those people who have lost their all, and expend it for a fanciful town planning scheme. It is a blow to democracy. The people should have a chance to build the homes they want."[22] It was evident that Hawkins was giving voice to a popular sentiment, for he rode the tide of suspicion and discontent to a victory in the mayoralty election on April 24.

DESPITE PUBLIC OPPOSITION, the provincial government forged ahead with its plans when it passed a bill that expanded the HRC's mandate and its powers. The commission became "responsible for both the physical and financial rehabilitation of the explosion's victims and the reconstruction of the devastated area."[23] On paper, the HRC's priorities seemed straightforward. However, the problems it faced were complex, myriad, and far-reaching. One of the commission's first moves was to announce it was accepting applications for financial relief from those who had suffered explosion-related losses. Payouts were available for medical care, transportation, funereal fees, and general living expenses. Because the formula the agency adopted for the living expense was based on income prior to December 6, high-income households—which also had relatively high expenses—were eligible to receive more money than were blue-collar or low-income individuals or families. This became a source of controversy and a flashpoint for public anger. Nonetheless, applications for compensation poured in by the thousands.

Many insurance companies refused to honour claims for personal or real property; standard insurance policies of the time covered loss due to fire but not explosion. Lawyers for the insurance companies argued the explosion in the harbour was the fault of the military and was war-related. That being the case, it followed that the government should be responsible for covering people's losses, not insurers. In the end, after four months of wrangling and discussion, the HRC and the insurance companies reached an agreement under which insurers paid householders and small businesses twenty cents on the dollar in compensation; large businesses got thirty-five cents on the dollar.

The HRC set up three new tribunals to deal with residents' claims. One was an appraisal board that considered losses of more than $5,000; the other two dealt with claims of less than $100 submitted by individuals and shop owners who had lost merchandise. Disgruntled Haligonians who sought financial relief were quick to test the new system and its limits. They filed more than 16,400 claims with a total value of $3.5 million. That is an average of about $210 per claim; a dollar went much further in 1917 than it does today.

In order to catalogue and process such a huge volume of claims in an efficient and timely manner, the HRC enlisted local lawyers to act as judges. Each compensation claimant had a maximum of ten minutes to make his or her case. Those who argued persuasively collected a cheque on the spot. However, "few received the amount asked for, as a percentage of the total sum was nearly always deducted."[24] This was a further cause for disappointment, and it led to much grumbling and anger.

Rehabilitation Committee chair J. Harry Winfield was so frustrated with the carping and criticism that he lashed out, lecturing journalists on the difference between "rehabilitation" and "restitution."[25] In his regular job as general manager of Maritime Telegraph and Telephone, Winfield was unaccustomed to being in the public spotlight or suffering criticism. His comments inflamed an already volatile situation and opened Winfield and the HRC to still more criticism and to demands for increased transparency in the process. A letter writer to the *Herald* expressed some widely held frustrations when he demanded to know where all the money that donors far and wide had given for emergency relief in Halifax had gone. "Let us get done with all the 'log rolling' that is going on in the city for appointment of fat jobs to [the] commission." The letter-writer then went on to chide the committee for allotting money as if the people who applied for relief "were mendicants humbly approaching the Throne of Plenty and begging on bended knees a few dollars out of the vast sums of money that have been contributed for their relief."[26]

NO LESS CONTENTIOUS than the scheme for processing property claims was the HRC's system for awarding cash sums to workers who had been injured by the explosion. Some had lost wages in the short term; others had suffered long-term disabilities and were unable to work, in some cases ever again.

Nova Scotia in 1917 was one of just two Canadian provinces with a Workmen's Compensation Board (WCB) system. The process, which was geared to the needs of working men, paid an injured worker up to fifty-five per cent of pre-accident salary.[27] Many of those who filed the paperwork for a WCB claim came up against the same sort of legal technicalities as did those who filed insurance claims. Because most workers had incurred their injuries in the explosion rather than as a direct result of being on the job, they failed to qualify for WCB benefits. The only option open to them was to seek payments and pensions from the HRC.

In addition to disabled workers, the applicants included—among others—widows, widowers who now had no one to care for their children, and orphaned children. The HRC was not part of the WCB system and had its own rules, regulations, and decision-making process. The HRC modelled its pension schedule on the one used by the Canadian military. Under that scheme, a widow with property worth less than

$3,000 was eligible to receive a pension of between forty-five and sixty dollars per month, with eight dollars more for every *living* child. Someone such as Mary Jean Hinch, who had lost her husband and ten children (but was pregnant at the time of the disaster), was eligible for a maximum of sixty-eight dollars per month for life.

SO INTENT WERE HRC officials on ensuring that no one defrauded the system that a bureaucratic thicket quickly grew up around the agency. HRC caseworkers set to work interviewing claimants, recording the details of their financial status, their biographical information, and the specifics of any medical conditions they or their family members were dealing with. The process was intrusive, and privacy concerns were minimal to non-existent.

A SINGLE HEADSTONE MARKS THE GRAVES OF MARY JEAN HINCH'S HUSBAND AND TEN CHILDREN, ALL OF WHOM DIED WHEN THE EXPLOSION LEVELLED THEIR VEITH STREET HOME. (COURTESY OF KRISTIN LIPSCOMBE)

In retrospect, it is understandable why the vetting and evaluation process for individuals was a source of irritation for those who came up against it and for liberal-minded members of the community; Judge Benjamin Russell was among this latter group. The former Member of Parliament for Halifax criticized the entire compensation process, which he said was plagued with "an overdose of business efficiency and social service pedantry."[28] Indeed, it was with an eye to ensuring that claimants were not able to achieve a financial windfall by living together or pooling their incomes that HRC examiners delved into the intimate details of claimants' personal lives. For example, "if a woman's morality came into question, she could lose her pension temporarily or permanently."[29]

Such bureaucratic intrusions into the circumstances of people who had suffered so much pain and who had incurred such horrific losses did not seem fair to many people. As a result, the mood of Halifax residents began to change.

CHAPTER 28

Toward a New "Normal"

Halifax, Nova Scotia, Mid-December 1917

In the first minutes, hours, and days of anguish after the explosion of December 6, the people of Halifax were in a state of numbed shock. However, as the realities of the situation became apparent, the despair that had gripped the city faded. Barely a week after the disaster, the first of several commercially produced booklets of photos of the ruins ("Single copies 50¢") went on sale. "By early 1918, three firms had produced about sixty-one different views of the explosion on post cards."[1] There was also an illustrated booklet entitled "Impressions of the Halifax Disaster," written by Lieutenant-Colonel Frederick McKelvey Bell, assistant director of medical services for the Canadian Armed Forces. Interest in the Halifax disaster was intense and it was widespread.

The air of crisis lessened as shipments of relief aid—food, clothing, medical supplies, and desperately needed window glass—flowed into Halifax. In fact, so much aid arrived that Cap Ratshesky appealed to relief agencies in Boston to stop sending such shipments. "Please send money instead," he asked.[2]

Life in Halifax was slowly starting to get back to a semblance of normal—or at least to the new "normal." By the morning of December 12, the
city's medical needs had begun to stabilize. A large number of doctors
from neighbouring communities were in town to volunteer their services,
and "altogether there was an abundance of professional help at hand."[3] As
a result, naval ships the USS *Tacoma* and the USS *Von Steuben* departed.
The relief team from Massachusetts also began preparing to hand off
operations of Bellevue Hospital to a volunteer team from Rhode Island. At
the same time, a fresh contingent of doctors and nurses from Maine were
busy setting up another hospital. Cap Ratshesky and his team finally had
time to tour Halifax's devastated North End, doing so in two new trucks
the state of Massachusetts had donated to the relief effort. Then at nine
o'clock on the morning of December 13, a Boston-bound train carrying
the volunteer members of the Massachusetts Committee on Public Safety's
emergency relief team left Halifax. Cap Ratshesky and his team of
Massachusetts volunteers departed from a profoundly different city than
the shattered one in which they had arrived on December 8. The New
Englanders were gone, but they were not forgotten.

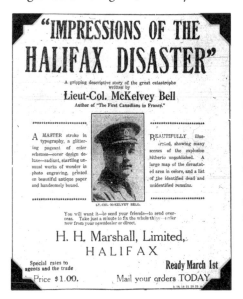

LIEUTENANT-COLONEL FREDERICK
MCKELVEY BELL, ASSISTANT DIRECTOR
OF MEDICAL SERVICES FOR THE
CANADIAN ARMED FORCES, WAS JUST ONE
OF THE RELIEF WORKERS WHO WROTE OF
THEIR EXPERIENCES IN THE WAKE
OF THE EXPLOSION. (ADVERTISEMENT
IN THE *HALIFAX HERALD*, 1918)

Following his return to Boston, Ratshesky would continue his successful business career, his political involvements, and his support for charitable causes. In 1930, President Herbert Hoover would appoint him as America's ambassador to Czechoslovakia, a post he held for two years. Ratshesky would die on March 15, 1943, at the age of seventy-seven; however, the good he did continued to live on—and does to this day—through the A.C. Ratshesky Foundation and the world-renowned Beth Israel Deaconess Medical Center in Boston.

Cap Ratshesky's contributions to the Halifax relief efforts would also come to be remembered each year at Christmas. In 1917, the people of Nova Scotia sent a huge Christmas tree to the city of Boston as a thank-you and a remembrance for the help the MCPS and the American Red Cross provided Halifax. In 1971 the Lunenburg County Christmas Tree Producers Association resurrected the gesture, and in 1976 the Nova Scotia government would take on responsibility for the practice, which has become a Yuletide tradition.

EVEN BEFORE LIFE RESUMED in Halifax, many people were demanding to know who had been responsible for the events of December 6. The day after the disaster the *Truro Daily News* was already calling for blood. "The party or parties responsible for such a needless collision with clear water, in broad daylight, should be hung in good old-fashioned style at the yard's arm."[4] The ever-excitable *Herald* seized ownership of the issue, demanding that authorities identify and punish whomever was responsible for the disaster. "If men higher up or lower down, through incompetency or duplicity, are to blame let it be known. If this was the work of the archenemy whose methods do not stop at killing women and children then the people want to know it. Halifax is deeply concerned in this. All of Canada is deeply concerned, and the people will not rest satisfied until the truth is known. We owe this much to the dead, the suffering wounded, and the friends who are left to sorrow."[5]

Initially, many people in Halifax assumed that German warships or Zeppelins had attacked the city. However, as the realization spread that the carnage and destruction were the result of an "accident" in the harbour, suspicions grew that German saboteurs had played a role or had even caused the disaster.

Halifax residents of German heritage wisely began keeping a low profile; a tide of anti-German hysteria and anger was rising. On December 10, acting on orders from the military authorities, Police Chief Frank Hanrahan had his police officers round up for questioning anyone they could find who had a German-sounding name.[6] Then on December 11, a Boston newspaper added fuel to the rumour mill when it reported that "a carrier pigeon wounded in the explosion of Thursday and with a message in German under its wing has been captured in a house in the burned area of Halifax."[7] Local newspapers picked up the same news report and fanned the fires of suspicion and outrage. "There are in Halifax today certain people of German extraction and birth whose citizenship in the Dominion has been respected since the war began, who have been allowed full freedom in our community to buy and sell, and to pursue their normal occupations," a *Herald* editorial thundered. "[They] have repaid us within the last few days by laughing at our distress and mocking our sorrow."[8]

No one knew what a German agent looked like, and so neighbours suddenly became suspicious of each other. Friends began looking twice at friends. Anyone with a tie to the *Imo* or the *Mont-Blanc* was suspect and paid a price. Harbour pilot Francis Mackey suffered persecution simply because he was an easy target. The Borden government in Ottawa was eager to divert attention from the roles federal bureaucrats and senior RCN officers had played in the run-up to the disaster in Halifax. As a result, Minister of Marine and Fisheries Charles C. Ballantyne and Admiral Charles Kingsmill, of the RCN, looked for scapegoats. Mackey, along with Captain Aimé Le Médec and Commander Evan Wyatt, filled the bill.

Many Halifax residents viewed Captain Aimé Le Médec with suspicion and hostility simply because he was French. The recent federal election campaign had raised awareness that French-speaking Quebeckers opposed Canada's involvement in the war. Never mind that Le Médec had never set foot in Quebec or that France was Canada's ally.

Commander Evan Wyatt was blamed for what had happened, in no small measure because of his own hubris and prickly personality, which put him into a position where his superiors deemed him to be expendable.

With both Captain From and pilot William Hayes being dead, the only person connected with the *Imo* who came under suspicion was the ship's helmsman. Johan Johansen was fortunate to have escaped death in the explosion. Newspaper reports quoting statements made by Francis Mackey gave credence to the notion there was "something erratic going on aboard the *Imo* just before the collision."[9]

Twenty-four-year-old Johan Johansen was the son of a mariner from Sandefjord, the same Norwegian port that was Captain From's hometown. Sandefjord was not a big place, and so it is likely that Johansen's father knew From or worked with him. If so, that familiarity could explain how Johansen came to be a member of the *Imo*'s crew. He had gone away to sea in 1907 at age fourteen and lived in the United States for five years. While there, Johansen had learned to speak English and briefly served as a quartermaster on an American navy ship. There was nothing in his maritime service record to indicate he had ever worked on a German ship or had any extended contact with Germans. However, "John" Johansen was fair-haired and Nordic. To mistrustful eyes in Halifax, he *looked* Germanic; there were not many Norwegians in Nova Scotia in 1917.

Johansen was also suspect because he had the *opportunity* to create havoc. His hands were on the wheel of the *Imo* when the ship crashed into the *Mont-Blanc*. The ensuing blast had wrecked the *Imo*'s bridge, killing

Captain From and pilot Hayes, and sending Johansen flying. Afterward, he was in shock, with glass fragments in his right eye and one of his knees swollen "to about three times the size of the other."[10] When sailors from a search party from HMS *Highflyer* rescued Johansen, he was in dire need of medical care.

After four days in the hospital's sick bay, on the morning of December 12, Johansen moved over to the American-run Bellevue Hospital, likely because he claimed to be living in Philadelphia or because he had made it known he had served for a time in the U.S. Navy. "Examination failed to disclose any serious trouble," Cap Ratshesky noted, "but for the purpose of observation, it was decided to keep him in the hospital twenty-four hours."[11]

It was here that the proverbial plot thickened. Soon after being admitted to Bellevue, Johansen was "observed limping toward a stairway."[12] One of the medical staff chased him back to bed, but that evening he tried to leave the building a second time. Intercepted by a volunteer nurse, Johansen offered the woman twenty-five dollars to let him "go home." She instead reported him to the military. When soldiers went through the young Norwegian's belongings, they found what they assumed were incriminating items. One was a book in Norwegian; the searchers mistook the text for German. They also found newspaper clippings about the explosion and some handwritten notes Johansen had made. It may well have been—and it would be understandable—that the young Norwegian had panicked after learning he was suspected of having murdered two men, seized control of the *Imo*, and then rammed her into the munitions ship *Mont-Blanc*.

Nonsensical though all of this was, the military arrested Johansen. "This man was regarded as a suspicious character at the hospital because he had asked for a newspaper and because he had tried to go out for a walk," Major-General Benson, the commanding officer of the local army garrison, would later explain.[13]

WHEN WAR BEGAN in Europe in July 1914, Canada had no civilian counter-intelligence capabilities. Given the country's physical location, its colonial history, and its lack of foreign involvements, there was no need for a cloak-and-dagger agency. However, events in Europe gave rise to "an impetus [for] the development of areas of intelligence expertise ... and domestic counter-intelligence [that] was stimulated above all by the fear of an intensive German campaign of sabotage mounted again the country."[14]

The Borden government called upon the Dominion Police, the Royal Northwest Mounted Police, military intelligence, and private detective agencies such as Pinkerton to serve as counter-intelligence agencies. Halifax being a garrison city and a vital wartime port, it was by default that the military was in charge of such activities there. So it was that with Johansen in the county jail, navy intelligence officers in Halifax began gathering information about him. As they did so, it soon became apparent there was nothing of value to be learned, certainly nothing that was significant or incriminating.

Word began circulating in the Allied intelligence community in North America that military officials in Halifax had nabbed a man who might be a German agent. On December 15, British military intelligence officials in New York City cabled Captain George Eldridge, the naval intelligence officer in Halifax, to ask if Johan Johansen "has cataract in left eye and is deaf."[15]

The information about the *Imo*'s helmsman that Eldridge sent to Captain Sir William Wiseman in New York, along with the requested photo, left no doubt that Johansen was not the man the British were seeking. "The description of the man is as follows: born September 1893 at Sandefjord, Norway. Parents Norwegian. Age 24. Height 5' 11". Complexion fresh. Hair fair. Clean-shaven. Weight 178 lbs. Strong build. Muscular. High cheekbones. Nose broad. Slightly turned up. Scar on index finger of left hand. General appearance that of a Norwegian."[16]

The fact Wiseman bothered to involve himself in the investigation into Johan Johansen's background is revealing. Wiseman was one of the key adjutants of Sir Mansfield Smith-Cumming, the first head of Britain's legendary Secret Intelligence Service (SIS)—a.k.a. MI5. Wiseman's purpose in being in New York was to grow the agency's network and its influence in North America.

As it happened, the British were not the only ones interested in knowing more about Johansen. Three days after Wiseman's query, a U.S. army intelligence officer in Baltimore, Maryland, contacted Halifax to ask for a detailed description and a photograph of one "John Johansen." The Americans were tracking a suspected German agent who was using that name or something similar.[17] It was all very tentative and speculative.

FEARS OF GERMAN SPIES and sabotage were real and warranted in all Allied countries during World War I. As a British observer had noted in the opening months of the conflict, "Systematic espionage is . . . and has been for many years a most cherished part of German war administration, developed with much forethought and with characteristic Teuton cunning."[18]

Prior to April 1917 and America's entry into the war, members of the German Foreign Office—the *Auswärtiges Amt*—who were stationed in the United States had "encouraged Germans to conduct sabotage activity for the benefit of Germany's war effort."[19] There was a substantial population of German immigrants in the country—more than eight million people. One German-language newspaper in New York City was selling 75,000 copies each day. Major urban centres such as New York, Milwaukee, and St. Louis all had sizeable German populations, and some smaller cities—Hoboken, New Jersey, for one—were almost entirely German.

A spy ring based in the German embassy in Washington was busy carrying out covert operations in New York City, the northeastern United States, and selected spots along the U.S.–Canada border. The Kaiser's agents were responsible for acts of sabotage across the United States—most notably the calamitous Black Tom explosion of July 30, 1916, in New York harbour. German agents and their hirelings also carried out a few attacks on Canadian targets. Most caused only minimal damage; the ineptitude of the perpetrators led to the foiling of others. For example, a plot to blow up the Welland Canal fell apart when the man hired to plant dynamite got into a dispute with the German agent who had recruited him. The agent refused to pay the man $2.57. The money was a day's wages that the would-be saboteur insisted were due. When the disgruntled man took his complaint to police, that put an end to any plot to blow up the Welland Canal.[20]

Any threat to Canada from German agents and saboteurs was more imaginary than real. The number of German immigrants to Canada, relatively speaking, was substantially lower than it was in the United States, and there were more and better targets for sabotage south of the border, especially in the New York City area.

Most of the German people who had come to Canada in the wave of immigration that washed over the country in the 1890s and early 1900s homesteaded on the prairies. Yet Canada's oldest cohesive German settlement was in Nova Scotia, where 2,400 Protestant farmers and tradesmen from southwest Germany had settled in the early 1750s. The majority of these newcomers had left Halifax to start their own community at Lunenburg. There were lots of Müllers, Schmidts, Schultzes, Hubleys, and Bauers in the provincial capital, but all were thoroughly "Canadianized" by the early decades of the twentieth century. There was not much sympathy for or loyalty to the Kaiser in Nova Scotia.

Similarly, despite the importance of the port of Halifax to the Allied war effort, there was surprisingly little German espionage activity happening here; in fact, there was and is no credible evidence that German agents were routinely at work in Halifax. This is not to say that German sympathizers were not listening and watching, or that German agents did not visit the port—or mused about doing so—from time to time. They were and they did.

In January 1915, for example, the British consul in Los Angeles reported having heard rumours that German agents were planning to sneak bombs aboard Allied troop ships that were leaving for Europe from Halifax and Saint John, New Brunswick. No such attacks ever occurred, and an investigation by Canadian police turned up no evidence of any such plot.[21]

In April of 1918, the American consul general in Halifax, one Arthur McLean, asked Justice Department officials to investigate two "suspicious people," local residents who *might* have been Americans. The pair had no visible employment, but McLean suspiciously noted that they seemed to be "well supplied with funds."[22]

THE UNCERTAINTY, FEAR, AND ANGER that was directed toward Halifax's German community was swirling in the background when the first public event was held in the city after the disaster. On the afternoon of Monday, December 17, morgue officials buried the charred remains of ninety-five unclaimed and unidentified bodies and bits of other bodies that searchers had recovered. Officials at the city's temporary morgue held a joint Roman Catholic–Protestant funeral service—the first of several such events—at Chebucto School. It was "a bright day as to weather, a day of deep blue sky and radiant sunshine, but cold," a *Herald* reporter who attended the service would write.[23] A crowd of more than 3,000 jammed the streets around the school, and "from every window of every house facing the mortuary looked down human faces."[24]

A CROWD OF MORE THAN 3,000 PEOPLE JAMMED THE STREETS AROUND
CHEBUCTO SCHOOL ON THE AFTERNOON OF DECEMBER 17 AS A MASS
FUNERAL WAS HELD FOR UNIDENTIFIED VICTIMS OF THE HALIFAX
EXPLOSION. (WILLIAM JAMES FAMILY FONDS, CITY OF TORONTO ARCHIVES)

Soldiers carried the numbered caskets up from the dim light in the school basement and out into the afternoon sunshine. There they arranged the caskets in rows on the snowy ground, just inside the wooden picket fence that surrounded the schoolyard. Atop each coffin lay a small cluster of flowers. In the crisp air, the solemn music the band of the 66th Princess Louise Fusiliers was playing sounded "strained and thin."[25] However, "The Funeral March" suited the moment.

The curious throng in their heavy winter coats and hats pressed forward, straining to see what would happen. Sombre faces pressed against the fence. The crowd stared in silence at the motley collection of caskets, which were of varying sizes and colours. Those holding the remains of the smallest victims, the toddlers and infants, were small and white. Those filled with "the broken bodies of men and women"[26] were of standard size and dark in finish. They city of Halifax had provided them.

When finally all the coffins were in place, in neat rows, the Protestant portion of the service began. As the band played the hymn "O God, Our

Help in Ages Past," the crowd joined in. The people sang as one in a low, restrained register. Then, with the last mournful strains of the music fading away, ministers from the city's Protestant churches spoke—Anglican, Baptist, Lutheran, Methodist, Presbyterian, and Salvation Army. They stood shoulder to shoulder on a makeshift wooden speaker's platform. Reverend Clarendon Worrell, the Anglican Archbishop of Nova Scotia, spoke the words that many of the onlookers—and those elsewhere in Halifax—had in mind on this day. "It's not by the hand of the Almighty these unfortunate human beings have suffered, but by the mistakes of others," Worrell intoned.

THE ROMAN CATHOLIC SERVICE ON THE AFTERNOON OF DECEMBER 17 FOR THE UNIDENTIFIED VICTIMS OF THE HALIFAX EXPLOSION. (WILLIAM JAMES FAMILY FONDS, CITY OF TORONTO ARCHIVES)

The funeral service at the Chebucto School morgue ended when the crowd raised their voices in singing the hymn "Abide With Me" and "God Save the King." The soldiers then loaded the caskets onto waiting trucks. One column of vehicles, a mass of mourners trailing in its wake, headed for Fairview Lawn Cemetery, the city's non-denominational burial ground; the other vehicles set off for Mount Olivet, the Roman Catholic cemetery. With daylight slipping away, there was not much time for committals. "'No such procession[s] had ever trod the streets of the city,' the *Morning Chronicle* would report, 'and the prayer of all people here, of all creeds or no creed must be 'God grant so sad a sight may never be witnessed here again.'"[27]

No such sentiment of compassion was on display at the gates of Fairview Lawn, where a cemetery official halted the funeral cortege. There had been "a mistake," he announced. "As the dead were unidentified, and therefore without estates or relatives to meet the cost of burial plots, Fairview Lawn could not accept them."[28]

The cemetery official redirected the trucks carrying the coffins to a nearby patch of unconsecrated ground where workers had dug a mass grave. This would be the final resting place of more than ninety-five innocent victims of the Halifax explosion. These unfortunate souls would endure one final indignity. Without dignity, identity is erased. And so it was.

CHAPTER 29

A s funeral services for unidentified victims of the Halifax explosion were under way at Chebucto School, a very different kind of public event was taking place in Courtroom #1 of the Halifax County Court House. The federal government's Investigation into the *Mont-Blanc* and *Imo* Collision—"the Wreck Commission inquiry," as people called it—was into its third full day of hearings.

"The setting was almost Dickensian. The Inquiry [had] convened in a large room with twenty-five-foot ceilings in the old courthouse on Spring Garden Road. The windows had been blown out by the explosion and were boarded up. Power was unavailable and the room was dimly lit with two oil lamps. [Presiding judge Arthur] Drysdale peered down through the gloom from an elevated Victorian pulpit flanked on either side by the master mariners who were to serve as his advisors."[1]

HALIFAX COUNTY COURT
HOUSE TODAY LOOKS MUCH
AS IT DID BACK IN 1917.
(KEN CUTHBERTSON)

Pilot Francis Mackey was in the witness box on the afternoon of December 17. After recovering from his wounds, he returned to work a few days after the explosion. Alexander Johnston, the deputy minister of Marine and Fisheries, had instructed the Halifax Pilotage Commission to take no actions related to the events of December 6 while the Wreck Commission inquiry was under way. Despite this, life was not easy for Mackey, who was obliged to sit through the daily proceedings of the inquiry. Judge Drysdale had ordered him to do so while other witnesses were barred from the courtroom when they were not testifying. Mackey, dressed in a dark suit with a bow tie tucked beneath his jowly chin, was out of his element in the courtroom. In his quarter century as a pilot, he had never before been involved in an accident inquiry. His record was spotless, and he insisted, "I've done nothing wrong."

Mackey had come to the opening session of the Wreck Commission believing the purpose of the proceedings was to discover the facts of what had happened in Halifax harbour the morning of December 6. Mackey had entered the witness box on December 17 and in good faith had answered the questions put to him by the various lawyers, who were "the cream of the Nova Scotia Bar."[2]

When prompted by Humphrey Mellish, the high-profile Halifax lawyer—and former law partner of Judge Drysdale—who was representing the *Mont-Blanc*'s owner, Mackey stated his contention that the collision of the *Mont-Blanc* and the *Imo* was entirely the fault of the Norwegian ship's master and her pilot. But not everyone accepted his interpretation of events.

Mackey was on the witness stand much longer than he ever anticipated, and while he was there, it dawned on him how naive he had been about the reasons for the inquiry. It had become an ersatz trial, with Mackey being the accused. He had not expected this, not in an inquiry that was supposedly being held to determine the facts of the collision of the *Mont-Blanc* and the *Imo*. However, the harbourmaster and harbour pilots pointed accusatory fingers at CXO Evan Wyatt and the senior naval officers who were responsible for ship traffic in the port. Wyatt blamed the harbour pilots and his military superiors. The senior naval officers blamed Wyatt and others who were involved in port operations. The corporate owners of both ships denied responsibility for anything.

In short, all the parties who were involved in the events of December 6 were intent on shifting blame for the collision of the two ships and for the explosion that followed. However, the public appetite for finding out who was responsible for the disaster—either the guilty party or a scapegoat— was incessant, and it happened that Francis Mackey was an easy target. "The blame-the-pilot theme was blatantly evident, and charges without foundation were quickly reported in the press as if proven."[3] Halifax newspapers reported on the inquiry as if it were a criminal trial. "Some

One Blundered—Who? Court May Decide" shouted the page one headline in the *Herald* on December 12, the day before the first witness testified at the inquiry. The tone for press coverage of the proceedings was set early. The news articles that appeared each day, rich in details, were often accusatory and even inflammatory, so much so that some witnesses complained to Judge Drysdale, who forwarded the complaints to officials in Ottawa. As a result, when Ernest Chambers, Canada's chief press censor, visited Halifax on December 14, he chided the media for their sensationalistic coverage of the inquiry. Chambers urged reporters to abstain from "publishing statements that might interfere with the successful prosecution of the official inquiry . . . and which might produce anxiety and misgiving among the community at large."[4]

While that was all well and good, the courtroom behaviour of Charles Burchell, the "able and colourful"[5] lawyer who was there to represent the interests of the corporate owner of the *Imo*, did nothing to dial back emotions or the press's zeal for incendiary headlines. Burchell revelled in the theatricality of the moment, and he was relentless in questioning Mackey about specific details of the events of December 6.

In addition to Burchell, six other lawyers were taking part in the inquiry proceedings: Crown Counsel William Henry; Humphrey Mellish; Andrew Cluney, representing the Nova Scotia Attorney General; Francis Bell, the city of Halifax; and T.R. Robertson, the Halifax Pilotage Commission. And Joseph Nolan, an attorney from New York, was there to assist Humphrey Mellish in representing the interests of the *Mont-Blanc*'s owner.

Reporters from the Halifax newspapers, who had staked their claims to prime seats in the spectator area, attended on each day of the inquiry. Surprisingly, few members of the public came; people were still grieving, or else they were busy picking up the pieces of their own lives. Although most Haligonians had already made up their minds about who was responsible for the disaster, readers eagerly read the detailed newspaper accounts of each day's inquiry proceedings.[6] On December 17, Charles Burchell's relentless cross-examination of Francis Mackey was the focus of reports on the day's proceedings.

It was clear to one and all that, "for better or worse," Burchell was the dominant figure at the inquiry.[7] He made it clear that in his opinion the disaster was the result of the negligence of Captain Le Médec and pilot Francis Mackey. As Burchell set about proving that, he led witnesses in their testimony, browbeat others, and scoffed at testimony he disliked. At one point, when Commander Wyatt was on the witness stand, Burchell got into a heated exchange with the CXO that ended with the chagrinned lawyer admitting he was guilty of trying to bully Wyatt and introduce hearsay evidence. At another point, in a moment of hyperbole, Burchell referred to Captain Le Médec as a "crazy Frenchman." Burchell attempted to qualify his words, but there was no disguising his true feelings or his intentions.

The lawyer took advantage of the fact that because a Wreck Commission inquiry was not a formal trial, the atmosphere was relatively relaxed and the lawyers were able to bend the formal rules of evidence. It also served Burchell's purposes that Judge Drysdale and the other legal counsel involved—save the visiting American—knew each other on a first-name basis. Everyone in the courtroom certainly knew Charles Burchell.

At age forty-two, the Cape Breton native had been practising law in Halifax for a dozen years. "Although he was a superb all-around lawyer, in an adversarial confrontation such as the Inquiry [Burchell] was a street-fighter. To put it in the kindest possible way, he gave a virtuoso performance at the Inquiry."[8]

At one point on the afternoon of December 17, while questioning Francis Mackey, Burchell paused to ask the witness if he had heard bells ringing in the distance. When Mackey insisted he had not, Burchell advised Mackey that the bells had been tolling for unidentified victims of the explosion. "I want to ask you now," Burchell persisted, "knowing that this is the hour for the funeral, if you're willing to admit frankly that you have been deliberately perjuring yourself for the last two days?"[9]

"No," replied Mackey.

After asking twice more if Mackey was telling the truth, Burchell changed tack. He asked the pilot if he had a drinking problem. Was he someone "who frequently gets drunk?"

Again, Mackey said, "No."

That was the only answer the pilot could offer. He dreaded that if the Wreck Commission fingered him as having been negligent, it would destroy his reputation and end his career. That was something both lawyer Charles Burchell and Wreck Commissioner Captain Louis Demers seemed intent on doing. Mackey was equally determined to resist. With a wife and six children to support and bills to pay, Mackey desperately wanted to continue working as a harbour pilot. Doing so was his life, and so Mackey struggled to make a favourable impression on Judge Arthur Drysdale, the man who was presiding over the inquiry.

ARTHUR DRYSDALE WAS A MAN of strong opinions. Sometimes too strong. In his younger years, he was a top-notch trial lawyer; however, his tendency to make enemies for no reason sometimes proved problematic for him. Drysdale, who could be as arrogant as a lord, held most of his legal colleagues "more or less [in] contempt," as one of them put it.[10]

A native of the hamlet of New Annan, sixty miles northwest of Halifax, Drysdale was twenty-five when he answered his 1882 call to the bar. After practising law for nine years, he embarked on a political career, winning election to the provincial assembly as the Liberal member for Hants County. He held that seat for sixteen years, serving in the cabinet of Premier George H. Murray, 1901–1907, before retiring from politics to take up his judicial appointment.

"Arthur Drysdale was a good-looking man of strong physique," a colleague said of him. "His manner was abrupt and discourteous. He was fond of rough horse play both before and after he went on the Bench."[11] Drysdale's idea of fun was to creep up behind a male friend, seize hold of the man's collar and tie, and tear off the items in one fell swoop—the wing collars of dress shirts of the day being detachable.

Drysdale's "intellect was incisive, well-balanced and of quick perception,"[12] and he was by all accounts a competent judge; however, his ascension to the bench did not end his shenanigans. Typically, one day while he was presiding over a civil trial, Drysdale became frustrated; unable to

hear the testimony of the defendant, who was a short, soft-spoken man, Drysdale shouted, "Go home, Sonny!" When to the surprise of everyone in the courtroom, the man did so, Drysdale promptly ruled against him; in effect, by walking away it was as if the man had pleaded *nolo contendere*—no contest. The man's lawyer was so outraged that he demanded Drysdale himself pay the judgment. To the surprise of everyone, the judge complied. Even he seems to have understood that there were limits to his antics.

JUDGE ARTHUR DRYSDALE, WHO PRESIDED OVER THE WRECK COMMISSION INQUIRY, WAS A MAN OF STRONG OPINIONS. (NOVA SCOTIA ARCHIVES)

Arthur Drysdale presided over the Wreck Commission inquiry into the Halifax explosion because in addition to his judicial duties in Nova Scotia, he sat as a regional judge in the Admiralty Division of the now-defunct Exchequer Court of Canada. That court heard cases involving ships, nautical disputes, and accidents in which there was loss of life or significant property damage.[13] The collision of the *Mont-Blanc* and the *Imo* in Halifax harbour qualified on all counts.

Prior to the opening session of the Wreck Commission, Drysdale had conferred with Crown Counsel William Henry, and he met with Captain Louis Demers and Captain Walter Hose every day the inquiry was in session. Demers, who carried a reputation for being "all business," brought to the proceedings the same preconceptions he had voiced in his private conversations with Drysdale.

Captain Hose, the judge's other nautical advisor, also had set ideas about who was responsible for what had happened on December 6. Naval officers often served as advisors in such inquiries, but the decision to allow Hose to be involved in these proceedings was ill-advised. Hose's competence as a naval officer was not at issue; his impartiality was. The fact the captain was second-in-command in the port of Halifax should have raised questions about his possible conflict of interest. A *Herald* editorial asserted, "Captain Hose Should be Under Investigation and Not an 'Investigator' in the Halifax Disaster."[14] Halifax mayor Peter Martin, being of the same mind, fired off a telegram to Prime Minister Borden asking that he remove Hose from his involvement in the Wreck Commission inquiry.[15] That request was in vain. With Borden's blessing, Charles C. Ballantyne, the minister of Marine and Fisheries, responded to Martin's letter. In his curt note, he explained that because Hose had not written the regulations that governed Halifax harbour operations, he was not in a conflict of interest position.[16]

Ballantyne's logic was questionable. In the minds of objective observers, Hose's demeanour throughout the inquiry—like the behaviour of Judge Drysdale and Wreck Commissioner Demers—raised questions about his impartiality. It was evident from day one of testimony that the agendas and personalities of Hose and some of the other principals tainted the proceedings.

THE HASTE WITH WHICH the Wreck Commission inquiry was called and got under way—just seven days after the disaster—was a reflection of the sense of urgency of the unspoken political imperatives that were driving events. Thus, all the key figures who had survived the explosion of December 6 received subpoenas to provide testimony. Captain Le Médec of the *Mont-Blanc*, pilot Francis Mackey, and CXO Evan Wyatt were foremost among them.

For most of the first eight days of the inquiry, lawyers haggled over the details of the movements of the *Mont-Blanc* and the *Imo* in the minutes prior to the collision. The questions on these matters began on the morning of December 13, as soon as Captain Aimé Le Médec, the very first witness, took his place in the witness box.

Insisting that his grasp of English was tenuous, the captain answered questions through an interpreter. In the first of what would be two gruelling sessions on the witness stand, Le Médec answered questions for four and a half hours. Visibly nervous, he sat rolling and unrolling the handkerchief he clutched. Le Médec struggled to maintain his composure, speaking in an unemotional, matter-of-fact voice, even when the tone of the interrogation became accusatory, incriminating, and even mocking. This happened repeatedly as the various lawyers set about trying to poke holes in Le Médec's version of events and find discrepancies between his story and pilot Mackey's. For example, Le Médec was replying to questions put to him by Charles Burchell when the lawyer asked, "Do you know how long the *Mont-Blanc* was at [Pier 6] before the explosion?"

The captain replied that he had no way of knowing. Because he had been across the harbour, on the Dartmouth shore, said Le Médec, he could not see if the ship had drifted up against the pier before it blew up. "If I could have seen it, I would no longer be in this world."

Burchell smirked. "[The Captain] was getting away so fast he didn't look back to see," he declared.[17]

Under questioning by Crown Counsel William Henry, Le Médec admitted he had received basic training in English when he studied for his captain's certificate. As a result, he knew more of the language than he let on. This revelation called into question the captain's truthfulness on other matters. "I said I didn't speak English here because I can't make me understood," said Le Médec. "I know sufficient English to understand the pilot."[18]

Linguistic abilities—or lack of them—also became a topic of interest and provided Charles Burchell with an opportunity to ridicule Francis Mackey. In his cross-examination of the pilot, Burchell questioned him on how he had communicated with Captain Le Médec on the bridge of the *Mont-Blanc*. Mackey explained that he had done so using a combination of hand signals and a few French nautical terms. When Burchell asked Mackey to repeat some of the French words he knew, Mackey obliged. He did passably well until Burchell asked him if he could recall what words appeared on the face of the telegraph on the *Mont-Blanc* and other French ships. Mackey knew that *tout* meant "full speed" and *demi vitesse* was "half-speed."

"Spell it," Burchell demanded.

"I don't know if I can spell it correctly," said Mackey.

"Spell the first part."

"*D-E-M-I*," said the pilot.

"And the other word?

"I think it is '*T-A-S-S-E*.'"[19]

Mackey's attempt at spelling the French term for half-speed prompted laughter from those in the courtroom who knew he unknowingly had spelled the French word for a small cup: *une demitasse*. In mocking Mackey's lack of knowledge of the French language, Burchell had made an important point about the pilot's credibility. *Res ipsa loquitur*, as the Latin

legal phrase advises: "The thing speaks for itself." Without further comment, Burchell moved on to ask Mackey a series of questions about the
events of December 6. When the lawyer asked Mackey to draw a sketch
showing the positions of the two ships at the time, the pilot did his best.
However, he was no artist and his rough drawing did not correspond to
evidence given by some other witnesses. But Mackey held firm; he insisted
his drawing was accurate and that he was telling the truth. Undeterred,
Burchell persisted in his efforts to intimidate Mackey, asking what his
reaction would be "if all the witnesses on shore" said that he had misrep-
resented the positions of the two ships.

"I would stick to my own line," Mackey insisted.[20]

FRANCIS MACKEY WAS NOT the only witness to endure harsh treatment on the witness stand. When Peter B'Jönnas, the second officer of the
Imo, was testifying, he was vague and answered numerous questions by
saying he could not remember or had not been paying attention. Wreck
Commissioner Demers had little patience for B'Jönnas' lack of insights.
When he failed in his efforts to draw from the Norwegian sailor the kind
of information he wanted, Demers grew frustrated and snarled that it
appeared B'Jönnas did "not take much notice of anything."[21]

The wreck commissioner was equally short with Johan Johansen. As
the lawyer for the ship's owner, Charles Burchell had intervened to have
Johansen released from jail and returned to hospital. When the Imo's
helmsman appeared at the inquiry, like Peter B'Jönnas, he had few definitive answers to the questions that were put to him. Exasperated by this,
Demers scoffed. "For a man with an ambition to become an officer, you
seem to take little notice of what goes on around you."[22]

Neither B'Jönnas nor Johansen reacted to Demers' taunts, nor did
they push back when questioning from the various lawyers grew insistent.
Not all of the inquiry witnesses were as compliant. In the course of the

first eight days of hearings, Commander Evan Wyatt's name came up repeatedly. There was much speculation about what the CXO would have to say when he appeared on the witness stand.

Testimony given by Wyatt's superior, Captain Frederick Pasco, the day before Wyatt was due to testify was damning. Pasco all but accused Wyatt of incompetence. In response to questions posed by Crown Counsel Henry and Charles Burchell, the acting superintendent of the Naval Dockyard opined that the presence of barrels of benzol on the deck of the *Mont-Blanc* had been a key factor in the seriousness of the fire that broke out on the ship after the collision with the *Imo*. The *Mont-Blanc*, he explained, had been dangerously overloaded. "I'm surprised the people on the ship didn't leave in a body [in New York]."

Pasco recalled that in his previous command, at Sydney, he had not seen the need to spell out rules or guidelines to prevent ships packed with explosives from entering the harbour or from violating "the rules of the road." The reason was simple: common sense dictated that there was no need for such precautions. The captain said he was taken aback to discover that things were different in Halifax. "It certainly didn't occur to me that a ship would be coming up a harbour like a piece of fireworks ready to be exploded."[23]

The implications of Pasco's words were clear: in his opinion, Wyatt, as the CXO and the officer in charge of traffic in the port of Halifax—should never have allowed the *Mont-Blanc* into the harbour. The fact that such a dangerously overloaded ship was permitted to do so was reflective of the serious problems that plagued the port of Halifax. For one, the muddled structure of the naval command led to turf battles and petty bickering between senior naval commanders and between navy officials and civilian authorities. For another, both the pilots and the staff in the CXO's office were lax when it came to enforcing the naval regulations that governed shipping. The subsequent testimony from other witnesses highlighted the fact that "naval authorities had long since discarded the notion that intense monitoring was necessary or even desirable in a port where it was considered reasonable to expect that the normal rules of the road would be obeyed by all."[24] That seemed reasonable, and it was the case in most ports. But Halifax was different. It would come out that relations between the pilots' office and the CXO were dysfunctional. What is more, neither Commander Wyatt nor Mate Terrance Freeman, the examining officer who had reviewed the *Mont-Blanc*'s cargo manifest, had much experience dealing with munitions.

Pasco revealed that in the days after the disaster, federal bureaucrats and senior RCN commanders in Ottawa had moved to ensure there would be no repeat of the events of December 6. Admiral Kingsmill had introduced new regulations that tightened up the rules governing ship traffic in Halifax harbour. The timing of the move was ill-advised. It amounted, ipso facto, to a tacit admission that there had been serious problems with operations in the port of Halifax. None of the participants in the Wreck Commission inquiry who were in a position to raise this issue did so—not Judge Drysdale, not his nautical advisors, and none of the lawyers. Instead, they focused on Commander Evan Wyatt and challenged him to explain his own conduct and his perceived failure to deal with the issues that were plaguing the harbour. Wyatt, it seemed, had a lot to answer for.

SOME MEMBERS OF THE *MONT-BLANC* CREW AT THE WRECK INQUIRY. (NOVA SCOTIA ARCHIVES)

CHAPTER 30

FAIR PLAY AND GOATS

Halifax County Court House, January 1918

It was not in Commander Evan Wyatt's character to be docile or deferential. After all, he was an Englishman, a gentleman, and an officer, and all that those attributes entailed. Headstrong and self-confident, he had little patience for his inferiors or for those who did not accord him the respect he felt he was due. Wyatt's hauteur was on full display when he stepped into the witness box at the Wreck Commission inquiry on January 23. Attired in his Royal Navy uniform, three gold bars with loop proudly displayed on his sleeve, the commander was a model of military spit and polish, and he was in a defiant mood.

When Crown Counsel William Henry asked Wyatt if he had been aware of William Hayes' plan to take the *Imo* out of Halifax on the morning of December 6, Wyatt shook his head. He explained that no one—not the pilot, the agent for the *Imo*, nor anyone on the RCN guard ship stationed in the harbour—had told him the Norwegian vessel had not sailed as scheduled on the afternoon of December 5. Wyatt complained about the recalcitrance of the port's civilian harbour pilots. The commander made no secret of the fact he could not have cared less what the pilots thought of him. What irked him was that he had no authority to discipline the pilots when they failed to keep him informed of their activities or to follow his orders. On several occasions, Wyatt had complained about this in his conversations with the superintendent of the Naval Dockyard, Captain Martin. In the time-honoured tradition of the military, Wyatt had "covered his butt," stating his concerns in no fewer than three letters that he sent to his commanding officer. "For months and months I saw an accident or collision was coming," Wyatt noted "and I did not wish to be made the goat—you can call it intuition or what you like, but that was my idea."[1] Now, in the aftermath of just such an accident, Wyatt was face to face with the consequences of his dysfunctional relationship with some of the harbour pilots and of Captain Martin's failure to back him.

"So the responsibility for the *Imo* going out that morning would be upon the pilot in your opinion?" William Henry asked Wyatt.

"Absolutely," he replied.[2]

Wyatt's insistence on blaming William Hayes for the collision of the *Mont-Blanc* and the *Imo* did not sit well with Burchell. When it came time for the lawyer to cross-examine Wyatt next morning, he glared at the commander. Burchell demanded to know if Wyatt felt it was *proper* to have made "a charge against a dead man which is unfair and unwarranted [and] would be very much against British fair play."

"Neither unfair nor unwarranted, seeing as it's an absolute fact," Wyatt shot back.[3]

The thrust of Burchell's question cut deep, for it called into question the commander's claim to be "an officer and a gentleman." This was an issue he already felt touchy about after having endured the indignity of Admiral Kingsmill's admonishing him for allegedly being "ungentlemanly" and delinquent in making alimony payments to his first wife back in England.

The rancour between Burchell and Wyatt continued throughout the CXO's initial three hours in the witness box. Wyatt was determined to defend himself and his reputation. Charles Burchell was no less determined to paint the commander as an incompetent bungler whose failure to do his job had helped foster dangerous conditions in Halifax harbour. He had no shortage of ammunition to do so, most of it being rooted in Wyatt's own failings.

Having come to court without a lawyer, Wyatt acted as his own counsel. That he was in over his head became abundantly clear when Burchell asked him if he knew about the new shipping regulations for the port, the ones Captain Pasco had mentioned in his testimony. When Wyatt admitted that, yes, he knew about these regulations, Burchell pounced. If that was so, he asked, was the CXO also aware of a near collision between two ships in the Narrows on the previous day? A Halifax newspaper had reported a near accident involving an inbound oil tanker and an outbound ship that was carrying munitions. In truth, neither vessel carried cargo that posed much of a threat even if an accident had happened, but the timing of the episode could not have been worse for Wyatt or his superiors in Ottawa. Both Admiral Kingsmill and Minister Ballantyne felt embarrassed, and both were incensed that the RCN looked incompetent yet again. Kingsmill immediately telephoned Captain Pasco to demand an explanation.

In reply to Burchell's questions, Wyatt denied any responsibility for the incident. He pointed out that he had been in court when it happened. "Is it up to me when anything goes wrong wherever I am?" he snapped.[4]

Wyatt's testy response was less than convincing. It only served to further embolden Burchell, who persisted in hectoring the commander in hopes of causing him to lose his temper. In that, the lawyer succeeded. When Burchell asked Wyatt if he was responsible for ship traffic in Halifax harbour, Wyatt was evasive until finally his anger got the better of him.

He lashed out by attempting to shift to Captain Martin any blame for problems in the harbour and for the dysfunctional relationship between the pilots and the CXO's office. To buttress his claim that the superintendent of the Naval Dockyard was the one who was at fault, Wyatt referred to carbon copies of the three letters of complaint he had sent to Martin.

The captain, who was in Ottawa at the time and unavailable to testify in person, replied to the accusation in a telegram he sent to Halifax. In it, Martin denied that the CXO had ever raised with him any concerns about his relationship with the harbour pilots. Martin also claimed he had never received any letters about this from Wyatt.

CAPTAIN EDWARD MARTIN HAD FALLEN ILL WITH CANCER WHEN THIS PHOTO WAS TAKEN IN 1921. HE DIED NOT LONG AFTERWARD. (CANADIAN WAR MUSEUM)

William Henry, ever dutiful, pursued the matter. Unfortunately, by the time he finally uncovered evidence that supported Wyatt's version of events, it would be too late to do anything with it. The inquiry was over, and Judge Drysdale had already rendered his decision. Since the existence of the letters was "a subsidiary phase of the matter, which [did] not really affect the responsibility for the collision,"[5] that was the end of the matter. The damage to Wyatt's reputation was done. Burchell had succeeded in discrediting the CXO, casting doubt on his version of events and even making him appear pompous and worthy of ridicule. Wyatt had sealed his own fate and scuttled his naval career. "By implicating his superior, [he] had put himself beyond the pale."[6]

Wyatt's superiors had heard more than enough. On January 26, mere hours after his third and final appearance at the inquiry, word came from Ottawa that Wyatt was out as CXO for the port of Halifax. He was officially "on leave" and discharged from active duty; his services "were no longer required." When a newspaper reporter contacted Admiral Kingsmill for further comment, the head of the RCN initially seemed taken aback. His surprise was genuine; his political masters had not informed him of their decision to cashier Wyatt, or else he was surprised that the minister had announced the news without alerting him. Either way, Kingsmill was chagrinned. "The truth is that Ottawa does not take Admiral Kingsmill any too seriously," an *Evening Mail* editorial scoffed. "He is jokingly referred to as the man who was created an admiral for losing a ship [and] is more famous in the capital for his social than his naval exploits."[7] Some observers speculated that Prime Minister Borden himself had orchestrated the changes in Halifax. That may well have been so, for Borden was eager to deflect attention and blame for the disaster away from his newly elected government and from the RCN. The revelations that had come out of the Wreck Commission inquiry all but dictated that he would act. The media and the public were demanding sweeping changes in the senior ranks of the RCN, and the service's already frayed reputation was in danger of unravelling entirely. Morale within the ranks was suffering.

Kingsmill scrambled to confirm the news that Commander Evan Wyatt had been relieved of his duties as CXO for the port of Halifax. At the same time, the admiral announced the reassignment of Captain Pasco to another temporary posting at Saint John, New Brunswick. Captain Martin, the superintendent of the Naval Dockyard, was moving to Kingston, Ontario, to help make arrangements for the temporary move of the Naval College to the Royal Military College. A senior officer from Esquimalt was coming east to succeed Martin in Halifax.

While Kingsmill insisted these redeployments were routine, most observers felt that Kingsmill was trying to defuse the embarrassment of Martin's duplicity in the matter of the letters and his apparent indifference to the operational deficiencies in the Halifax harbour. Wyatt lost his job; Martin disappeared in a paper shuffle. He and Admiral Kingsmill were friends, and it would emerge many years later that Martin actually alerted officials in Ottawa to Wyatt's concerns about his differences with Halifax's harbour pilots; however, federal bureaucrats had done nothing to correct the situation, and Kingsmill was eager to keep this quiet. As military historian John Griffith Armstrong has said, it was "a sorry mess of apparent intrigue and cover up."[8]

That issue aside, the prevailing view among senior navy officers, federal bureaucrats, and senior officials in the Borden government was the same one that William Henry had expressed in memos he sent to Deputy Minister Johnston: "The harbour regulations [in Halifax] were sufficient . . . to safeguard the port."[9] In effect, Henry accepted the notion that common sense and the internationally recognized nautical rules of the road *should* have been enough to ensure that ship traffic would move safely into and out of Halifax harbour. Thus, it followed that the senior naval officers in the port— Canadian and British—bore no responsibility for the events of December 6, even though they were responsible for ensuring that the pilots and masters of ships moving into and out of the port complied with those rules and with existing regulations. The irony, of course, was that Evan Wyatt, who had voiced his fear of being made "the goat" when an accident happened, ended up in that sacrificial role. Unfortunately for him, he was "too clever by half." His own hubris ultimately put him into position to serve as a scapegoat.

It speaks volumes that in the wake of the explosion, Captain Pasco had ordered that a new signal station be set up at the entrance to the

Narrows, and he had hastily drawn up—and Ottawa had quietly approved—the new regulations that now governed the movement of munitions ships in Halifax harbour. Whenever such a ship arrived in the examination anchorage off McNabs Island, it was now obliged to stay put until the channel that led to Bedford Basin was clear of all other traffic. Whenever a munitions ship was leaving port as part of a convoy, it was now obliged to do so at the tail end of the procession; no incoming traffic was allowed to move until the munitions ship was out of the harbour.

There is no record of Evan Wyatt's reaction to these changes. He had other more pressing matters on his mind just then, for as he was about to discover, a new, even more traumatic ordeal than his public humiliation at the Wreck Commission inquiry lay ahead for him. The same was true for Captain Le Médec and pilot Francis Mackey.

THE LAST WITNESS to testify at the Wreck Commission inquiry did so on January 29, 1918. Ironically, that same morning a fire broke out on a wharf in the city's new South End ocean terminal, where workers continued to unload ammunition from the SS *Picton*, the cargo ship that had suffered serious damage in the explosion on December 6. The rumour that another munitions ship was ablaze in Halifax had sparked a minor panic. Officials ordered the evacuation of several schools, and some South End residents fled their homes. Fortunately, dock workers were able to douse the fire before any real harm occurred. However, the incident ratcheted up the public's unease and embarrassed, yet again, the naval officers who were in charge of operations in the harbour. This latest scare also underscored the urgency of the decision Judge Drysdale was about to render.

He had heard from sixty witnesses during the fourteen days the inquiry was actually in session. (In fact, the inquiry stretched over forty-eight calendar days, but that interval included a one-month break, December 21 to January 21.) The accumulated documentation from the inquiry consisted of depositions from dozens of additional witnesses, seventy exhibits, and more than 1,700 pages of verbatim testimony.

In letters he sent to Deputy Minister Alexander Johnston, William Henry expressed the politically unpopular opinion that the RCN and Commander Wyatt were blameless in the events that had triggered the explosion on December 6, 1917. He also stated that had he found the testimony given by Captain Le Médec and pilot Mackey to be consistent and credible. As Henry saw it, responsibility for the collision of the *Imo* and the *Mont-Blanc* lay with the captain and pilot of the *Imo*, and Halifax harbour pilots also wore some of the blame. In his summation at the inquiry, Henry confided that initially "I did not understand, [n]or did anybody until the matter was gone into further, that the pilots had been systematically neglecting the[ir] duty for several months."

Judge Drysdale saw things differently after conferring with Captain Hose and Wreck Commissioner Demers. Even before Henry and the other lawyers involved in the inquiry had delivered their closing statements, Demers had formulated his own conclusions, and "the crusty sailor's influence was actually paramount in the inquiry's outcome."[10] He articulated his views in two lengthy memos in which he "rather astonishingly placed moral considerations above rules of maritime law," as military historian John Griffith Armstrong would point out. "To the Wreck Commissioner's mind, the weighing of evidence required no great effort of deliberations."[11]

Demers offered no comment on Captain Martin's failure to remedy the problems that plagued the administration of Halifax harbour, but he was critical of the Pilotage Commission and urged that the federal government take immediate action to reform it. That was the prompt Marine Minister C.C. Ballantyne needed to seize the moment and announce the creation of a Royal Commission to look into all aspects of the role of pilots in the operation of Halifax harbour. Hearings got under way on

February 5, but the results were already a foregone conclusion. Commission chair Thomas Robb was a Ballantyne crony who was ready to deliver a report tailor-made for the minister's political purposes. Just two months after its creation, the commission would bring forward thirty-two recommendations to impose wholesale changes to Halifax's pilotage system and bring it under federal control. [12]

As for Judge Drysdale's rulings in the wake of the Wreck Commission inquiry, they were astonishing for at least two reasons. For one, he released his findings on February 4, a mere six days after the last session of the proceedings—and there was a weekend in there. For another, the judgment was but a single page of text that took him only a few minutes to read. Drysdale concluded that the *Mont-Blanc* was entirely to blame for the collision. With that in mind, he recommended some corrective measures, four of which were key. Drysdale opined (1) that Francis Mackey should face criminal charges and lose his pilotage licence; (2) that the French government should cancel Captain Aimé Le Médec's master's ticket; (3) that RCN senior officers should discipline Commander Evan Wyatt; and (4) that they should censure pilot Edward Renner (who had guided the tramp steamer that had preceded the *Mont-Blanc* though the Narrows on December 6), [13] as well as the Halifax harbour pilots in general. How exactly naval authorities would discipline civilian pilots was unclear.

MANY PEOPLE WHO had followed the Wreck Commission hearings puzzled over Judge Drysdale's findings, but the public and the local media were supportive; a *Herald* editorial praised Drysdale's decision as being "vitally important to the people of this city and the whole country." [14] Those who had already taken to assailing Francis Mackey on the street with shouts of "Murderer!" applauded when Halifax police chief Frank Hanrahan, acting on orders from the provincial Attorney General, detained the pilot as he was leaving the courtroom after hearing Judge

Drysdale read his findings. Hanrahan took personal delight in apprehending Mackey. The chief's son, Frank Jr., was sweet on pilot William Hayes' daughter Agnes, and the two would eventually marry; Halifax in 1918 was a small, tightly knit community.

Hanrahan personally arrested Captain Le Médec on a downtown street and arrested Wyatt at his home early next morning. All three defendants faced manslaughter charges in connection with the deaths of pilot William Hayes and Captain From. The courts set bail for Le Médec at $10,000 and at $6,000 each for Mackey and Wyatt. When la Fédération des Syndicats de Capitaines au Long Cours de France, the French sea captains' association, appealed to the government in Paris to intervene on Le Médec's behalf, the French consul in Halifax posted most of the money to arrange the captain's release.

Initially, at least, because his pilot's licence was suspended and he was not working, Mackey did not have enough money for his bail; neither, apparently, did the local pilots' association. Mackey remained in jail until a friend—county sheriff James Hall, who was also a member of the Halifax Pilotage Commission's executive board—came forward to bail him out.

On the morning of February 5, Le Médec, Mackey, and Wyatt were all at the courthouse for the start of the preliminary hearing into the charges against them. Crown Prosecutor Andrew Cluney was in the middle of questioning a witness when Evan Wyatt's father-in-law breezed into the courtroom. Walter Brookfield, one of Halifax's most prominent and wealthiest citizens, announced he was there to post bail for his son-in-law, stating that "he was a busy man and hadn't much time to spare."[15]

Once Brookfield had posted bail for Wyatt, he departed, as did the commander. When the Crown prosecutor suggested Wyatt might want to hear the evidence to be given, the commander sniffed. "I'm not interested in the collision in the slightest degree."[16] Like his fellow defendants, Wyatt continued to insist he had done nothing wrong. He also asserted that the civil authorities in Halifax had no jurisdiction to arrest him; he was, after all, a British naval officer. Aimé Le Médec advanced a similar argument, insisting that those same authorities had no right to arrest him because he was a captain in the French merchant marine. Despite this, with the charges against Le Médec, Mackey, and Wyatt headed for trial on March 7, Mackey's lawyer took a bold gamble. He petitioned the Supreme Court of Nova Scotia for a writ of habeas corpus, one of the oldest remedies available to a defendant who stands unjustly accused. If a judge chooses to issue such a writ, the defendant wins release from custody on the grounds the charges against him or her are without merit.

In this case, the judge who considered the matter was Supreme Court Justice Benjamin Russell, one of Nova Scotia's most senior magistrates. Sixty-eight years old and a former lawyer and Liberal MP, he was a founder of the Dalhousie University law school and taught there for many years. After deciding to exclude much of the testimony from the Wreck Commission, Russell sifted through evidence from the preliminary hearing and considered new testimony given by a witness in the *Mont-Blanc* owner's civil suit against the owner of the *Imo*. Captain John Makiny, the master of the armed naval tug *Nereid*, had witnessed the collision of the *Imo* and the *Mont-Blanc*. His testimony about the events of that day was clear and concise, and after reading the transcript, Russell concluded "that so far from being negligent or careless, as charged in the information, the defendant [Mackey] had taken every possible care to prevent the collision which was about to be caused by the conduct of the *Imo*."[17]

Russell's decision to dismiss the charges against Mackey and order the release of both the pilot and Captain Le Médec touched off a storm of public protest and a barrage of angry newspaper editorials. The provincial Attorney General appealed the ruling to the Supreme Court of Canada but was unsuccessful. That put an end to the legal proceedings against Mackey and Le Médec.

The captain wasted no time in returning home to Brittany. After a bit of downtime, in August 1918 he resumed his career with the CGT. Le Médec would continue serving as master of various ships until early 1931, when he retired at age fifty-three and began drawing a pension of 600 francs per month. On March 16, 1931, he would learn he had been named a Knight in the National Order of the Legion of Honour—un Chevalier de la Légion d'Honneur. The award, France's highest order for military and civil distinction, salutes those who have performed at least twenty years of public service or twenty-five years of professional activity with "eminent merits"— that is, for performing one's job flawlessly and exceptionally. The Chevalier is the lowest of the five levels of the Legion of Honour, and while retiring merchant marine sea captains often receive the honour, that Le Médec did so confirms the fact that his service record was not marred by anything that had happened in Halifax. The captain would quietly live out his life, dying on March 7, 1955, at age seventy-seven. Family members would bury Le Médec's body in a small cemetery not far from his Brittany home.

JUDGE RUSSELL'S RULING also derailed the criminal case against Evan Wyatt. Despite this, the provincial Attorney General forged ahead with efforts to prosecute him. It would prove to be a wasted effort. With Judge Russell presiding, the trial jury took only "a few minutes" to find Wyatt not guilty.[18]

Despite this, his naval career was over. The Canadian Navy List for October 1916 to June 1918 would include the news that as of May 3, 1918, Commander Evan Wyatt's appointment with the Naval Service of Canada had been "terminated." As a matter of standard operating procedure, the Admiralty in London offered him an opportunity to return to duty in the Royal Navy; however, Wyatt had no desire to suffer further humiliation, and so he accepted a designation of having been "discharged to the shore" and a three-month war service gratuity of $540.[19] The money was small succour. The pronouncement that his services were "no longer required" surely must have been bittersweet for Wyatt. Yet despite the embarrassment and indignities he had suffered, there was at least some measure of compensation: he would no longer be on the hot seat or in the public eye.

Wyatt and his wife, Dorothy, would soon move to the Boston area, where they settled in the suburb of Newton. There, in November 1918, Dorothy gave birth to a son they named Samuel. Evan Wyatt returned to work with the United Fruit Company, serving as the master of ships that carried cargoes of bananas from the Caribbean to the United States.

Wyatt would also work for a time in banking, and when he retired in 1951 at age seventy-three, he and his wife would relocate to Sarasota, Florida. It was there that Wyatt would die on March 2, 1967. Revealingly, the brief obituary that appeared in the local newspaper would make no mention of Commander Wyatt's RN naval career or of his role in the great Halifax harbour explosion of 1917; some things were best forgotten.

Dorothy Wyatt would die in 1979 and would be buried next to her husband in Sarasota Memorial Park Cemetery.

UNLIKE HIS CO-ACCUSED and even with the dismissal of the criminal charges against him, leaving Halifax was never an option for Francis Mackey. All his roots were there, and at age forty-six, he wanted to resume his work as a pilot; he had a wife and six children to support. But Mackey was a marked man. As his biographer, Janet Maybee, has so eloquently explained, "The minister of marine, Charles C. Ballantyne, refused to restore the licence Mackey had voluntarily surrendered upon the laying of criminal charges against him."[20] The reason for the minister's intransigence, although unstated, was obvious: with Wyatt and Le Médec having departed, Mackey was "the only useful scapegoat left in Halifax."[21]

By continuing to point the finger of blame at the harbour pilot, Ballantyne succeeded in diverting public and media attention away from any questions about the responsibility of the Borden government and the RCN for the Halifax disaster. As a result, Mackey would spend four years and his life savings in the effort to clear his name, recover his pilot's licence, and recoup $17,000 in lost wages. He succeeded in the first two endeavours, but not on the latter. What is more, by the time he recovered his pilot's licence and returned to work in 1922, his travails had left his life turned upside down. Mackey's wife, Lillian, would die two years later at the still-young age of forty-seven. Family members were convinced the stress of her husband's ordeal was a significant factor in her early death.

Mackey would remarry in September 1925 and would work until 1937, when he finally retired. Francis Mackey would die on December 31, 1961 at the age of eighty-nine.[22]

THE CIVIL SUIT BETWEEN the owners of the *Mont-Blanc* and the *Imo* took a long time to wend its way through the courts. The process had begun on January 10, 1918, when the CGT filed suit against the South Pacific Whaling Company for $2 million in damages plus costs. The *Imo*'s owner promptly counterclaimed for the same amount. Since the case involved ships, it was a matter for the Exchequer Court of Canada. That meant Judge Arthur Drysdale would preside over the trial. Common sense and the duty to act fairly should have prompted Drysdale to recuse himself from the case; however, it was not in his character to do so. Drysdale stubbornly forged ahead. When, for reasons unknown, the plaintiff's lawyer failed to object, the outcome of the trial was a foregone conclusion, especially after both parties agreed to allow into evidence all the testimony from the Wreck Commission inquiry. Only one additional witness testified at the civil trial, and that was the aforementioned Captain John Makiny. It was his testimony that had helped convince Judge Russell to grant pilot Francis Mackey's petition for a writ of habeas corpus. Judge Drysdale was unmoved. He reprised his inquiry ruling. In a decision he handed down on April 27, 1918, Drysdale reiterated his view that the collision of the *Imo* and the *Mont-Blanc* was the fault of the pilot and captain of the French ship. Judgment for the defendant with costs, he decreed.

Five days after Drysdale's ruling, the CGT's lawyer filed an appeal with the Supreme Court of Canada. It took a year for the five judges who heard the legal arguments to reach a verdict. When they did so, their inconclusive ruling said more about the political situation in Canada at the time than it did about the merits of the litigants' legal arguments. Two English-speaking judges sided with Drysdale when they rejected the appeal, while two French-speaking judges upheld it. It fell to Justice Francis Anglin to break the tie; however, he ruled that the captains and pilots of both vessels had been at fault in the December 6 collision.[23] In rendering what in effect was a non-decision, the Supreme Court passed the case to the Judicial Committee of the Privy Council in London for final resolution.

PRIOR TO 1949, the Judicial Committee of the Privy Council, a board of the British Privy Council, served as a court of final appeal for Canada. Created by acts of the British Parliament in 1833 and 1844, that tribunal consisted of jurists who had held high judicial office in Britain, along with a sprinkling of Commonwealth judges. This august group exercised jurisdiction over all colonial courts, including the Supreme Court of Canada.

When in 1875 Canada's federal government established that court as the highest in the land, the justice minister of the day tried unsuccessfully to abolish appeals to the Privy Council; as a compromise, Canada and Great Britain agreed that Ottawa would be free to regulate the kind of appeals that Canadian courts referred to London for judgment. This arrangement remained in effect until 1949 when the Supreme Court of Canada became the country's ultimate legal arbiter. All of this was the legal backdrop when in January 1919 Charles Burchell, acting on behalf of the owner of the *Imo*, appealed the Supreme Court of Canada's ruling to the Privy Council.

The court heard the legal arguments over a five-day period in February 1920. Four judges in their black robes and powdered wigs sat with two nautical advisors as they listened to the lawyers, weighed the evidence, and pondered the relevant legal issues. On March 22, 1919, they handed down their nineteen-page decision. "Their Lordships are clearly of the opinion that both ships are to blame for their reciprocal neglect . . . to have reversed and gone astern earlier than they did," wrote Lord Atkinson. "They are therefore of the opinion that the judgment appealed from should be affirmed."[24]

Those were the final words in the long legal battle over the collision of the *Mont-Blanc* and the *Imo*. In the end, the courts convicted no one of any crime, and the owner of neither ship collected financial compensation for losses suffered. The legal debate about who had been negligent was finished, although the question of who had been *responsible* remained unresolved. "For most people it was a real muddle, and they found it difficult to blame one ship or the other."[25]

CHAPTER 31

"BIG MEN ARE NOT OVERWHELMED BY BIG IDEAS"

Halifax, Nova Scotia

On April 12, 1918, the *Halifax Herald* published its "reconstruction number." Four months after the fact, it revisited the story of the disaster that had devastated half the city and claimed so many innocent lives.

The newspaper reprinted the names of "the known and determined dead" along with articles devoted to the theme "how Halifax may gain thru [*sic*] the disaster." The overriding message was that despite its travails, the city was being reborn and would continue to prosper. However, a full-page editorial cautioned that "unless the planning and redevelopment (not merely reconstruction) of the devastated and adjacent area is taken in hand at once, on broad and comprehensive lines, it will be almost impossible to secure any improvement in the future."[1] The *Herald* would step forward as a cheerleader for work of the Halifax Relief Commission and the notion that "big men are not overwhelmed by big ideas, which are often the most and not the least practical."[2]

The impetus to rebuild Halifax and the ongoing war effort remained the prime focus for municipal officials and the city's business leaders. Regardless, there was no escaping the reality that many residents of the devastated North End were still struggling to recover and to rebuild their lives. Providing ongoing medical care for the most seriously injured explosion survivors was a major challenge; many of these people remained hospitalized. Others who had sustained wounds—physical, emotional, or both—but who remained mobile continued to battle their pain. For some, the heartache would never end. That was especially true for those who had lost their eyesight. The Halifax School for the Blind, with help from the American Red Cross, launched a major fundraising drive. When in the spring of 1918 the school began offering classes in reading and writing Braille, forty-one people enrolled; most of them were adult women who had to relearn basic life skills that enabled them to care for themselves and their families, and in at least a few cases, to find or return to work. When the Red Cross in Halifax staged a July 1918 auction to raise money for blind relief programs, among the items up for sale were handicrafts created by ten of the women who were blinded in the December 6 explosion.

The *Halifax Herald*, like other local newspapers, continued to stoke the fires of public outrage with its coverage of the legal proceedings that followed the disaster and with controversies that arose over the HRC's administration of pension and compensation monies; financial claims flooded into the commission's offices, along with more than 10,000 pension applications. However, the bureaucratic wheels sometimes turned too slowly, especially when claimants were impatient to see their cases settled so they could move on in their lives.

The Richmond neighbourhood remained a snow-covered wasteland in the early months of 1918. It was only with the coming of spring that work crews finally resumed the grim job of searching for the dead.

Initially, the HRC moved to repair or rebuild houses for individual property owners. Workers repaired 3,000 dwellings in the first seven weeks after the disaster. However, such a pace was unsustainable. When the administrative process proved to be unwieldy and impractical, the demands from those who were desperate to receive compensation from the HRC grew louder by the day. Negotiating hundreds of such agreements for lost property was both time consuming and complicated.

HRC chairman T. Sherman Rogers seized the idea of having a "city planning expert" direct the resurrection of the North End. "We're going to make that part of the city as convenient as the south and west ends, with the same conservative atmosphere, so that people in all stations of life will build their homes there in the future," he announced.[3]

The provincial government had given the HRC wide-ranging authority to develop a master plan for North End revitalization. "For 30 years, the agency maintained control over building and zoning of 325 acres of Halifax's devastated North End."[4]

The HRC had the power to expropriate property without even notifying the owner directly, and it was able to go about its business with little public input or oversight. Not surprisingly, this proved highly controversial, as did the HRC's decision to retain the services of an urban planning expert to direct the rebuilding of the North End.

SCOTTISH-BORN THOMAS ADAMS was a leading proponent of "the garden city movement," an innovative approach to city building that was the brainchild of Sir Ebenezer Howard (1850–1928). His visionary zeal was the product of an era in which humanity placed its faith in science and technology to solve all the world's problems; anything seemed possible. Howard's idealistic nineteenth-century ideas about green spaces and sustainable urban environments would not seem out of place today. He envisioned cities in which the residents would live in harmony with nature.

Thomas Adams bought Howard's messianic vision to North America in October 1914 when he accepted a three-year appointment as the town planning advisor with a Canadian government agency called the Commission of Conservation. Prime Minister Sir Wilfrid Laurier, inspired by the progressivism of President Teddy Roosevelt, had created the commission in 1909 to advise Canadian governments on the best ways to promote conservation and make optimum use of natural resources.

When a commission official suggested to HRC chairman T. Sherman Rogers that Thomas Adams might be the ideal person to devise a grand redevelopment plan for Halifax, Rogers agreed. Offered the job, Adams leapt at the opportunity. Never one to think small, he suggested the HRC expropriate even more land in Halifax's North End, enough to accommodate a grand model community the likes of which the world had never seen.

Rogers, wary of trying to do too much and of further stirring up any more anti-HRC sentiments, informed Adams that the agency would not expropriate any more land. Undeterred, Adams forged ahead nonetheless. His ambitious master plan had three overarching aims: "to realign streets in the area for better drainage and transportation; to build both emergency and permanent houses; and to convert Fort Needham into a scenic park" that would be as nice as the one at Point Pleasant in Halifax's South End.[5]

Adams' main priority soon became the construction of the new housing Halifax so urgently needed. The planner was intent on replacing temporary apartment complexes with a planned neighbourhood that would be functional, durable, and aesthetically pleasing. He proposed to bring this vision to life in what residents would come to call "the Hydrostone district." This was a portion of Merkelsfield, a level area atop Fort Needham hill.

The Hydrostone name has a quaint, even cryptic, ring to it, but its origin was prosaic. The district drew its name from the material that workers used to construct most of the 328 new houses as well as shops and offices in the planned community. Hydrostone was the trade name for a kind of patented cement block made by a Chicago-based company. The pressure-moulded blocks resembled the cement blocks that today are ubiquitous on new home-building sites in Canada and across North America. Hydrostone blocks were relatively inexpensive, fire-resistant, easy to manufacture, relatively light, and simple to work with, and they could be finished with a visually attractive facing of granite dust or sand. The machinery to make these blocks was set up on a site in nearby Eastern Passage, on the Dartmouth side of the harbour. Once it was humming at full capacity, the factory turned out 4,000 blocks daily. By September 1918, work on the Hydrostone housing was under way in earnest.

New housing also began to rise phoenix-like among the blackened ruins of streets on the east-facing slope of Fort Needham hill. The HRC did not expropriate properties here, and so redevelopment on these streets occurred on an ad hoc basis. "The Relief Commission expected that it would seed the slopes of Fort Needham with houses, [and] then private investment would take over. But the North End was depopulated, and many North Enders had horrible memories of the area, were superstitious, and refused to move back."[6]

About 600 of the new homes that property owners erected on the streets of the old Richmond neighbourhood copied the designs of houses in the Hydrostone area; others were one-offs. In that regard, the streets-capes on the Fort Needham hillside were eclectic in appearance and, for better and worse, were somewhat reminiscent of the pre-explosion Richmond neighbourhood. The same was true of the new construction on the waterfront. Work there continued apace on the Naval Dockyard and on a huge new shipyard that would "employ 3,000 men, attract new industries, and make the North End a veritable human hive of activity," or so the *Herald* insisted. In August 1918, Halifax issued more than $560,000 in building permits, a record number for the city.

However, despite all the new construction that was happening and the optimism that prevailed in some quarters, it was not all smooth sailing for Halifax's rebirth. "The scarcity of labor is proving to be a handicap," the *Herald* lamented, "and there will be thousands of dollars of work left unfinished when the winter sets in."[7] Paradoxically, in the summer of 1919, tensions rose over the HRC's practice of hiring of non-union workers. At the same time, conflicts between the HRC and the Town Planning Board continued to escalate, and Thomas Adams' relationship with the HRC frayed as commission members grew increasingly skeptical about the planner's "greater vision for the entire city."[8]

In the end, Adams' enthusiasm for Halifax's redevelopment initiatives inevitably waned, as did his involvement. He was disillusioned and frustrated that his grand vision for the city had proved to be too grand—or was it "grandiose"? At the same time, the high tide of idealism that in 1909 had prompted the federal government to create the Commission of Conservation ebbed in the cynicism of the post-war world. It died entirely in 1921 when the commission disbanded. Canadians were preoccupied with other concerns that seemed more pressing than quixotic plans for garden cities.

Almost 620,000 veterans who had returned home were finding that reintegration into civilian life was not always easy. In addition, the country was coming to grips with the realization that 61,000 Canadians had died in the war—plus another 2,000 who had perished in the Halifax explosion—while another 173,000 servicemen and -women had come home wounded. Then there was the great Spanish influenza outbreak of 1918–1919. Troops brought the virus home from overseas. Worldwide, the epidemic claimed 20 million lives; in Canada, 50,000 people fell victim, many of them young people in the prime of life.

Under the circumstances, it is not surprising that Thomas Adams' priorities also changed. He went in search of new opportunities and found them in 1921 when he began teaching at the Massachusetts Institute of Technology in Cambridge, Massachusetts. Two years later, Adams accepted a commission to develop a regional master plan for New York City. The planner's involvements in Halifax and in Canada ended, but his legacy would endure.

ALTHOUGH THE FIRST residents had moved into the Hydrostone district in 1919, it would take four years for all the construction in the neighbourhood to be completed. By then, 2,000 people were living here. The legislation that had created and enabled the HRC granted the agency ownership of Hydrostone houses for thirty years. In 1949, the agency would begin selling the houses to residents. Money from the sales and from the rents that were being collected went into the kitty to help fund pensions the HRC provided to survivors of the Halifax explosion.

THE WORK OF THE Halifax Relief Commission continued in the two decades between the world wars of the last century. Following the death of T. Sherman Rogers in 1928, Major H.B. Stairs succeeded him as commission chairman. At the time, the agency employed seven staff. They spent most of their time administering the meagre forty-dollar monthly pensions that accident survivors were collecting. Writing in a 1946 report, HRC secretary-comptroller William Tibbs, an army veteran who had lost part of an arm in the Great War, explained the agency's rationale for awarding pensions. "[They] were not granted solely for the damage to the Human Machine, but on the extent to which injuries were disability as regards former occupation."[9]

The purchasing power of HRC pensions inevitably declined with each passing year, and so the commission routinely dealt with—but only occasionally granted—pensioners' requests for advances or for emergency money. The pleas to increase the monthly payouts were endless; at the same time, with more than 1,000 people receiving money, the long-term solvency of the $30-million pension fund was a constant concern. However, by 1950, the actuarial tables gave HRC administrators the confidence to accede to the demands for pension increases. After thirty-three years, the number of explosion survivors still collecting monthly pensions was dropping steadily. By January 1976, with just sixty-five names still on the rolls and $1.5 million remaining in the fund, the HRC disbanded; the Canadian government assumed responsibility for administering the remaining pensions. In 2004, only three people were still on the rolls. Today, the last of those explosion survivors is long gone, and that chapter in the history of the great Halifax harbour explosion of 1917 has come to its inevitable ending.

ASPECTS OF THOMAS ADAMS' grand plan had pointed the way toward the future for Halifax's North End and for the entire city. Integral to Adams' vision were two new arterial streets that diagonally traversed the North End. Dartmouth Avenue—as its name suggests—was intended to provide access to a bridge that Adams in his mind's eye saw spanning the Narrows one day. It would carry people and vehicles high above the spot where on December 6, 1917, the *Mont-Blanc* and the *Imo* had collided with such monumental consequences.

In the late 1960s, Adams' vision became a reality when the city of Halifax built the A. Murray MacKay Bridge. This 2,427-foot, four-lane crossing, which links Halifax and Dartmouth, opened to traffic on July 10, 1970. The "new bridge," as locals call it, is one of two huge suspension bridges that span the harbour. The other, the 2,500-foot-long Angus L. Macdonald Bridge, had opened in 1955 two miles to the south.

Another important component of Thomas Adams' plans called for the creation of a park in the 15.6-acre hilltop greenspace atop Fort Needham hill. The view from up there is commanding, for it overlooks the city, Bedford Basin, and the Narrows. Like the building of a bridge to Dartmouth, a Fort Needham park was one aspect of his master plan for Halifax that would remain unfulfilled until long after his 1940 death.

The HRC deeded the property to the city in 1942 on the condition that it be used as a parkland into perpetuity. However, it was not until after 1948 that the commission got around to creating a park there. By this time, soil erosion had ravaged the hillside; there were weeds growing everywhere, and rubble littered the site. The HRC set about beautifying the greenspace that over the next ten years, with financial assistance and help from the province and the people of Halifax, would become Fort Needham Memorial Park.

In 1983, the province announced funding for a memorial bell tower. A group of citizen volunteers calling themselves the Halifax Explosion Memorial Bells Committee raised additional money and took ownership of the initiative, which culminated in the installation of a carillon of ten bronze bells in a newly erected commemorative tower designed by Halifax architect Keith Graham. The dramatic cragginess of the structure's profile evokes memories of the ruins of buildings that fell victim to the 1917 explosion. At the same time, the lofty towers reach upward to the heavens and the promise of renewed hopes.

The bells installed in the memorial tower were originally donated by explosion survivor Barbara Orr, who lost her entire family in the explosion. For many years, the bells had hung in the belfry of United Memorial Church on nearby Kaye Street. However, in the mid-1960s, the bells had to be taken down for structural reasons and had remained homeless until they found new purpose.

A dedication ceremony for the Fort Needham Memorial Bell Tower took place on June 9, 1985. Later that same year, on December 6—the sixty-eighth anniversary of the great Halifax harbour explosion—a time capsule filled with explosion-related artifacts was sealed inside the tower, with the intention that it would be opened in 2017, on the centenary of the disaster.

Each year on December 6, those who remember the disaster that devastated Halifax attend a memorial service at the Fort Needham bell tower. The hymns are the same ones sung at the funeral service for the unidentified dead on December 17, 1917, and at services in the churches of Halifax and Dartmouth on New Year's Day 1918. The bells of the memorial tower—now numbering fourteen, after four additional bells were added to the carillon in 1990—chime out "O God, Our Help in Ages Past" and "Abide With Me." The tolling bells and somber voices that waft over Halifax's historic North End and over that nautical bottleneck that is the Narrows serve as a timeless reminder of the 2,000 innocent souls who were lost so tragically in the great Halifax harbour explosion of 1917, Canada's worst disaster.

EACH YEAR ON DECEMBER 6, A MEMORIAL CEREMONY FOR THE VICTIMS OF THE HALIFAX HARBOUR EXPLOSION OF 1917 IS HELD AT THE FORT NEEDHAM MEMORIAL BELL TOWER. (COURTESY OF KRISTIN LIPSCOMBE)

ACKNOWLEDGEMENTS

When I began my research into the great Halifax harbour explosion of 1917, I had no idea of how much work lay ahead. At first glance, the story seemed simple enough: two ships had collided in Halifax harbour, and disaster ensued. However, the more I read and the more people I spoke with, the bigger and more complex the story became. It was akin to an onion. Each time I peeled away one layer, there was another, and then another. The details sometimes were poignant enough to bring tears to my eyes.

The trail I followed in piecing together the research for this book took me from Canada to the United States and on to England, France, and Norway. Along the way, I received information, kind words, and no end of encouragement from scores of people. I owe special thank-yous to my editor Patrick Crean, HarperCollins (Canada); my agent, Richard Curtis, New York; genealogical researcher Liv Marit Haakenstad, Hamar, Norway; Anne-Marie Pocreau, a grand-niece of Captain Aimé Le Médec, the SS *Mont-Blanc*; and my loving wife, Marianne Hunter, who understood and excused my all-too-frequent absences from family events and social gatherings so that I could "work on the book."

I also owe debts of thanks to scores of other people without whose help I could not have completed my research. Among them are the following individuals:

CANADA: Major John Griffith Armstrong, Ottawa, ON; Dianna Bristol, Kingston, ON; Jeff Brown and Paul Boyle, Halifax Professional Fire Fighters Association—IAFF Local 268; Marjorie Bousfield, Kingston, ON; Virginia Clark, Halifax, NS; John Colwell and Andrew Colwell, Halifax, NS; Marilyn and John Elliott, Halifax, NS; Ingrid Gagnon, Kingston, ON; Alice Gibb, London, ON; William Glover, editor, *The Northern Mariner*, Winnipeg, MN; Prof. Grant W. Grams (Concordia University of Edmonton), Edmonton, AB; Frank Hanrahan, Ottawa, ON; Larry Harris, senior graphic designer, Queen's University, Kingston, ON; Philip L. Hartling, archivist, and the staff at the Nova Scotia Archives, Halifax, NS; Janet Kitz, historian, Halifax, NS; Janice Landry, Halifax, NS; Kristin Lipscombe, freelance photographer, Halifax, NS; Blaine Marks, town clerk/manager, Burgeo, NL; Roger Marsters, marine curator, and Derek Harrison, director of volunteers and educational programs, Maritime Museum of the Atlantic, Halifax, NS; Janet Maybee, Francis Mackey biographer; Walter McCall, Windsor, ON; Patricia MacDonald, copy editor, Sydney, NS; Alexandra McEwen, reference librarian, and the staff of the National Library and Archives Canada, Ottawa, ON; David More, historian, Kingston, ON; Prof. Emeritus Graeme Mount (Laurentian University), Sudbury, ON; Gary O'Donnell, Halifax pilot, Atlantic Pilotage Authority, Halifax, NS; Laurel Parson, assistant archivist, General Synod Archives, Anglican Church of Canada, Toronto, ON; Prof. Henry Roper (University of King's College), Halifax, NS; Alan Ruffman, nautical historian, Halifax, NS; Britton C. Smith, nautical historian, Kingston, ON; Michael Vollmer, yacht designer, Burlington, ON; Diane Walker, Jackson family historian, Halifax, NS; and Joel Zemel, Evan Wyatt biographer, Halifax, NS.

FRANCE: Nancy Chauvet, Iconographic Collection documentalist, Association of French Lines, Le Havre; M. Alain Croce, Martigues; and Danielle Quer, secretary, SGA/DMPA/SHD, Division Centre West–Lorient.

NORWAY: Hjørdis Bondevik and Per Gisle Galåen, the Norwegian Maritime Museum, Oslo; Prof. Nikolai Brandal (Oslo University), Oslo; Arne Torbjørn From, Sandefjord; Dag T. Hoelseth, historian, Oslo; Gunnhild Holmen, National Library of Norway, Oslo; Jan Erik Ringstad, curator NMF, Commander Chr. Christensen's Whaling Museum, Sandefjord; Rolleiv Solholm, chief editor, the *Norway Post*, Oslo; and Renathe-Johanne Wågenes, executive officer, digital archive, Regional State Archives in Bergen.

UNITED KINGDOM: Abi Coates, Hayle Library, Hayle, Cornwall; Ann Foreman, Hayle, Cornwall; George Hay, National Archives, London; Ian Pearce, Great Ayton, North Yorkshire; Kimberley and the Teesside Archives staff, Exchange House, Middlesbrough; Damian Saunders, Reading, Berkshire; and Elizabeth Wells, archivist/records manager, Westminster School, London.

UNITED STATES: Thomas Boghardt, senior historian, U.S. Army Center for Military History, Washington, DC; Stephanie Call, Jewish Heritage Center, New England Historic Genealogical Society, Boston, MA; Cecily Dyer, Library & Archives, Brooklyn Historical Society, Brooklyn, NY; Heather Glasby, archivist, Research Services (RE-PA) National Archives at Philadelphia, PA; Hal Harmon, reference librarian, Sarasota County Library System, Sarasota, FL; Thomas P. Jabine, Serial and Government Publications Division, Library of Congress, Washington, DC; Caitlin Jones, reference archivist, State Library of Massachusetts; Janet Lindenmuth, Widener Law

School library, Wilmington, DE; Jeff McNamara, nautical historian, Brooklyn, NY; Annie Tummino, archivist and scholarly communication librarian, SUNY Maritime College, Throggs Neck, NY; Kim Van Wagenen, Bountiful, UT; and Prof. Michael Warner, command historian, U.S. Department of Defense, Washington, DC.

SELECT BIBLIOGRAPHY

NON-FICTION

Armstrong, John Griffith, *The Halifax Explosion and the Royal Canadian Navy: Inquiry and Intrigue* (UBC Press, 2002).

Beed, Blair, *1917 Halifax Explosion and American Response* (Nimbus Publishing, 1999).

Bird, Michael J., *The Town That Died* (McGraw-Hill Ryerson, 1962).

Blum, Howard, *Dark Invasion: 1915, Germany's Secret War and the Hunt for the First Terrorist Cell in America* (Harper, 2014).

Chapman, Harry (Ed.), *Dartmouth's Day of Anguish* (Dartmouth Historical Society, 1992).

Dupuis, Michael, *Bearing Witness: Journalists, Record Keepers and the 1917 Halifax Explosion* (Fernwood Publishing, 2017).

Durflinger, Serge Marc, *Veterans with a Vision: Canada's War Blinded in Peace and War* (UBC Press, 2010).

Erickson, Paul, *Historic North End Halifax* (Nimbus Publishing, 2004).

Flemming, David D., *Explosion in Halifax Harbour: The Illustrated Account of a Disaster That Shook the World* (Formac, 2004).

Hébert Boyd, Michelle, *Enriched by Catastrophe: Social Work and Social Conflict after the Halifax Explosion* (Fernwood Publishing, 2007).

Hill, Allan Massie, *It Happened to Me* (Thorn Press, 1942).

Hopkins, Helen Burbidge, *Take My Hand: A Casual Stroll Through the Life of Helen Hopkins* (Express Printing, 2000).

Horwood, Joan, *The Great Halifax Explosion, Dec. 6, 1917* (Avalon Publications, 1976).

Kitz, Janet F., *Shattered City: The Halifax Explosion and the Road to Recovery* (Nimbus Publishing, 1990).

Kitz, Janet F., *Survivors* (Nimbus Publishing, 1992).

Kitz, Janet, and Joan Payzant, *December 1917: Re-visiting the Halifax Explosion* (Nimbus Publishing, 2006).

Larabee, Ann, *The Dynamite Fiend: The Chilling Story of Alexander Keith Jr., Nova Scotian Spy, Con Artist, & International Terrorist* (Nimbus Publishing, 2005).

Le Queux, William, *The German Spy System from Within* (Hodder & Stoughton, 1915).

Mac Donald, Laura M., *Curse of the Narrows: The Halifax Explosion of 1917* (Walker and Co., 2005).

Mahar, James, and Rowena Mahar, *Too Many to Mourn* (Nimbus Publishing, 1998).

Metson, Graham (Ed.), *The Halifax Explosion: December 6, 1917* (McGraw-Hill, 1978).

Mildon, Catherine M., *Exploded Identity: A Saga of the Halifax Explosion* (Trafford, 2005).

Monnon, Mary Ann, *Miracles and Mysteries: The Halifax Explosion, December 6, 1917* (Lancelot Press, 1977).

Mount, Graeme, *Canada's Enemies: Spies and Spying in the Peaceable Kingdom* (Dundurn Press, 1993).

Prince, Samuel H., *Catastrophe and Social Change, Based Upon a Sociological Study of the Halifax Disaster* (Columbia University, 1920).

Raddall, Thomas, *Halifax: Warden of the North* (Doubleday and Company, 1965).

Rasky, Frank. *Great Canadian Disasters* (Longmans Green & Company, 1961).

Ratshesky, Abraham C., *Report of the Halifax Relief Expedition December 6 to 15, 1917,* Massachusetts (Halifax Relief Expedition, 1918).

Remes, Jacob A.C., *Disaster Citizenship: Survivors, Solidarity and Power in the Progressive Era* (University of Illinois Press, 2016).

Report of the Royal Commission Appointed to Inquire Into and Report Upon the Pilotage System and Its Administration at the Port of Halifax, Nova Scotia.

Robinson, Ernest Fraser, *The Halifax Disaster, December 6, 1917* (Vanwell Publishing, 1997).

Robinson-Mushkat, S. William, "City at a Critical Juncture: Halifax's Town Planning Board at the End of the Progressive Era, 1911–1924," unpublished master of arts thesis (St. Mary's University, 2010).

Ruffman, Alan, and Colin D. Howell, *Ground Zero: A Reassessment of the 1917 Explosion in Halifax* (Nimbus Publishing and Gorsebrook Research Institute, 1994).

Smith, Marilyn Gurney, *The King's Yard: An Illustrated History of the Halifax Dockyard* (Nimbus Publishing, 1985).

Snow, Pauline, *Worse Than War: The Halifax Explosion* (Four East, 1992).

Zemel, Joel, *Scapegoat: The Extraordinary Legal Proceedings Following the 1917 Halifax Explosion* (SVP Productions, 2012).

MICROFICHE

Sheldon, Joseph, *A Bolt from the Blue* [microform] (Cox Bros., 1918).

Smith, Stanley K., *Heart Throbs of the Halifax Horror* [microform] (G.E. Weir, 1918).

ARTICLES

Adams, Thomas, "The Planning of the New Halifax," *The Contract Record*, August 28, 1918, pp. 680–683.

Armstrong, John Griffith, "Letters from Halifax: Reliving the Halifax Explosion Through the Eyes of My Grandfather, a Sailor in the Royal Canadian Navy," *The Northern Mariner*, October 1988, pp. 55–74.

Baker, Howard, "When Hell Came to Halifax," *History Today*, December 2002, pp. 42–43.

Chambers, Rear Admiral M. Bertram, "Halifax Explosion" *The Naval Review*, 1920, Vol VII, No. 3.

Gilligan, Edmund, "Death in Halifax," *American Mercury* Vol. 43, No. 170 (February 1938), pp. 175–181.

Glasner, Joyce, "On the Front Lines of Disaster," *Canada's History*, December 2007-January 2008, pp. 16–24.

Ingram, Katie, "Truth Is the First Casualty," *Halifax Magazine*, December 2015, pp. 26–28.

MacLeod, M., "Helping Unheeded: Newfoundland's Relief Effort and the Historiography of the Halifax Explosion, 1917," *Nova Scotia Historical Review*, Vol 2, No. 2, 1982.

Maybee, Janet, "The Persecution of Pilot Mackey," *The Northern Mariner*, Vol. XX, No. 2 (April 2010), pp. 149–173.

McAlister, Chryssa, T. Jock Murray, and Charles Maxner, "The Halifax Explosion of 1917: An Oculist Experience," *Canadian Journal of Ophthalmology*, Vol. 43, No. 1 (2008), pp. 27–32.

McAlister, Chryssa, T. Jock Murray, and Charles Maxner, "The Halifax Explosion (1917): Eye Injuries and Their Care," *British Journal of Ophthalmology*, June 2007, pp. 832–835.

Moore, Oliver, "A Day of Blinding Fire, a Life of Stunning Success," *Globe and Mail*, September 14, 2009, p. A-3.

Morton, Suzanne, "The Halifax Relief Commission and Labour Relations during the Reconstruction of Halifax, 1917–1919," *Acadiensis: Journal of the History of the Atlantic Region*, Vol. XVIII, No. 2 (Spring 1989), pp. 73–93.

Rasky, Frank, "The Day Halifax Exploded," *Liberty Magazine*, May 1959, pp. 143–165.

Richardson, Evelyn M., "The Halifax Explosion, 1917." *The Nova Scotia Historical Quarterly*, Vol. 7, No. 4 (December 1977), pp. 305–330.

Rockwell, Fred, "Flying Babies, Shards of Glass, and a Bucket of Eyeballs," *Globe and Mail*, December 1, 2007, p. F-12.

Scanlon, Joseph, "Source of Threat and Source of Assistance: The Maritime Aspects of the 1917 Halifax Explosion," *The Northern Mariner*, No. 4 (October 2000), pp. 39–50.

Smith, Douglas, "The Railways and Canada's Greatest Disaster: The Halifax Explosion, December 6, 1917," *Canadian Rail*, November-December 1992, pp. 201–213.

Wright, H. Millard, "The Other Halifax Explosion," *Bedford Magazine*, July 18–20, 1945.

PHOTOS

Roe, Harold T., The Halifax catastrophe: forty views showing extent of damage in Canada's historic city as the result of terrific explosion on Thursday, December 6, 1917, which killed 1,200 men, women, and children; injured 3,000; and rendered 6,000 homeless, causing property damage of nearly $50,000,000 (Royal Print & Litho, 1917).

Weir, Gerald E., Devastated Halifax: views of the greatest disaster in the history of the American continent, caused by the explosion that followed the collision of the French munition ship *Mont-Blanc* and the Belgian relief ship *Imo* in Halifax harbour, December 6, 1917 (G.E. Weir, 1917).

West House Museum, Halifax, 09:06, December 6, 1917: a photo-documentation of the Halifax explosion (West House Museum, 1977).

CHILDREN'S AND YOUNG ADULT LITERATURE

Beveridge, Cathy, *Chaos in Halifax* (Ronsdale Press, 2004).

Dixon, Michael, and Peter Hawkins (illustrations), *The Halifax Explosion* (McClelland & Stewart, 1997).

Glasner, Joyce, *The Halifax Explosion: Surviving the Blast That Shook a Nation* (Altitude Publishing, 2003).

Haworth-Attard, Barbara, *Irish Chain* (HarperTrophy Canada, 2002).

Lawson, Julie, *No Safe Harbour: The Halifax Explosion Diary of Charlotte Blackburn* (Scholastic Canada, 2006).

McKay, Sharon E, *Penelope: Terror in the Harbour* (Penguin Books, 2001).

Robinson, Ernest Fraser, *The Halifax Disaster, December 6, 1917* (Vanwell Publishing, 1987).

Walker, Sally M., *Blizzard of Glass: The Halifax Explosion of 1917* (Square Fish, 2014).

FICTION

Burrill, Janet C. *Dark Clouds of the Morning: A Historical Novel* (Word Alive Press, 2011).

Lotz, Jim, *The Sixth of December* (PaperJacks, 1981).

MacLennan, Hugh, *Barometer Rising* (Collins, 1941).

MacNeil, Robert, *Burden of Desire* (Seal Books, 1992).

McKelvey, Bell F., *A Romance of the Halifax Disaster* (Royal Print and Litho, 1918).

Smallwood, Bill, *Lives of Courage, 1912–1932* (Borealis Press, 2008).

Tattrie, Jon, *Black Snow* (Pottersfield Press, 2009).

ONLINE RESOURCES

Baker, Janet, Profile of Archibald M. MachMechan, *Dictionary of Canadian Biography*, http://www.biographi.ca/en/bio/macmechan_archibald_mckellar_16E.html.

Brandal, Nik, and Ola Teige, "The Secret Battlefield, Intelligence and Counter-intelligence in Norway during the First World War," https://uio.academia.edu/NikolaiBrandal/Papers.

Canadian Broadcasting Corporation (CBC) Digital Archives: The Halifax Explosion, http://www.cbc.ca/archives/topic/the-halifax-explosion.

CBC Halifax Explosion website, a large interactive website about the explosion: www.cbc.ca/halifaxexplosion.

Francis Mackey, Canadian Broadcasting Corporation recorded interview, October 3, 1967, Nova Scotia, Archives and Records Management, AR 1267-1269,1958,http://www.cbc.ca/archives/entry/mont-blanc-pilot-francis-mackey-recalls-halifax-1917-explosion.

HalifaxExplosion.net features images and reading material related to the Halifax explosion and the early RCN.

Halifax explosion 100th anniversary website: www.halifax.ca/halifaxexplosion.

Halifax Public Library, "Explosion in Halifax Harbour," December 6, 1917: www.halifaxpubliclibraries.ca.

Historica Minutes: "The Halifax Explosion," https://www.historicacanada.ca/content/heritage-minutes/halifax-explosion.

Maritime Museum of the Atlantic Halifax Explosion web page: https://maritimemuseum.novascotia.ca/what-see-do/halifax-explosion.

National Film Board documentary (1991), *"Just One Big Mess": The Halifax Explosion, 1917,* http://www3.nfb.ca/objectifdocumentaire/index.php?mode=view&language=english&filmId=30.

Nova Scotia Archives Halifax Explosion Book of Remembrance, a database of victims with 1,950 names, https://novascotia.ca/archives/remembrance/.

Perkins School for the Blind archives: www.perkinsarchives.org/halifax-disaster.html.

Scanlon, Joe, "The Halifax Explosion," Canadian Risk and Hazards Network, Winter 2014: www.crhnet.ca.

White, Ja mes, "The Garrison Response to the Halifax Disaster, December 6, 1917" (unpublished research paper, Parks Canada, 2014). Accessible online at https://h mhps.ca/pdf/The-Garrison-Response-to-the-Halifax-Disaster_James_White_Preliminary_Report_2014-04-09.pdf.

ENDNOTES

INTRODUCTION

1. Testimony of Captain Frederick C.C. Pasco, *Imo* vs *Mont-Blanc*, Vol. 1, p. 519.
2. www.cbc.ca/archives/entry/two-ships-collide-and-halifax-reels. See also p. 291 of *Ground Zero: A Reassessment of the 1917 Explosion in Halifax Harbour*, edited by Alan Ruffman and Colin D. Howell (Nimbus Publishing/Gorsebrook Research Institute, 1994). (Cited hereafter as *Ground Zero*.)
3. Bronfman, Charles, *Distilled: A Memoir of Family, Seagram, Baseball, and Philanthropy* (HarperCollins, 2016), location 2843 in Kindle edition. It is clear that many other people share Bronfman's opinion of Coleman's prominent role in the Halifax explosion story. In June 2017, the Halifax Transit authority announced that more than half of the 11,000 Haligonians who voted in a poll to choose names for Halifax's two new passenger ferries chose to name one of the boats in Coleman's honour.
4. *Halifax Chronicle Herald*, December 6, 2013.
5. MacMillan, Margaret, *The War That Ended Peace: The Road to 1914* (Random House, 2013), p. xxxi.

CHAPTER 1

1. Bird, Michael, *The Town That Died* (Nimbus Publishing, 2011), p. 2. (Cited hereafter as Bird.)
2. *Investigation: Mont-Blanc and Imo Collision at Halifax, December 1917*, p. 39. (Cited hereafter as Wreck Commission Inquiry.)
3. Ibid., p. 40.
4. The Statue of Liberty-Ellis Island Foundation, www.libertyellisfoundation.org/ship-result.
5. Commander Odiarne Coates' Royal Navy service record, National Archives of the United Kingdom, ADM 196/43/32.
6. Bird, op cit., p. 3.
7. Ibid., p. 4.
8. Email from Anne-Marie Pocreau to author, August 20, 2015.

9. Ancestry.ca, confirmed by Legion of Honor citation.

10. Bird, op cit., p. 5.

CHAPTER 2

1. *Brooklyn Daily Eagle,* July 31, 1916, p. 4.

2. Ibid.

3. *Ground Zero,* op cit., p. 297.

4. For more information on the history of the explosives, see the article "High Explosives: The Interaction of Chemistry and Mechanics" by William C. Davis, *Los Alamos Science,* No. 2 (Spring Summer 1981), pp. 48–75.

5. *New York Times,* July 31, 1916, p. 4.

6. Bolotenko, George, "Wartime Explosions in Archangel, 1916–1917," *The Northern Mariner,* Vol. XXI, No. 4 (October 2011), pp. 377–405.

7. *New York Times,* July 31, 1916, p. 4.

8. Tucker, Gilbert N., *The Naval Service of Canada: Its Official History,* Vol. I (Minister of National Defence, Ottawa, 1962), p. 229.

9. Testimony of Edward Flower, *Imo* vs *Mont-Blanc,* Vol. 1, p. 638, lines 4–39.

10. In 1917, steering orders on ships were "helm orders"—hence the person at the ship's wheel was known as the "helmsman." This system was a holdover from the days of sailing ships. As historian Michael Bird explains in his book *The Town That Died,* when the helmsman of the *Mont-Blanc* turned the ship's wheel to starboard, the ship's rudder moved in the opposite direction, to port. This also caused the ship's bow to turn to port. Today, the system has changed and ships are steered like automobiles. As Bird notes, "The wheel to starboard or port send[s] both rudder and bows in the same direction" (p. 8).

CHAPTER 3

1. Mac Donald, Laura, *Curse of the Narrows: The Halifax Explosion of 1917* (HarperCollins, 2005), p. 3. (Cited hereafter as Mac Donald.)

2. Raddall, Thomas, *Halifax: Warden of the North* (Doubleday and Company, 1965), p. 2. (Cited hereafter as Raddall.)

3. Bird, op cit., p. 30.

4. "The Humanitarian Years," the Museum Exhibit Galleries, Herbert Hoover Presidential Library and Museum website.

5. Two other children died in their infancy.

6. Email from Arne From to author, January 12, 2017.

7. From's patent number was 1329. Found online at www.arkivverket.no/URN:NBN:no-a1450-ru10051001120046.jpg.

8. Gudrun was born February 2, 1900, and immigrated to the United States in 1932. Magnhild was born in 1901, and died in 1984. She reportedly made her living as a professional tennis player.

9. Norway's 1910 census, http://digitalarkivet.arkivverket.no/en-gb/ft/sok/1910.

10. The knot is a unit of speed equal to 1 nautical mile (1.852 kilometres) per hour, approximately 1.151 miles per hour. Twelve knots is 14 miles per hour or 22 kilometres per hour.

11. Quotation derived from a news report in the *Philadelphia Commercial News* that was referenced in the *Halifax Morning Chronicle*, December 17, 1917, p. 9. (Cited hereafter as *Philadelphia Commercial News*.)

12. Re Admiralty Case #927, District Court of Delaware, *Schmaal* vs. *Steamship* Imo.

13. *Philadelphia Commercial News*, op cit.

14. This number includes 383 Norwegian ships sunk by German torpedoes and 54 that German mines sank. Total tonnage was 987,816. Source: *A List of Neutral Ships Sunk by the Germans—8 August 1914 to 26 April 1917*. National Archives of Australia, Series A5954, CVS192/34.

CHAPTER 4

1. Archibald MacMechan interview with Captain Percy Newcombe, Halifax Disaster Records Office, Nova Scotia Archives, MG1, Vol. 2124, #207.

2. Armstrong, John Griffith, *The Halifax Explosion and the Royal Canadian Navy: Inquiry and Intrigue* (UBC Press, 2002), p. 20. (Cited hereafter as Armstrong.)

3. Borden was the last Canadian prime minister to be knighted (in 1915); in deference to "the Nickle Resolution" of 1917, no others have been so honoured.

4. Raddall, op cit., p. 2.

5. Between Ive's Point, at the north end of McNabs Island, and the breakwater located at Point Pleasant, in the city of Halifax's residential South End.

6. Testimony of George R. Smith, *Imo vs Mont-Blanc*, p. 615, line 6; p. 617, line 4.

7. Ibid., p. 615.

8. Ibid., pp. 615, 617. Smith also stated that he had received a phone call at home that evening from "the examining officer of the *Niobe*." The man had called with a question about another ship, and in that same conversation, he asked about the status of the *Imo*. Smith advised him that the Norwegian ship would not be leaving until next morning.

CHAPTER 5

1. Email from Gary O'Donnell, Halifax pilot, Atlantic Pilotage Authority, to author, November 9, 2016.

2. Kipling's 1922 poem "Song of the Cities" reads "Into the mist my guardian prows put forth / Behind the mist my virgin ramparts lie / The Warden of the Honour of the North / Sleepless and veiled am I!"

3. Bird, op cit., p. 25.

4. Rules and Regulations for the Port of Halifax and Office of Harbour Master, Order-in-Council, October 14, 1896.

5. In 1917, the daily activities of harbour pilots were governed by the Pilotage Act of 1873.

6. Armstrong, op cit., p. 22.

7. Report of the Royal Commission Appointed to Enquire Into and Report Upon the Pilotage System and Its Administration at the Port of Halifax, NS," February 27, 1919, p. 8.

8. "Time Machine: What Life in Canada Was Like Before the First World War," *Globe and Mail*, June 26, 2014.

9. Testimony of Commander Evan Wyatt, *Imo* vs *Mont-Blanc*, Vol. II, p. 1227.

10. Bird, op cit., p. 174.

11. Testimony of Captain Edward Martin, Wreck Commission Inquiry, Vol. II, p. 1613.

12. Testimony of Commander Evan Wyatt, Wreck Commission Inquiry, Vol I, p. 1681.

CHAPTER 6

1. Testimony of Francis Mackey, *Imo* vs *Mont-Blanc*, Vol. 1, p. 136.

2. Cable from Wells to Rear Admiral Bertram M. Chambers, December 3, 1917, NSS 37-25-8.

3. Testimony of Mate Terrance Freeman, *Imo* vs *Mont-Blanc*, Vol. II, p. 1162.

4. CBC radio interview of Francis Mackey by Bob Cadman (1958), CBC Radio Collection, Nova Scotia Archives, Ar1267-69.

5. According to Bird, op cit., p. 11, Mackey and his host lit up cigars and enjoyed an after-dinner smoke. However, like some other aspects of Bird's gripping account of the Halifax explosion, the truth of his words is questionable. Mackey may well have offered a cigar to the Frenchman, but it is unlikely he would have accepted it. Le Médec was uneasy with the cargo his ship was carrying and would not have taken the chance.

CHAPTER 7

1. *New York Times*, December 7, 1917, p. 2.

2. MacNeil, Robert, *Wordstruck* (Viking, 1989), p. 15. (Cited hereafter as *Wordstruck*.)

3. MacLennan, Hugh, *Barometer Rising* (McClelland and Stewart, 1958), p. 6. Of all the fictional accounts of the Halifax explosion written over the years, MacLennan's novel is widely regarded as the best. The book, a Canadian literary classic, is still in print almost six decades after it was written. (Cited hereafter as *Barometer Rising*.)

4. Ibid., p. 235.

5. Erickson, Paul A., *Historic North End Halifax* (Nimbus Publishing, 2004), p. 65.

6. *Wordstruck*, op cit., p. 15.

7. Blakeley, Phyllis, *Glimpses of Halifax, 1867–1900*, Publication #9, Public Archives of Nova Scotia (Mika Publishing, 1973), p. 212.

CHAPTER 8

1. Catalogue of the British National Archives, ADM/340/149/26. The notations in Wyatt's service record indicate he had been "serving on HMS *Niobe* since 25/8/14."

2. Email from Elizabeth Wells, archivist and records manager, Westminster School, to author, April 14, 2016.

3. *Times of London*, "Pay in the Navy" by Admiral Charles Beresford, November 19, 1912, p. 14. Beresford, a rival of Admiral John Arbuthnot "Jackie" Fisher, First Admiral of the Fleet, seldom missed an opportunity to chide Fisher for the way he was running the Royal Navy.

4. Williamson, Jeffrey G., "Structure of Pay in Britain, 1710–1911," *Economic History Review*, Vol. 40, Issue 4, pp. 561–570. It is difficult to translate 1914 British pounds into today's dollars, but the generally accepted multiplier is 97. Using that measure, a Royal Navy lieutenant's annual salary of £292 in 1914 today would be about $33,000 Canadian or $28,000 U.S.

5. *London Gazette*, October 25, 1907, p. 7125.

6. Edwin Izod and his wife, Ellen, had two sons and two daughters. Madeline (b. 1881) was the second youngest of the children. Her father's company, Edwin Izod and Son, was one of twenty-one corset makers in Portsmouth in the early years of the twentieth century. Fashioned from twelve separate shaped pieces and forty whalebone strips, the garments gave the wearer an hourglass figure. A steam-moulding process that Edwin Izod developed in 1868 involved placing a corset, wet with starch, on a steam-heated copper torso form until it dried into the desired shape. The end product was a beautiful, stylish garment in which "the fabric and bones are adapted with marvelous accuracy to every curve and undulation of the finest type of figure," as an advertisement in the July 1879 edition of *The Ladies' Gazette of Fashion* proclaimed. For a more comprehensive account of the Izod family's business activities and accomplishments, see Zemel, Joel, *Scapegoat: The Extraordinary Legal Proceedings Following the 1917 Halifax Explosion* (SVP Productions, 2012), p. 408n. (Cited hereafter as Zemel.)

7. Ibid., p. 16.

8. Ibid.

9. Ibid.

10. Ibid., p. 279.

11. Armstrong, op cit., p. 161.

CHAPTER 9

1. Armstrong, John Griffith, "Letters from Halifax: Reliving the Halifax Explosion through the Eyes of My Grandfather, a Sailor in the Royal Canadian Navy," *The Northern Mariner*, October 1988, p. 60. (Cited hereafter as "Letters from Halifax.")

2. *Barometer Rising*, op cit., p. 142.

3. Mahar, James, and Rowena Mahar, *Too Many to Mourn: One Family's Tragedy in the Halifax Explosion* (Nimbus Publishing, 1998), p. 6. (Cited hereafter as *Too Many to Mourn*.) Written by Mary Jean Hinch's son, this revealing book is the definitive account of the Jackson family's devastating losses, ordeal, and survival.

CHAPTER 10

1. For many years, the name of the ship was unknown. Those who wrote about the Halifax explosion alluded to the vessel simply as "the American freighter" or as "a tramp steamer." It was military historian John Griffith Armstrong who identified the *Clara*. He writes on p. 141 of his book *The Halifax Explosion and the Royal Canadian Navy*: "RCN intelligence files indicate that she was no 'tramp' steamer but almost certainly the New York–registered *SS Clara*, a former Austro-Hungarian merchant ship owned by the United Sates Shipping Board Emergency Fleet."

2. National Archives of Canada, File #9704-244, Part 1. This "List of Licensed Pilots on Active Duty," dated December 26, 1917, included the names of fourteen Halifax harbour pilots. Interestingly, the list included the name of Francis Mackey, the pilot of the ill-fated *Mont-Blanc*. An explanatory paragraph the writer added to the bottom of the document explains: "Frank Mackey is the only pilot holding any certificate other than a pilots [*sic*] license, which is a Master's Certificate." The information provided on Edward Renner indicated that his record was "Good"; however, there was a cryptic notation in the "Accidents" column that he had been involved in a "Slight one at No. 2 Pier, liability not recorded." No further details on this incident were given.

3. Bird, op cit., p. 15.

4. Ibid.

5. *Barometer Rising*, op cit., p. 141.

6. Testimony of Lieutenant Arthur Adams, *Imo* vs *Mont-Blanc*, pp. 688–689.

7. Martin, John P., *The Story of Dartmouth* (Dartmouth, 1957), pp. 515–516.

CHAPTER 11

1. Testimony of John Makiny, April 1, 1918, Appeal Book, p. 12.

2. *Barometer Rising*, op cit., p. 142.

3. Bird, op cit., p. 21.

4. Ibid., p. 443, l. 29; p. 444, l. 31.

5. Ibid., p. 446, ll. 8–26.

6. When the Canadian naval ship HMCS *Niobe* foundered off Cape Sable in 1911, it was Horatio Brannen and his crew who went to her assistance. They hauled the ship off the rocks and patched her up so that she could make it to Halifax for repairs in the dry dock.

7. Testimony of Walter Brannen, *Imo* vs *Mont-Blanc*, Vol. 1, p. 480, l. 6; p. 481, l. 8.

8. According to Armstrong, op cit., p. 33, Horatio Brannen's reported comment was that the *Imo* "was going as fast as any ship he ever saw" in the channel. His words have been paraphrased for narrative effect.

9. Testimony of Walter Brannen, *Imo* vs *Mont-Blanc*, Vol. 1, p. 481, ll. 20–23; p. 487, ll. 40–43.

10. A 1958 Francis Mackey interview with CBC Radio, aired October 3, 1967. CBC Archives, www.cbc.ca/archives. (Cited hereafter as Mackey interview with CBC Radio.)

11. Testimony of Francis Mackey, *Imo* vs *Mont-Blanc*, Vol. 1, p. 148, ll. 25–27.

12. Bird, op cit., p. 21.

13. Testimony of Francis Mackey, *Imo* vs *Mont-Blanc*, Vol. 1, p. 142, l. 44; p. 143, l. 43.

14. Bird, op cit., p. 22.

15. Testimony of Francis Mackey, *Imo* vs *Mont-Blanc*, Vol. 1, p. 136, ll. 2–10.

16. Testimony of Captain Aimé Le Médec, *Imo* vs *Mont-Blanc*, Vol. 1, p. 45, ll. 22–24.

17. Testimony of Francis Mackey, *Imo* vs *Mont-Blanc*, Vol. 1, p. 137, ll. 10–12.

CHAPTER 12

1. Testimony of Francis Mackey, *Imo* vs *Mont-Blanc*, Vol. 1, p. 138, ll. 21–27.

2. For a detailed discussion of the effect of the maneuvering by Captains From and Le Médec, see Armstrong, op cit., p. 35.

3. Ibid., p. 35.

4. Testimony of Francis Mackey, *Imo* vs *Mont-Blanc*, Vol. 1, p. 137, ll. 40–41.

5. Testimony of Peter B'Jönnas, *Imo* vs *Mont-Blanc*, Vol. 1, p. 81, l. 40.

6. Testimony of Johan Johansen, *Imo* vs *Mont-Blanc*, Vol. I, p. 428.

7. Bird, op cit., p. 34.

8. *Barometer Rising*, p. 151.

CHAPTER 13

1. Testimony of Peter B'Jönnas, *Imo* vs *Mont-Blanc*, Vol. 1, p. 81.
2. Testimony of Captain Aimé Le Médec, *Imo* vs *Mont-Blanc*, Vol. 1, pp. 38–39.
3. *Barometer Rising*, op cit., p. 151.
4. Testimony of Mate Herbert Whitehead, *Imo* vs *Mont-Blanc*, Vol. 1, p. 650.
5. Armstrong, op cit., p. 36.
6. Mackey interview with CBC Radio, op cit.
7. Testimony of Francis Mackey, *Imo* vs *Mont-Blanc*, Vol. 1, p. 137.
8. Testimony of Captain Aimé Le Médec, *Imo* vs *Mont-Blanc*, Vol. 1, p. 39.
9. Bird, op cit., p. 36.
10. Testimony of Jean-Baptiste Glotin, *Imo* vs *Mont-Blanc*, Vol. 1, p. 105.
11. Testimony of Francis Mackey, *Imo* vs *Mont-Blanc*, Vol. 1, p. 131.
12. Testimony of Able Seaman George Abbott, *Imo* vs *Mont-Blanc*, Vol. 1, p. 478

CHAPTER 14

1. *Barometer Rising*, op cit., p. 151.
2. *Halifax Herald*, January 12, 1912, p. 1. The writer of that news report described the fire as being "the most disastrous conflagration that has visited Halifax in many years."
3. Testimony of Herbert Whitehead, *Imo* vs *Mont-Blanc*, Vol. 1, p. 651.
4. Armstrong, op cit., p. 37.
5. Testimony of Alphonse Serré, *Imo* vs *Mont-Blanc*, Vol. 1, p. 304.
6. "Death . . . advanced, roaring over the water," *Halifax Mail-Star*, December 4, 1972, p. 7.
7. Mackey interview with CBC Radio, op cit.
8. A kipper is a whole herring that has been sliced in half from head to tail, gutted, salted or pickled, then smoked. Kippers were once a breakfast staple in Great Britain, but today they are considered a delicacy.
9. Bird, op cit., p. 49. Military historian John Griffith Armstrong, whose 2002 book *The Halifax Explosion and the Royal Canadian Navy* provides a definitive account of the RCN's involvement in the disaster, has praised British journalist Michael Bird's account—in his 1962 book *The Town That Died*—of the heroic efforts of Lieutenant-Commander Tom Triggs and Captain Horatio Brannen to pull the *Mont-Blanc* away from Pier 6.
10. Testimony of Herbert Whitehead, *Imo* vs *Mont-Blanc*, Vol. 1, p.651.
11. Testimony of Charles Mayers, *Imo* vs *Mont-Blanc*, Vol. 1, p. 68.
12. Gilligan, Edmund, "Death in Halifax," *American Mercury*, February 1938, p. 176. (Cited hereafter as Gilligan.)

CHAPTER 15

1. *Barometer Rising*, op cit., p. 152.
2. *Ground Zero*, op cit., p. 276.

3. The Halifax fire department was started in 1765. From 1768 to 1894, the all-volunteer, part-time service was known as the Union Engine Company. By 1894, some of the firefighters were being paid, and the service was renamed the Halifax Fire Department. By 1918, the department had evolved as the needs of the city of Halifax changed, and the city's firefighters were full-time professionals.

4. According to fire-engine historian Walter McCall of Windsor, ON (author of the 2005 book *100 Years of American LaFrance*), *Patricia* was a 1913 American LaFrance Type 12 Triple Combination Pumper. "Ordered in 1912, it was shipped from the American-LaFrance Fire Engine Co. factory in Elmira, NY, to Halifax on 6 February 1913. The first LaFrance motor pumper delivered in Canada, it was powered by a 100-horsepower six-cylinder motor, which drove an 800 Imperial gallon-per-minute rotary gear pump. Bearing factory serial #249, it was named the *Patricia*—which was lettered on its long hood." McCall email to the author, July 19, 2016.

5. Landry, Janice, "When the Bell Calls: The Last Alarm," *Halifax Magazine*, November 2012. Halifax.mag/cover/the-last-alarm.

6. Yarmouth County Museum and Archives, YMS-1-699. A copy of this letter can be accessed on the Canadian Broadcasting Corporation's website: www.cbc.ca/halifaxexplosion/he3_shock/he3_shock_feature_letter_bellew.htm.

7. Pasco began his naval career aboard HMS *Wolverine*, a Jason-class three-masted wooden screw corvette. The ship became flagship of the Royal Navy's "Australia Station" and was eventually handed over to the Colony of New South Wales as a training ship for the New South Wales Naval Brigade and New South Wales Naval Artillery Volunteers.

8. For more information on Sydney's importance as a WWI naval port, please see "Sydney, Nova Scotia, and the U-Boat war, 1918" by Roger Sarty and Brian Tennyson, *Canadian Military History*, Vol. 7, No. 1, 2012.

9. Testimony of Captain Frederick C.C. Pasco, Wreck Commission Inquiry, p. 1040.

CHAPTER 16

1. "Letters from Halifax," op cit., p. 61.

2. *Halifax Evening Mail*, December 13, 1917, p. 1.

3. Raddall, Thomas, *In My Time: A Memoir* (McClelland & Stewart, 1976). Online excerpt at www.cbc.ca/halifaxexplosion/he3_shock/media/raddall.pdf.

4. Halifax explosion reminiscence of Jean Holder, December 6, 1985. Nova Scotia Archives, MC27, Vol. 9, p. 1.

5. Testimony of Commander Evan Wyatt, *Imo vs Mont-Blanc*, Vol. 1, pp. 569–570.

6. *Canadian Encyclopedia*, www.thecanadianencyclopedia.ca/en/article/status-of-women.

7. Ibid.

8. *Halifax Mail-Star*, December 6, 1972, p. 11.

9. Wikipedia lists Vincent Coleman's age as forty-five. However, the Halifax Explosion Remembrance Book lists his age as forty-two, while a genealogical website shows his birthdate as being 1877, meaning he was forty at the time of his death.

10. "Vincent Coleman and the Halifax Explosion," Maritime Museum of the Atlantic, December 6, 1917, https://maritimemuseum.novascotia.ca.

CHAPTER 17

1. USS *Tacoma* deck log, December 6, 1917, p. 6, RG 24-Bureau of Naval Personnel, Entry 118 GT, Logs of U.S. Ships and Stations, 1801-1946.
2. *New York Times*, December 9, 1917, p. 5.
3. Gilligan, op cit., p. 177.
4. *Barometer Rising*, op cit., p. 154.
5. MacMechan, Archibald, *The Halifax Explosion: December 6, 1917* (McGraw, Hill, Ryerson, 1978) p. 14. (Cited hereafter as MacMechan.)
6. *Halifax Mail-Star*, October 6, 1967.
7. Kitz, Janet, *Shattered City: The Halifax Explosion and the Road to Recovery* (Nimbus Publishing, 1989), p. 37.
8. *Halifax Herald*, December 7, 1917, p. 1.
9. Kitz, op cit., p. 63.
10. The exact number of people who died in the Halifax explosion will never be known for certain. There was no accurate count of the number of people who were actually living in Halifax in December 1917. In addition, no traces of the bodies of some victims—how many is impossible to say—were ever found. Such was the nature and intensity of the explosion.
11. "Letters from Halifax," op cit., p. 61.
12. *Halifax Morning Chronicle*, December 13, 1917.
13. *Halifax Daily Echo*, December 12, 1917.

CHAPTER 18

1. Johansen interview, *Philadelphia Bulletin*, February 18, 1918.
2. Ibid.
3. *Ground Zero*, op cit., p. 37.
4. Mackey interview with CBC Radio, op cit.
5. Kitz, op cit., p. 31.
6. Mackey interview with CBC Radio, op cit.
7. Ibid.
8. Testimony of Walter Brannen, *Imo* vs *Mont-Blanc*, Vol. 1, p. 486.
9. Testimony of Captain Frederick C.C. Pasco, *Imo* vs *Mont-Blanc*, Vol. 1, p. 1041.
10. "Letters from Halifax," op cit., p. 61.
11. Ibid., p. 63.
12. Ibid.
13. Armstrong, op cit., p. 62.
14. For a more complete account of this incident, please see Armstrong, op cit., pp. 39–40, 44–45.
15. Report of Lieutenant C.A. McLennan, n/d, MD6 86-2-1, NAC, RG 24, Vol. 4548, as cited in Armstrong, p. 58.

16. Mac Donald, op cit., p. 98.

17. Armstrong, op cit., p. 60.

CHAPTER 19

1. Prince, Samuel H., *Catastrophe and Social Change: Based Upon a Sociological Study of the Halifax Disaster* (Ph.D. thesis, Columbia University, 1920), p. 29. (Cited hereafter as Prince.)

2. Bird, op cit., p. 80.

3. *Toronto Star*, December 11, 1917, p. 18. Kendall became captain of the RMS *Empress of Ireland* in May 1914. Just a few weeks later, on the night of May 29, the passenger ship sank in the St. Lawrence River after colliding with the SS *Storstad*, a Norwegian coal freighter that was equipped with an ice-breaking bow. The damage to the *Empress of Ireland's* hull was so extensive that the ship sank in just fourteen minutes, taking 1,012 passengers and crew to the bottom with her. Kendall was thrown from the bridge when the ship keeled over; however, he survived and was eventually cleared of all charges in the disaster. The sinking of the *Empress of Ireland* was, and remains, Canada's worst ever maritime disaster.

4. MacMechan, op cit., p. 57.

5. Ibid.

6. Jean Holder reminiscence, Halifax Disaster Relief Office, Nova Scotia Archives MG27, Vol. 9, No. 4. (Cited hereafter as Jean Holder reminiscence.)

7. Ibid.

8. Ibid.

9. Rockwell, Fred, "Flying Babies, Shards of Glass, and a Bucket of Eyeballs," *Globe and Mail*, December 1, 2007, p. F-12.

10. *The Canadian Churchman*, February 25, 1943, p. 125.

11. The Titanic deck chair that Rev. Cunningham was given is now on display at the Maritime Museum of the Atlantic in Halifax.

12. Rev. Henry Cunningham, personal narrative, as told to Archibald MacMechan, director, Halifax Disaster Record Office, Nova Scotia Archives, MG1, vol. 2124, no. 130.

13. Ibid.

14. Ibid.

15. *Halifax Mail-Star*, December 6, 1972, p. 7.

16. Ibid.

17. Ibid.

18. Ibid.

19. Remes, Jacob, *Disaster Citizenship: Survivors, Solidarity and Power in the Progressive Era* (University of Illinois Press, 2016), pp. 771–772, Kindle edition. (Cited hereafter as Remes.)

CHAPTER 20

1. *Globe and Mail*, June 26, 2014.

2. Halifax explosion reminiscence of Rev. Henry Cunningham, Nova Scotia Archives, MG1, no, 2124, 138a.

3. *Halifax Herald*, December 7, 1917, p. 2.

4. Anonymous [Rear Admiral Bertram Chambers], "Halifax Explosion," *Naval Review* Vol. 7, No. 1 (1920), p. 446. (Cited hereafter as Chambers.)

5. Ibid.

6. Kitz, op cit., p. 53.

7. Monnon, Mary Ann, *Miracles and Mysteries: The Halifax Explosion: December 6, 1917* (Lancelot Press, 1977), p. 122.

8. Ibid., pp. 122–123.

9. Anonymous account written by a sister at Mount St. Vincent convent, Nova Scotia Archives, MG1, Vol. 2124, No. 19.

10. *Halifax Morning Herald*, "News of Shipping and Trade," December 5, 1917, p. 10.

11. Chambers, op cit., p. 448.

12. Remes, op cit., p. 755.

13. Ibid.

14. MacMechan, op cit., p. 64.

15. McMurray, Mrs. Alexander, "Memories of 1917 Explosion disaster," *Halifax Chronicle Herald*, December 6, 1974, p. 11. (Cited hereafter as McMurray.)

16. Ibid., p. 66.

17. Dakin's Solution, also called Dakin's Fluid, or Carrel–Dakin Fluid, is an antiseptic solution containing sodium hypochlorite. First used during World War I to cleanse battlefield wounds, Dakin's Solution was developed by English chemist Henry Drysdale Dakin and French surgeon Alexis Carrel. Stronger germicidal solutions, such as those containing carbolic acid (phenol) or iodine, damage healthy cells or lose their potency in the presence of blood serum. The solvent action of Dakin's Solution on dead cells hastens the separation of dead from living tissue. Dakin's Solution is prepared by passing chlorine into a solution of sodium hydroxide or sodium carbonate. The solution is unstable and cannot be stored more than a few days. The Carrel–Dakin treatment consists of the periodic flooding of an entire wound surface with the solution.

18. MacMechan, op cit., p. 67.

19. Ibid., p. 66.

20. McMurray, op cit., p. 11. Dr. Tooke was serving in the Canadian Army Medical Corps in 1917.

21. Baker, Howard, "When Hell Came to Halifax," *History Today*, December 2002, p. 43. Identified by Bird, op cit., p. 149.

CHAPTER 21

1. Mac Donald, op cit., p. 89.

2. Richardson, Evelyn, "The Halifax Explosion," *Nova Scotia Historical Quarterly*, Vol. 7, Nos. 1–4, 1977, p. 312.

3. Fraser, R.L., *The Atlantic Advocate*, January 1967.

4. *Toronto Star*, December 20, 1917, p. 8.

5. *Toronto Globe*, July 3, 1918, p. 1.

6. *Halifax Herald*, December 8, 1917, p. 1.

7. Remes, op cit., pp. 577–582.

8. Lieutenant Garnet Colwell had escaped serious injury. He was in the attic of the quartermaster's storehouse at the Wellington Barracks when the explosion occurred. The roof collapsed, but apart from a few bruises he had suffered, the young Colwell was unhurt.

9. MacMechan, op cit., p. 50.

10. Halifax City Hall homepage, www.halifax.ca/facilities/cityhall.php.

11. *Dictionary of Canadian Biography*, Vol. XV (1921–1930), www.biographi.ca/en/index.php.

12. MacMechan, op cit., p. 50.

13. Ibid., p. 33.

14. MacMechan, op cit., p. 323.

15. Ibid., p. 50.

16. Beed, Blair, *1917 Halifax Explosion and American Response* (Nimbus Publishing, 1999), p. 19.

17. MacMechan, op cit., p. 51.

18. Ibid.

19. Smith, Douglas, "The Railways and Canada's Greatest Disaster: The Halifax Explosion, December 6, 1917," *Canadian Rail*, November–December 1992, p. 202.

20. Rear Admiral Chambers' message to the secretary of the navy, December 6, 1917, as quoted in Bird, op cit., p. 85.

21. Minutes of Emergency Committee meeting, December 6, 1917, p. 1, Halifax Municipal Archives, Halifax County Council Minutes, 1916–1917.

22. MacMechan, op cit., p. 52.

23. Ibid.

24. Armstrong, op cit., p. 69.

25. Ibid.

26. MacMechan, op cit., p. 54.

27. Ibid., p. 55.

28. Ibid.

29. Lines from a poem written by one of the sisters of St. Joseph's School and Convent, Nova Scotia Archives, MG1, Vol. 2124, #17.

30. MacMechan, Archibald, "Morgue at Chebucto School," Halifax Disaster Relief Office, Nova Scotia Archives, MC1, Vol. 2124, #203, #282d.

CHAPTER 22

1. Being a Royal Navy veteran, Pasco remembered that the warships HMS *Natal* and HMS *Bulwark* had both been lost as a result of accidental internal explosions. *Bulwark* was at anchor near Sheerness off the coast of Kent on November 26, 1914, when she was destroyed by a blast that claimed the lives of 736 crewmen. *Natal* suffered a similar fate when on December 30, 1915, she blew up in the Scottish port of Cromarty. That accident killed more than 390 crewmen and civilians.

2. Testimony of Captain Frederick C.C. Pasco, *Imo* vs *Mont-Blanc*, Vol. 1, p. 1042.

3. Ibid.

4. Ibid.

5. Ibid.

6. Bird, op cit., p. 118.

7. Bird, op cit., p. 128

8. *Hartford Courant*, December 18, 1917, p. 10.

9. Dupuis, Michael, *Bearing Witness: Journalists, Record Keepers and the 1917 Halifax Explosion* (Fernwood Publishing, 2017), p. 7. (Cited hereafter as Dupuis.)

10. Ingram, Katie, "Truth Is the First Casualty," *Halifax Magazine*, December 2015, p. 26.

11. Dupuis, op cit., p. 12.

12. Kingsmill to Chambers, February 14, 1918, File 350, NAC, RG 6 E, Vol. 621, reel T-102. As quoted in Armstrong, op cit., p. 120.

13. *Halifax Herald*, December 12, 1918, as quoted in Bird, op cit., p. 130.

14. *Toronto Globe*, December 12, 1917, p. 1.

15. *Toronto Star*, December 11, 1917, p. 18.

16. *Hartford Courant*, December 24, 1917, p. 4.

17. Armstrong, op cit., p. 115.

18. Major Avery DeWitt, letter to Halifax Disaster Record Office, as quoted in Glasner, "On the Front Lines of Disaster," *Canada's History*, December 2007-January 2008, p. 20.

19. MacMechan, op cit., p. 72.

CHAPTER 23

1. For the complete list of ships and boats, please see "Ships of the Halifax Explosion" on the Maritime Museum of the Atlantic home page at https://maritimemuseum.novascotia.ca/research/ships-halifax-explosion.

2. HMS *Highflyer*'s logbook, December 6, 1917, www.naval-history.net website.

3. Maybee, Janet, "The Persecution of Pilot Mackey," *The Northern Mariner*, Vol. XX. No. 2 (April 2010), p. 159.

4. Ibid., p. 153.

5. Canada Shipping Act 1906, Part X, Chapter 13, pp. 179–180. Found online at https://archive.org/stream/revisedstatuteso03cana#page/2058/mode/2up.

6. Armstrong, op cit., p. 119.

7. Kerr, Donald, "Another Calamity: The Litigation," *Ground Zero: A Reassessment of the 1917 Explosion in Halifax Harbour* (Nimbus Publishing-Gorsebrook Research Institute, 1994), p. 365. (Cited hereafter as Kerr.)

8. A copy of the statement, which was included in a news article written by *Herald-Journal* reporter J.V. Keating, can be found in Dupuis, op cit., p. 126.

9. Armstrong, op cit., p. 117.

10. William Henry to Alexander Johnston, December 22, 1917, LAC, RG 12, Vol. 2827, File 9704-244, two volumes, Part 1. As quoted in Zemel, op cit., p. 84.

CHAPTER 24

1. U.S. Bureau of Naval Personnel, RG 24, Entry 118, the USS *Tacoma*, December 6, 1917, GT Logs of Ships and Stations, 1801–1946.

2. Scanlon, Joseph, "Source of Threat and Source of Assistance: The Maritime Aspects of the 1917 Halifax Explosion," *The Northern Mariner*, No. 4 (October 2000) p. 45.

3. Ratshesky founded the Beth Israel Hospital in Boston in 1916. In 1996 it merged with New England Deaconess Hospital to form the Beth Israel Deaconess Medical Center, the nationally renowned teaching hospital of Harvard Medical School. Among independent teaching hospitals in the United States, Beth Israel Deaconess Medical Center consistently ranks in the top three recipients among biomedical research funding from the National Institutes of Health.

4. *Boston Post*, December 8, 1917.

5. Prince, op cit., p. 32.

6. Halifax Harbour Pilotage Log of Captain Nicholas LaMont Power, MBE, January 1, 1906, to November 27, 1954. Unpublished.

7. Hervey Jones, personal narrative, Halifax Disaster Record Office, Nova Scotia Archives, MG1, Vol. 2124, #161.

8. Ibid.

9. *Sandefjord Blad*, February 4, 1918, p. 2.

10. *Halifax Chronicle Herald*, December 6, 1967, p. E3.

CHAPTER 25

1. Kitz, op cit., p. 71.

2. Hopkins, J. Castell, *The Canadian Annual Review of Public Affairs* (War Series, 1918), pp. 646–656.

3. Zweig, Eric, "The NHL's First Game?" http://ericzweig.com. In Toronto, the Ontario Hockey Association had begun its 1917–1918 season the night of December 14 with an HRC benefit game in which the defending Allan Cup senior amateur team, the Dentals (a University of Toronto team made up of dental students and recent alumni), played the Hamilton Tigers.

4. *Boston Globe*, December 17, 1917, p. 9.

5. *Halifax Herald*, December 17, 1917, p. 1.

6. MacMechan, op cit., p. 74.

7. Report of the Superintendent of Neglected and Delinquent Children (1919), Province of Nova Scotia, p. 110.

8. For more information on the life and career of E.H. Blois, please visit www15.pair.com/buchanan/genes/docs/ernblois.html.

9. Mac Donald, op cit., p. 232.

10. *Halifax Morning Chronicle*, December 12, 1917.

11. Ibid.

12. The Halifax Explosion Book of Remembrance is accessible online at https://novascotia.ca/archives/remembrance.

13. Kitz, op cit., p. 101.

CHAPTER 26

1. *Boston Evening Transcript*, December 7, 1917.
2. Ratshesky, Abraham C., "Report of the Halifax Relief Expedition, December 6–15, 1917" (Wright and Potter Printing Company, 1918), p. 7. (Cited hereafter as Ratshesky.)
3. *Boston Herald*, December 8, 1917.
4. Ratshesky, op cit., p. 9.
5. Ibid.
6. Ibid., p. 10.
7. Borden, Robert L., *Robert Laird Borden: His Memoirs* (MacMillan Company, 1938), p. 764.
8. *Boston Herald*, December 9, 1917.
9. Ratshesky, op cit., p. 11.
10. Ibid.
11. *Boston Herald*, December 9, 1917.
12. Ibid.
13. Ibid.
14. Ratshesky, op cit., p. 13.
15. *Too Many to Mourn*, op cit., p. 206.
16. Ibid.
17. It was not until December 20 that a crew of workmen, who were clearing away rubble and recovering bodies from the ruins of houses that had stood on Veith Street, recovered the charred and broken remains of Mary Jean Hinch's family: her husband, Joe, age fifty; daughters Helen, two; Margaret, five; Annie, five; Mary, twelve; Helena, seventeen; and Clara, nineteen; and sons Ralph, three; James, eight; Joseph, nine; and Thomas, fifteen. All were buried in a common grave at Halifax's Mount Olivet Cemetery.
18. *Too Many to Mourn*, op cit., p. 167.
19. Ibid., p. 173.
20. Jean Holder reminiscence, op cit., p. 6.
21. Call, Stephanie, "How Can We Ever Forget Massachusetts?: Abraham Ratshesky and the 1917 Halifax Relief Effort," *American Ancestors*, Winter 2016. (Accessible online at www.american-ancestors.org/Browse/Publications/AAM-Vol-17-No-1.)
22. *Boston Post*, December 9, 1917, p. 5.
23. The unabashedly patriotic song "Over There," written by George M. Cohan in 1917, was popular with the American military and the public during both world wars. Today, "Over There" is best remembered for the line in its chorus that announces "The Yanks are coming."

CHAPTER 27

1. Armstrong, op cit., p. 69.
2. Ibid., p. 105.
3. Chambers, circular to Naval Ottawa, Admiralty, C-in-C North America and West Indies, December 9, 1917, NSS 1048-48-1, Vol. 3, NAC RG 24, Vol. 3774. As quoted in Armstrong,

op cit., p. 105. In fact, the first post-disaster convoy, made up of thirty-three ships, sailed out of Halifax on December 11 with a patched-up HMS *Highflyer* serving as the naval escort.

4. Hervey Jones, personal narrative, Halifax Disaster Record Office, Nova Scotia Archives, MG1, Vol. 2124, #161.

5. The election became unnecessary when the Liberal candidate dropped out. As a result, two Unionist candidates—one of whom was Halifax mayor Peter Martin—were acclaimed to office.

6. Bird, op cit., p. 149.

7. McAlister, C., J. Murray, H. Lakosha, and C. Maxner, "The Halifax Disaster (1917): Eye Injuries and Their Care," *British Journal of Ophthalmology*, June 2007, pp. 832–835.

8. Armstrong, op cit., pp. 96–97

9. *Boston Post*, December 11, 1917.

10. Ibid., p. 96.

11. Ibid., p. 23.

12. Documents about the alcohol theft are posted online at http://halifax.ca/Archives/explosion-sources.php#Theft.

13. MacMechan, op cit., p. 68.

14. Kitz, op cit., p. 137.

15. *Halifax Herald*, January 7, 1918.

16. Ibid., p. 140.

17. Massachusetts State House, MS Coll 90, Folder 13. As quoted in Mac Donald, op cit., p. 237.

18. *Toronto Star*, January 21, 1918, p. 15. The Halifax Board of Trade and the Board of Control, which was the paid executive of city council, had urged the mayor to invite the provincial and federal governments to get more involved in long-term relief efforts in the city, especially in relation to the disbursement of relief funds. When Nova Scotia premier George H. Murray came out in support of the idea, a meeting of officials from the city and both senior levels of government was held on December 28. Less than a month later, on January 22, 1919, Parliament passed a bill establishing the Halifax Relief Commission (HRC). For more information on the HRC, please visit the Nova Scotia Archives website (https://archives.novascotia.ca).

19. Nova Scotia Archives website: https://memoryns.ca/halifax-relief-commission-fonds.

20. *Halifax Herald*, April 10, 1918, pp. 1–2.

21. Ibid.

22. Kitz, op cit., p. 188.

23. Morton, Suzanne, "The Halifax Relief Commission and Labour Relations During the Reconstruction of Halifax, 1917–1919," *Acadiensis: Journal of the History of the Atlantic Region*, Vol. XVIII, No. 2 (Spring 1989), p. 73.

24. Ibid., p. 147.

25. *Halifax Herald*, January 5, 1918.

26. *Halifax Herald*, January 7, 1918.

27. Ontario was the first Canadian province to adopt a system of compensation for workers who were seriously injured on the job. The Ontario Workmen's Compensation Act of 1914 was the first Canadian statute and served as a model for provincial legislation in Nova Scotia (1915),

British Columbia (1916), Alberta (1918), and New Brunswick (1918). Working women were an afterthought in the Workmen's Compensation scheme, if they were ever thought of at all.

28. Johnstone, D. "The Tragedy of Halifax, 1917," Nova Scotia Archives, MFM, Microfilm J735.

29. Kitz, op cit., p. 180

CHAPTER 28

1. Kline, Bernard, "Post Cards of the 1917 Explosion," *Ground Zero*, op cit., p. 140.

2. *Boston Evening Transcript*, December 10, 1917.

3. Ratshesky, op cit., p. 17.

4. Kitz, op cit., p. 151.

5. *Halifax Herald*, December 10, 1917.

6. *Halifax Herald*, December 10, 1917, p. 1.

7. *Boston Evening Transcript*, December 11, 1917.

8. *Halifax Herald*, December 12, 1917.

9. *Gazette* (Montreal), December 17, 1917.

10. *Imo vs Mont-Blanc* file, National Library and Archives Canada File NSS 37-25-8, Exhibit MBR/19, p. 22. (Cited hereafter as NL&A.)

11. Ratshesky, op cit., p. 17.

12. Ibid.

13. *Imo vs Mont-Blanc* file, NL&A File NSS 37-25-8, Exhibit MBR/19, p. 22.

14. *Canadian Encyclopedia* home page, "Intelligence and Espionage."

15. *Imo vs Mont-Blanc* file, NL&A, NSS 37-25-8.

16. Memo from Naval Central Office, Halifax, Nova Scotia, to Captain Sir William Wiseman, c/o British Naval Attaché, New York City, December 21, 1917. NL&A, NSS 37-25-0. The fact that "Willie" Wiseman was involved in the investigation into Johan Johansen's background is significant. Wiseman, New York–based in December 1917, was one of the key agents in the service of Sir Mansfield Smith-Cumming, the first head of Britain's Secret Intelligence Service (SIS)—a.k.a. MI5.

17. Captain L. Demers to Captain H.C. Craig, Baltimore, MD, January 2, 1918. NL&A, File 9704—244, Pt. 1, Record Group 12, Acc. 2827.

18. Le Queux, William, *The German Spy System from Within* (Hodder & Stoughton, 1915), p. 1.

19. Grams, Grant W., "Karl Respa and German Espionage in Canada During WWI," *Journal of Military and Strategic Studies*, Vol. 8, No. 1 (Fall 2005).

20. Blum, Howard, *Dark Invasion: 1915, Germany's Secret War and the Hunt for the First Terrorist Cell in America* (Harper, 2014), p. 162.

21. Mount, Graeme, *Canada's Enemies: Spies and Spying in the Peaceable Kingdom* (Dundurn Press, 1993), p. 42.

22. Ibid., p. 42.

23. *Halifax Herald*, December 18, 1917, p. 3.

24. Ibid.

25. MacMechan, Archibald, Halifax Disaster Record Office, Nova Scotia Archives, MG 1, Vol. 2124, #282d.

26. *Halifax Herald*, December 18, 1917, p. 3.

27. Kitz, op cit., pp. 108, 110.

28. Bird, op cit., p. 157.

CHAPTER 29

1. Kerr, op cit., p. 369.

2. Kerr, op cit., p. 369.

3. Maybee, Janet, *Aftershock: The Halifax Explosion and the Persecution of Pilot Francis Mackey* (Nimbus Publishing, 2015), p. 44. (Cited hereafter as *Aftershock*.) Historian Janet Maybee's authoritative book details for the first time the previously untold tragic story of Mackey's ordeal and of his long, costly fight to clear his name.

4. E.J. Chambers to Willoughby Gwatkin, December 18, 1917, NAC File 350, RG 6E, Vol. 621, Reel T-102. As quoted in Armstrong, op cit., p. 124.

5. Armstrong, op cit., p. 122.

6. When Ernest Chambers, Canada's chief wartime press censor, visited Halifax on December 14, he conferred with General Benson, the commander of the city's garrison, about security and censorship issues. Benson and other military leaders were upset with press coverage of events in the city and of the proceedings of the Wreck Commission. As a result, when Chambers met with journalists, local as well as visiting, he pointed out to them what censorship measures were appropriate in the circumstances. The meeting produced limited results. Even the *Halifax Herald* obligingly toned down its inflammatory rhetoric, at least for a few days. However, the newspaper's editors continued to give the daily sessions of the Wreck Commission front-page coverage and to make use of headlines that stirred emotions and fuelled conspiracy theories. For example, a headline in the December 17 edition of the newspaper asked, "Did Another Hand Than Pilot's Direct *Imo*'s Course?"

7. Kerr, op cit., p. 370.

8. Ibid., p. 369.

9. Kitz, op cit., p. 158.

10. Graham, Justice R.H., "Honourable Arthur Drysdale," Nova Scotia Archives, MG100, Vol. 136, #17.

11. Ibid.

12. *Halifax Daily Echo*, October 21, 1922, p. 1.

13. The Exchequer Court of Canada, which was inaugurated in 1875, was inspired by the Court of Exchequer in England, both in its name and its jurisdiction. The Exchequer Court of Canada initially dealt with matters of revenue and in all civil cases in which the Crown was the plaintiff or petitioner. The Exchequer Court of Canada was abolished in 1971, when the Federal Court of Canada came into existence.

14. *Halifax Herald*, January 10, 1918.

15. Halifax mayor Peter F. Martin, telegram to Prime Minister Robert Borden, January 13, 1918, NL&A, File NSS 37-25-3, Vol. 1.

16. Minister of Marine and Fisheries Charles C. Ballantyne to Prime Minister Robert Borden, NL&A, File NSS 37-25-3, Vol. 1.

17. Testimony of Captain Aimé Le Médec, *Imo* vs *Mont-Blanc*, Vol. 1, p. 40.

18. Ibid., p. 887.

19. Ibid., pp. 162, 167.

20. "As marked by pilot Mackey," testimony of Pilot Mackey, *Imo* vs *Mont-Blanc*, Exhibit M B R/17, Vol. 1, pp. 178–182.

21. Kitz, op cit., p. 156.

22. Ibid., pp. 160–161.

23. Testimony of Captain Frederick C.C. Pasco, *Imo* vs *Mont-Blanc*, Vol. 1, p. 1043.

24. Armstrong, op cit., p. 162.

CHAPTER 30

1. Testimony of Commander Evan Wyatt, *Imo* vs *Mont-Blanc*, Vol. 1, p. 1680.

2. Ibid., pp. 1095–1096.

3. Ibid., p. 1215.

4. Kitz, op cit., p. 165.

5. Armstrong, op cit., p. 234.

6. Ibid.

7. *Halifax Evening Mail*, February 1, 1918.

8. Armstrong, op cit., p. 203. Armstrong's book is the definitive account of the political and military intrigues that were playing out behind the scenes in Ottawa and Halifax as the Wreck Commission inquiry was under way.

9. Ibid., p. 187.

10. Ibid., p. 191.

11. Ibid.

12. *Toronto Globe*, March 18, 1918, p. 5.

13. Renner's piloting licence was later suspended; however, by October 1920 he was back on the job. Although he had admitted to guiding the American ship SS *Clara* up the wrong side of the Narrows on the morning of December 6, 1917, his punishment was relatively—and surprisingly—lenient.

14. *Halifax Herald*, February 7, 1918.

15. Ibid. The *Mail* article reported that "S.M. Brookfield" appeared at the courthouse. However, historian Joel Zemel in his book *Scapegoat: The Extraordinary Legal Proceedings Following the 1917 Halifax Explosion* writes that it was *not* the uncle of Wyatt's wife, Dorothy, who posted bail for him, but rather Walter Brookfield, Wyatt's father-in-law. It seems likely that the *Mail* reporter got the facts wrong.

16. Ibid.

17. Russell, Benjamin, *Autobiography of Benjamin Russell* (Royal Print & Litho, 1932), p. 270.

18. *Halifax Herald*, April 20, 1918.

19. Zemel, op cit., p. 289.

20. *Aftershock*, op cit., p. 158.

21. Ibid.

22. Ibid., p. 79.

23. *La Compagnie Générale Transatlantique* v. The Ship *"IMO,"* [1919] S.C.R. 644

24. The Ship *"IMO"* v. *La Compagnie Générale Transatlantique / La Compagnie Générale Transatlantique* v. *The Ship "IMO,"* UKPC 27. Found online at www.bailii.org/uk/cases/UKPC/1920/1920_27.html.

25. Kitz, op cit., p.159.

CHAPTER 31

1. *Halifax Herald*, April 12, 1918.

2. Ibid.

3. *Halifax Herald*, July 31, 1918.

4. Erickson, Paul, *Halifax's North End: An Anthropologist Looks at the City* (Lancelot Press, 1987), p. 58.

5. Ibid.

6. Ibid., p. 123.

7. *Halifax Herald*, September 5, 1918.

8. Robinson-Mushkat, S. William, "City at a Critical Juncture: Halifax's Town Planning Board at the End of the Progressive Era, 1914–24" (unpublished MA thesis, Saint Mary's University, 2010), p. 86.

9. Kitz, op cit., p. 199.

INDEX

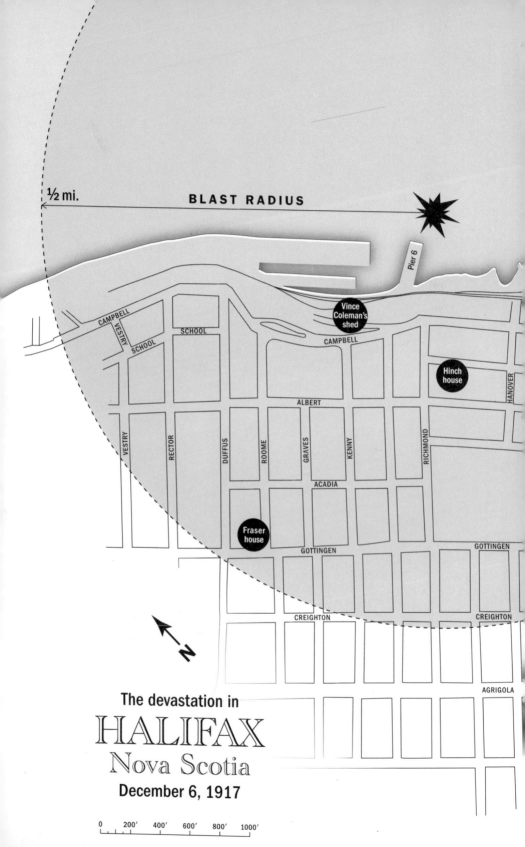

½ mi.

BLAST RADIUS

Pier 6

Vince Coleman's shed

CAMPBELL

VESTRY

SCHOOL

SCHOOL

SCHOOL

CAMPBELL

Hinch house

HANOVER

ALBERT

VESTRY

RECTOR

DUFFUS

ROOME

GRAVES

KENNY

RICHMOND

ACADIA

Fraser house

GOTTINGEN

GOTTINGEN

N

CREIGHTON

CREIGHTON

AGRIGOLA

The devastation in

HALIFAX
Nova Scotia
December 6, 1917

0   200'   400'   600'   800'   1000'